Understanding
Your Dog
FOR
DUMMIES®

by Stanley Coren and Sarah Hodgson

BICENTENNIAL

BICENTENNIAL

1807

®WILEY

2007

BICENTENNIAL

BICENTENNIAL

Wiley Publishing, Inc.

Understanding Your Dog For Dummies®

Published by
Wiley Publishing, Inc.
111 River St.
Hoboken, NJ 07030-5774
www.wiley.com

WILEY

About the Authors

Stanley Coren is best known to the public for his popular books on dogs and on general psychological issues. However, within the scientific world, he's also a highly respected scientist, a Professor of Psychology at the University of British Columbia, and a Fellow of the Royal Society of Canada.

His engaging writing style and his broad knowledge about the behavior of dogs and people have made his books *The Intelligence of Dogs, Why We Love the Dogs We Do, What Do Dogs Know?, How to Speak Dog, The Pawprints of History, How Dogs Think, Why Do Dogs Have Wet Noses?*, and *Why Does My Dog Do That?* all best-sellers. Roger Caras, President of the ASPCA, and himself a best-selling author of dog books, noted "Stanley Coren has an incredible gift — the ability to take the most complex matters and make it all seem so simple and clear." Perhaps this is why Coren was named Writer of the Year by the International Positive Dog Training Association and is a sought-after contributor to a number of national dog and pet magazines, including *Pets Magazine, Modern Dog, AnimalSense, Dog and Puppy Basics,* and *AKC Gazette.*

Many professional associations have recognized Coren's work with service dogs, and he's received awards from several major police dog organizations, including the California Canine Narcotic Dog Association and the British Columbia Police Canine Association. His work with and knowledge of dogs has often caught the attention of the media, and he's been the subject of feature articles in *People Magazine, USA Today, Time Magazine, Maclean's, US News & World Report, New York Times, Los Angeles Times, San Francisco Chronicle, Washington Post,* and others. His affable manner has also made him a popular guest with the broadcast media, and he's been featured on numerous television programs, including *Oprah, Larry King Live, Dateline, 20/20, Maurie Povich, Good Morning America, Charlie Rose,* and the *Today Show.* He currently hosts the national TV series *Good Dog!* in Canada.

Sarah Hodgson, president of Simply Sarah Incorporated, has been a trainer of dogs and their people in Westchester, New York, and Southern Connecticut for more than 20 years. She's the author of eight dog-training books, including *Puppies For Dummies, Dog Tricks For Dummies, Puppies Raising & Training Diary For Dummies, Teach Yourself Visually Dog Training, You and Your Puppy* (co-authored with James DeBitetto), *DogPerfect,* 2nd Edition, *PuppyPerfect,* and *Miss Sarah's Guide to Etiquette for Dogs & Their People.* In addition, Sarah has produced two videos, patented a dog training leash (the Teaching Lead), and invented many other products to simplify the shared lives of dogs and people.

Sarah is frequently featured as a dog training specialist on network television, radio, and print media, including *The New York Times,* NBC, CBS, Animal Planet (Disney syndicate), FOX, CNN, WOR, Hollywood Pets, *Parenthood* magazine, and others. She has worked with many famous persons' dogs, including TV personality Katie Couric, actors Richard Gere, Glenn Close, Chazz Palminteri, Chevy Chase, and Lucie Arnaz; business moguls George Soros, Tommy Hilfiger, Tommy Mottola, and Michael Fuchs; and sport greats Bobby Valentine and Alan Houston.

In addition, Sarah is a behavior consultant and education facilitator at the Adopt-A-Dog shelter in Armonk, New York, where she holds training and socialization programs, conditioning each of the dogs within a fully decorated home environment before their formal adoption. For more information on everything Sarah, visit her Web site at www.dogperfect.com.

Sarah also writes a weekly column and balances all with her top priorities: her family and pets!

Dedication

We dedicate our book to dogs . . . from all the ones we've loved, helped, and nurtured to the ones we look forward to knowing. You have filled our path with reason and given shape to our days and meaning to our life experience. Woof!

Authors' Acknowledgments

There are so many people who deserve gratitude: Nancy Shalek for steering the boat, Kelly for your editorial efforts that grace every page, and Mike who spearheaded this project from the beginning.

And as always, our friends and family. . . . You are our sideline crew and support team. We would never — could never — be so delighted with our life if it weren't for every one of you. Big hug!

Publisher's Acknowledgments

We're proud of this book; please send us your comments through our Dummies online registration form located at www.dummies.com/register/.

Some of the people who helped bring this book to market include the following:

Acquisitions, Editorial, and Media Development

Project Editor: Kelly Ewing

Acquisitions Editor: Michael Lewis

General Reviewer: Brad Phifer

Editorial Manager: Michelle Hacker

Editorial Supervisor and Reprint Editor: Carmen Krikorian

Editorial Assistant: Leeann Harney

Cartoons: Rich Tennant
(www.the5thwave.com)

Composition Services

Project Coordinator: Jennifer Theriot

Layout and Graphics: Joyce Haughey, Stephanie D. Jumper, Laura Pence, Heather Ryan, Alicia B. South

Anniversary Logo Design: Richard Pacifico

Proofreaders: Aptara, Susan Moritz

Indexer: Aptara

Publishing and Editorial for Consumer Dummies

    Diane Graves Steele, Vice President and Publisher, Consumer Dummies

    Joyce Pepple, Acquisitions Director, Consumer Dummies

    Kristin A. Cocks, Product Development Director, Consumer Dummies

    Michael Spring, Vice President and Publisher, Travel

    Kelly Regan, Editorial Director, Travel

Publishing for Technology Dummies

    Andy Cummings, Vice President and Publisher, Dummies Technology/General User

Composition Services

    Gerry Fahey, Vice President of Production Services

    Debbie Stailey, Director of Composition Services

Contents at a Glance

Table of Contents

Introduction

● ●

*P*repare yourself for a journey into the mind of a dog! No matter where you start in this book, each page illuminates some facet of your dog's life experience: from her unique personality, to how and why she either focuses on your directions or spirals into an independent cycle of what you may consider negative behavior. Though scientific information is the backbone of understanding your dog's behavior, our book is a far cry from a boring read! Upbeat and cleverly written, it brings science into the mainstream, using language everyone can understand and relate to. When you walk away from this book, your dog's behavior will no longer be a mystery — it will be common sense.

Another unique aspect of this book is that it seamlessly weaves two schools of thought together. Stanley Coren, a behavioral scientist who specializes in understanding how dogs think and act, meets Sarah Hodgson, a dog trainer who specializes in changing dog behaviors. Our union has been eye-opening for us, and we bring this magic to you. This book offers something unique: a dog's-eye view of everything human. This book reveals how the grace and willingness of puppyhood can either be nurtured to encourage cooperative behavior patterns, or distorted, resulting in extreme reactiveness, destruction, housesoiling, and so on. Whereas Stanley explains a dog's perception and experience, Sarah shows you how to use this knowledge to better your communication with your dog and immediately recognize a source of conflict or confusion.

Whether you're picking up this book out of a simple love for dogs, a drive to understand and communicate with your dog with more insight, or a tested affection for a puppy that has matured in unpredicted ways, we guarantee you'll not be let down. In addition to seeing the world from your dog's perspective, you'll develop an appreciation for her as you gather a toolbox of techniques to train your dog and/or repair misunderstandings. Be prepared to get hooked on everything dog, and above all else, enjoy the ride!

About This Book

Everyone envisions a great relationship with their dog, as though the outcome were guaranteed: Peaceful strolls, interactive play, calming feelings generated by a pet that brings harmony to family life and ails the angst of everyday life. If only it were as easy as wanting it to be so.

If you're feeling overwhelmed by the prospect of getting a dog or queasy about your responsibility for the dog you've already committed to, you can relax. This book helps you recognize not only why your dog behaves in the way she does, but in the most positive way to encourage her cooperation.

Conventions Used in This Book

We stuck to the following conventions throughout the book:

- ✔ To avoid any gender bias, we refer to dogs as both males and females throughout the text. Except for anything that strictly relates to behaviors that are specifically male or female, you can be sure that the information applies to your puppy, regardless of gender.

- ✔ Anytime we introduce a new or scientific term, we *italicize* it.

- ✔ Keywords in lists appear in **boldface.** Also, when we present a list of steps to perform, the action you need to take is boldface as well.

- ✔ Web sites and e-mail addresses appear in `monofont` to help them stand out in the text.

What You're Not to Read

Though we've weaved together insightful information throughout this book, you don't need to scour each page to learn more about your dog. After all, who has the time to read a nearly 300-page book these days? Read one chapter at a time or use it as a reference throughout your dog's life, knowing that every page you digest will enhance your overall understanding of him and thus improve your relationship.

Even as you read, you can skip bits if you're pressed for time. Sidebars (gray boxes of text) include interesting, but non-essential information. The Technical Stuff and Just For Fun icons also contain insightful, but not necessarily crucial, facts.

Foolish Assumptions

Here's what we assume about you, our dear readers:

✔ You know your dog has four paws and a tail, and you love her dearly.

✔ You either have a dog now, love dogs but don't have one now, or are about to get a dog.

✔ You don't want to get your PhD in animal behavior, but desperately want to know more about how your dog interprets life.

How This Book Is Organized

This book is divided into five parts, each one having its own insightful theme. Here's a quick rundown.

Part I: The Fascinating World of Dogs

In this first part, you find out about your dog's individual communication skills. Like teaching your language to a foreigner, we give you the tools to understand your dog's behavior and translate your thoughts into Doglish, their natural language.

Part II: Embracing Your Dog's Identity

Until you recognize that your dog, whether a mixed breed or purebred, has a distinct identity that makes her unique, her behavioral quirks can be puzzling — and, at times, frustrating. The first step in understanding your dog is to respect the honorable task she was originally bred for and to identify how these inbred impulses will influence her personality and behavior. We also address the dramatic influence of your dog's sensory experience, as well as the emotional life and specific needs of a growing puppy. Finally, we discuss the psychological needs of an aging dog, from the emotional shock at her own physical and sensory decline, to diet supplements that may help to slow the degenerative process.

Part III: Doggie Delinquency

Let the training begin! This part starts out examining the many positive tools and techniques available to people who train dogs, highlighting systems that are both effective and encouraging. If your goal is to have a dog who not only listens to you, but enthusiastically *chooses* your direction over other impulses, the chapters in this part point the way.

Part IV: Dogs Don't Misbehave: Misperceptions and Solutions

In this part, we target the array of frustrations most common to dog owners, from housetraining a puppy to rehabilitating a fearful or aggressive dog. Looking at each issue from your dog's perspective, we help you see that what you may consider a problem is often a simple case of misunderstanding, lack of exercise, or manageable stress.

Part V: The Part of Tens

Last but not least, we gather together the top-ten lists of the most common misperceptions and ways to communicate silently. Enjoy!

Icons Used in This Book

Throughout this book, you find icons that appear on the left side of the page and that point out different types of information. Here's a list of the various icons you may encounter:

This icon highlights useful tidbits and helpful advice.

These friendly reminders won't let any of the important information slip by.

"Warning, Warning!" Need we say more?

This icon alerts you to facts and technical information that may not be essential, but they're interesting to know all the same.

Take note of this icon. Though it may not contain crucial details, it does highlight a fun fact that's good to know.

Where to Go from Here

The neatest thing about this book is that you can jump in any-where. It's a no-rules reference for anyone who is getting or sharing their life with a dog. Look to the table of contents, flip to the index, or simply shut your eyes and open to any page. You'll find great topics to read about and new stuff to learn on every page.

Of course, this isn't to say that you shouldn't read our book cover to cover, but it's not a prerequisite! No matter where you start, remember that, like children, your dog is a very unique and moti-vated being who, above all else, wants to be involved in your life experience.

Part I

The Fascinating World of Dogs

The 5th Wave   By Rich Tennant

"I think he's just displaying normal pack instincts."

In this part . . .

Everyone who takes responsibility for a dog has a vision of how they'd like their dog to act: from polite to protective, from mellow to athletic, from interactive to aloof. The vision and reality, however, can sometimes differ measurably. Suddenly, an adorable puppy morphs into a maturing dog with thoughts of her own and mannerisms that may not line up with anyone's expectations.

In this part, you grow to appreciate your dog as a unique individual, fully equipped by evolution and centuries of selective breeding with her own set of ideals and inner drives. This part gives you the understanding you need to enjoy, cope with, or change your life with your pet.

Chapter 1

A Dog for Life: Dog Psychology 101

*T*here is no greater gift you can offer your dog than to understand her: to walk a mile in her paws. Though money can buy a lot of dog biscuits and squeak toys, and those obedience classes will encourage greater responsiveness to you, a lot more is going on behind the scenes than the simple recognition of the command "Sit." This chapter starts you on the journey discovering the mystery that is your dog.

Is Your Dog a Wolf in Sheep's Clothing?

Well, yes and no. Though we go more in-depth in this part, suffice it to say that dogs approached domestication at their own speed. There was no cosmic moment when some brave young boy (or girl), holding a wolf pup, approached their father and said, "Please, Dad, can we keep it?" Domestication was a slow evolutionary process that involved the gradual progression from curious wolves that drew closer to our campfire, to the marked physical changes that characterize dogs we know today.

People and dogs: Parallel evolution

Our relationship with dogs began during a time when survival was our only focus. Centered on staying alive, dogs provided personal protection and hunting assistance.

For eons, dogs and humans evolved in parallel: During the agricultural era, we modified our selection process to produce dogs who would cull the varmint population and others who would herd livestock. As kingdoms grew, massive dog breeds were shaped by a process of manual selection to guard the castles and aid in wars. And so on and so on until today, when there are more than 400 different dog breeds that populate our globe, all developed for particular tasks.

There is only one problem: Except for a few instances, any dog's special talents are rarely needed. But don't tell your dog: It would be too depressing. He thinks his abilities are still in high demand.

To know your dog, however, still requires you to understand his original breeding, and respect that his genes are still guiding his behaviors today. (For more on this topic, see Chapter 6.)

Personality

In Chapter 5, you discover how to identify your dog's temperament and how it shapes her understanding of the world you share. For example, a dominant dog assesses everyone who enters, whereas a timid dog hides under the table when the doorbell rings. Embracing your dog's personality helps you in your effort to orchestrate a training program to normalize your life together.

Unlike people who learn by listening, your dog is much more attuned to nonverbal communication, from how you hold your body (especially in moments of tension or stress) to where you focus your eyes. Learning your dog's language will help you understand her behavior and be understood in kind.

If you consistently look at your dog, she may interpret your interest as a need for leadership. Remember this little jingle: The more you look at your dog, the less she'll look to you.

Dog's devotion to people was hard-wired upon domestication. Your dog is the only species that will look to and take direction from another species (that's us) as if it was their own.

Sensory overload

To really consider life from your dog's perspective, you need a new nose. Dogs rely most heavily on their sense of smell to interpret even the minor aspects of their surroundings, such as when another animal may have passed through or even the stress hormone of a visitor in your home.

In your dog, our strongest scent, sight, is blurred and limited. Your dog can only recognize a limited range of colors and is more attuned to the motion of an object than its particulars. Dogs don't rely on the recognition of fine details of objects, but rather they were born to be hunters with the motto, "If it moves it might be food, and I'll chase and catch it!"

There is also a big difference in dog's hearing abilities, which can be traced to the evolution of our separate species. Humans are more sharply attuned to the sound of other human voices, whereas dogs are capable of hearing higher frequencies and fainter sounds. Because dogs evolved from hunters, their hearing is more attuned to the sounds that their potential prey might make.

In today's society, your dog's sensory strengths are rarely appreciated. An apartment dog is admonished each time he alerts to the sound of a footstep; hounds are scolded for getting into the trash; and all breeds are reprimanded for chasing the family cat. In our world, dogs are on sensory overload yet are expected to ignore everything. In Chapter 7, you can experience the world from your dog's perspective and also find out about new tasks that are being set for dogs that take advantage of their special sensory skills.

Age Influences

Whether you have a puppy or older dog, you can appreciate that time and experience will make a difference in your dog's behavior. A young puppy, who is often interpreting many of life's nuances for the first time, watches your actions carefully and is influenced by how you behave. An older dog, however, who has studied many human responses, may be less influenced by your activities — unless they're unusual or unexpected.

In Chapter 8, our puppy chapter, we highlight the way a puppy's mind develops and the ideal lessons to introduce at every stage. Further, we stress the critical importance of early socialization and how encounters with various people and places can change your dog's life — forever.

Dogs age too quickly. Though many of their life processes mirror ours, their timeline accelerates at ten times our rate. By age 3, your dog is a mature adult, by 7 most have reached middle age, and by 10, many are heading into their twilight years. It's a reality that can't be ignored or avoided.

In Chapter 9, you can find out how your dog's internal processes function throughout maturity and what you can do to ease their emotional adjustment. Like humans, physical changes are often accompanied by feelings of defensiveness and fear.

Influencing Your Dog's Learning

Dogs love to learn and feel connected to group activities. How you develop as a teacher and translator directly affects their enthusiasm for learning and, in turn, for life. Think of each lesson and highlighted word as though you were teaching a foreigner your language. "Sit," "Wait," "Down," and "Good" get lifted beyond mere command status, to verbal directions that show your dog how to act in everyday situations.

In Part III, we lay out all the tricks of the trade, exploring learning influences and emotional responses. In addition, we help you make sense of the different schools of thought about how to teach your dog and compare the differences between them — for example, shaping versus modeling.

There is no one approach to encouraging good behavior: Each dog is unique and may respond better to one technique than another. A clearly orchestrated attempt to educate yourself and understand the different methods available will keep your training effort fresh and alive. We also examine exactly how your dog assimilates new information and how you may use this understanding to further influence her behavior.

Though a dog can recognize up to 165 different directions, your goals need not be so lofty. In Chapter 12, we outline six directions that are most useful for navigating your life together (see Table 1-1). After you have these directions firmly planted in your dog's memory bank, they form the foundation for controlling your dog's behavior. Their use reassures your dog of her place in your family and her vital inclusion in your world. There is no greater gift you could offer your dog than that.

Table 1-1   Six Directions That Make a Difference

Word Cue	Daily Uses
Follow	When walking about town or off your property, or to encourage attention in your home
Wait-okay	To get your dog to stop and check in before entering or exiting your home or new buildings, as well as when you cross the street and approach stairs

Word Cue	Daily Uses
No (and other derivations, such as Not now, Leave it, Don't think about it)	To alert your dog that any given impulse is not in her best interest (for example, stealing food, chasing an object or animal, and so on)
Stay	Enforces impulse to control; ideally used when you need your dog to be still or to relax
Down (and Settle down)	Directs your dog into a submissive, relaxed pose or to her bed
Come	The human phrase equivalent of the word "Huddle"

Ain't Misbehaving!

No matter how livid you feel when your dog disobeys you or damages prized possessions, you won't influence her routines until you sit down and listen to her side of the story. Sure, your half-eaten shoes cost $95 dollars, but to your dog, its enticing aroma (perfume YOU) was impossible to pass by. In this section, we lead you through the most common frustrations, from housebreaking to anxiety-driven behavior and on to darker issues such as aggression, in our efforts to shape your ability to respond in a manner that your dog understands.

Why dogs act out

Just as people do, many dogs act out when they feel misunderstood, restless, or needy. If you walk around claiming that your dog is reacting out of spite, then, in your mind, her every reaction will be tainted by that view, even though "spite" is not an emotion dogs have. If you keep shouting "Bad dog!" every time your dog makes a wrong move, what option does she have?

 Dogs, like children, are motivated by what gets attention. However, it often appears that dogs can't differentiate positive attention from negative. If an action gets a reaction — any reaction — it will get repeated.

Furthermore, negative attention can be misperceived as being rough play or confrontation. Thus, a dog who steals from the counter may feel *prize envy* when her people react uproariously. A smart dog will simply wait until their people have left the room, and then (minus competition) carry the prize off to a more secluded space.

In Chapter 13, we examine how a dog learns to misbehave and just what can be done to reverse this trend.

Dissecting daily frustrations

Though you may have a real issue with some of your dog's behavior, it's unlikely that she does. Though a pee-stained carpet can raise your blood pressure, from her point of view the carpet is just as absorbent as the grass, and whether her accident was motivated by need or distraction, she did what came naturally.

Now, don't get distressed. We're not suggesting that you must live with a dog who urinates on the carpet, or jumps on company, or chews your slippers, but recognizing that your dog's behavior isn't motivated by spite, vengeance, or guilt can ease your frustration.

Chapter 13 addresses many of the most common complaints dog owners have about living with their dog, including barking, chewing, jumping, and housesoiling. Each behavior, though disruptive and aggravating, may be a perfectly normal sign of a dog that has bonded well and is trying to get along within the family unit. Although reorganizing her outlook may require some effort and intervention, the process usually takes less time and is less stressful than coping with the current frustrations that have become status quo.

When reality bites: Inside canine aggression

Aggression is the one behavior that sets a red flag down on any playing field. Though it's sometimes perfectly understandable, dogs are simply not allowed to bite human beings, unless of course they've been trained to such ends or are legitimately defending their territory. Dogs who bite are excluded from activities, relinquished to a shelter, or euthanized. Before your dog shows any signs of aggression, it is wise to understand what motivates him and do what you can to prevent it, either with your dog or other dogs you meet.

Chapter 15 takes a look at the different types of aggression, noting what may prompt such reactions. You also can discover what you can do to prevent aggression when it first appears.

No book for home use can address the needs of a dog that is exhibiting a full-blown aggressive response and threatening the safety of family members. Although we give you the means to recognize the nature of your dog's behavior, and even some ways to deal with it, if your dog has seriously bitten someone, or is really scaring you because he is threatening to bite, you must seek professional advice.

Chapter 2

Understanding Your Dog

. . . .

. . . .

*O*ur goal in this chapter, and as a whole, in the entire book, is to help you understand your dog from his vantage point: to discover what it must feel like to be a dog and to understand your role and capacities to shape your dog's behavior after you've developed empathy for his experience.

Your dog is not merely a four-footed person in a fur coat. Your dog is also not a wolf in disguise. Though some proponents of dog psychology emphasize the common ancestry between dog and wolf, your dog is more than a tamed version of any of its wild descendants, be it wolf, jackal, fox, coyote, or dingo. Your dog and these other canine species do share a lot of characteristics, both in physical makeup and behavior, but then humans share a lot of physical and behavioral characteristics with apes, which doesn't mean that we *are* apes (although we do know a guy that we have our suspicions about).

 Wolves and dogs are part of the larger group *Carnivora* (animals that are meat eaters and mostly live by hunting). Though each has a secondary classification specifying its distinctions, all are categorized by biologists as *canines* and members of the same biological family *Canidae*.

How Dogs Came to Be Dogs

If you were to line up all animals in the order in which they were domesticated, you would see that dogs lead the pack. In fact, dogs were brought into human's circle well before they even knew how to grow their own food.

Recent evidence, based on actual fossil substantiation, suggests that dogs were domesticated between 14,000 and 17,000 years ago which is much earlier than sheep (11,000 years ago) or cats (7,000 years ago). Domestication seems to have occurred at different times in different places, with dogs first domesticated in Asia and Russia, and then separately in the Middle East, Europe, and North America.

In the beginning

Dogs and humans naturally formed an everlasting relationship. Both species were hunters that lived and survived through a dependency on a close-knit hierarchical group. The main advantage humans had over canines, in fact, was the ability to learn and reason. In comparison to others in the animal kingdom, canines are intellectually advanced.

Although the wild ancestors of dogs were efficient and daring pack hunters, they also scavenged when the opportunity arose. Scavenging about human campfires proved fruitful and was certainly less dangerous than hunting (especially if you usually hunted some of the larger hoofed animals that could kick, gore, and hurt you).

When the opportunity regularly presented a free meal, wolf packs would locate a nearby den and take advantage of these leftovers.

Such leftovers were often dumped just outside the camp or village in heaps that archeologists call *middens*. For the wolves, middens were a veritable buffet of free food that was being continually renewed.

What sensible wolf would rather hunt when such easy pickings were available? And perfectly happy to oblige, the humans appreciated the value of having another species about that would make use of their waste, thereby keeping their camp both varmint and odor free.

Now perhaps if the relationship had just stopped there, no further domestication would have occurred. However, humans and canines share another important similarity—namely, both are territorial.

Wild canines came to view the area around the camp as their territory. As a result, when a threatening wild animal or a marauding band of strangers came close to the encampment, the canines created a commotion. The noise gave enough warning for the inhabitants of the camp to rally some form of defense, which was especially useful at night. As a result of the vigilance of these canines, the lives of the nearby humans became much safer.

First move, wolves

Domesticating dogs wasn't simply a matter of some Stone Age man's finding a wolf pup and bringing it home where it would be fed, sheltered, and treated like a dog. It may sound surprising, but the first stages of domestication were probably done by the wolves, themselves.

The only wolves that could benefit from discarded food were those that could comfortably coexist with humans. If a particular wolf was aggressive or threatening, he was simply killed by the human residents as a matter of safety. This process began the genetic elimination of the most destructive individuals. Animals that were friendlier and less fearful could stay closer to the settlement. In addition to free meals, such closeness provided them protection from predators that preferred to avoid human contact. When these friendlier canines began to interbreed, they ultimately generated a race of animals that were much more dog-like. In these new animals, the genes for tameness were predominant.

Domestication takes more than simply taming a wild animal. A tame animal allows a human to care for it and accepts human presence and control to some degree. A domesticated animal, however, is genetically modified. Humans exert control over its breeding patterns, which leads to an animal that is drastically different in both physical appearance and behavior than its wild ancestors. Certainly, no one would ever mistake a Pekingese or a bulldog for a grey wolf based on what they look like and how they act.

Don't try to tame a wolf

Research shows that instantaneous domestication is just not possible. Researchers have often tried hand feeding wolf puppies from birth and rearing them with a human family, and the results have been far from satisfactory.

In virtually all the scientific studies, as the wolf cubs matured, they became more wolf-like in their behavior: The previously "tame" cubs began to stalk and hunt farm animals, other house pets, and even children, growing ever more socially dominant and challenging their people for control. Although, as a puppy, such tame wolves can learn basic obedience commands, they stop responding to them when they're adults and begin challenging the authority and status of humans. Many reports tell of such supposedly domesticated wolves attacking and biting their handlers.

What happened next is best explained by some research done by the Russian geneticist Dmitry K. Belyaev, who was trying to re-create the domestication of dogs. He decided not to use wolves because, in many areas, evidence suggests that domestic dogs have interbred with wolves and any dog genes would contaminate the data. Instead, he used another canine species, namely silver foxes. Also, because silver fox fur is prized for making expensive garments, there was the potential for some economic benefits if he could domesticate these foxes and make them easier to raise on a farm.

The only form of genetic manipulation that Belyaev used was similar to what occurred naturally around prehistoric villages. He looked for the animals that were the most tame — the least fearful and aggressive. These animals were the only ones bred for successive generations. The most tame and friendly animals were bred with other tame and friendly animals, and after only six generations, noticeable differences existed between the tame and wild foxes. After 35 generations, this research created animals that looked and acted so much like a dog that they could be sold as pets and live in a human family. If you saw one of them walking down a street, you'd most likely believe that you were looking at some exotic breed of domestic dog.

What really happened to change a fox into a dog? Genetic changes aren't governed by a simple process. Because of the ways that our chromosomes are constructed, it turns out that if you want to change one specific feature genetically, you often end up changing other characteristics as well. That is exactly what happened when researchers began to breed foxes in a way that encouraged the genes associated with friendliness and tameness. It happens that these traits are linked to other genes so that selective breeding for tameness actually changed Belyaev's foxes physically and behaviorally. We now know that the resulting genetic mix actually changed the timing and rate of physical and psychological development in these new "dogs" so that they physically appear more dog-like as well.

Second move, humans

Because the wild canines hanging around the camp (see the preceding section) were more docile and friendly, some clever Stone Age person realized that if these canines would protect whole camps, why couldn't one protect an individual hut? Protection at a personal level. Hmmm. . . .

This development turned out to be a fortunate choice because, in the end, dogs would demonstrate other behaviors that would help keep early man (and his successors) alive, including

✔ Serving as a hunting partner to help find and then flush, run down, and capture game

✔ Assisting in herding flocks of animals

✔ Acting as a warrior or comrade-in-arms

✔ Participating in military actions or acting as an actual guard against attack

✔ Finding items by scent, including food, lost people, and property

Ever hear the expression, "It's a three dog night?" It came from Newfoundland where people would often tuck a dog or two under the covers to stay warm. Their expression was, "It's so cold, you're gonna need three dogs to keep you warm tonight!" But using dogs, whose body temperature is higher than humans, as a biological heat source isn't limited to this region of the world — all over the globe dogs are used to keep us warm.

Perpetual puppies

In truth, what the domestication process accomplished was to arrest dog development in a very puppylike state. In essence, domestic dogs are the Peter Pans of the canine world.

Which wild canines became dogs?

More than 30 different species of wild canines are candidates for the first animal that humans domesticated into a dog, but which species did humans actually take into their homes and make their closest animal companion?

DNA evidence suggests that the first wild canine that was domesticated was the grey wolf, though other types of wolves and also jackals, coyotes, wild dogs, dingoes, and even some varieties of fox got into the mix. As a result, any one dog may have a combination of genes from all these various members of the canine family. Researchers know this fact because domestic dogs can interbreed with any of these species (the exception being some of the common fox species, such as the red fox, which have the wrong number of chromosomes). The offspring from such matings are live, healthy, and fertile, which is usually taken as evidence that they're all the same species or, according to evolutionary theory, at least have a relatively recent common ancestor.

This research suggests that the dog at your side may be some random mix of genes, perhaps 40 percent wolf, 30 percent jackal, and 30 percent coyote, while another breed may be 60 percent wolf, 10 percent jackal, 15 percent arctic fox, and 15 percent dingo. No wonder so many different breeds have so many different physical appearances, behavioral styles, and personalities.

Neoteny refers to certain features normally found only in infants and young juveniles, but which in certain animals persist into adulthood.

If you look closely at Figure 2-1, you may note that many of the physical features of an adult domestic dog resemble those of a wolf puppy more than those of an adult wolf. Figure 2-1 shows common physical differences between wolves and dogs that come about because of neoteny. As you move down the arrow, you move farther away from adult characteristics and toward more puppylike features. Notice that at the very bottom of the figure, you see sort of a super puppylike dog whose features are even more immature than those found at all in wolves — at least beyond a newborn pup.

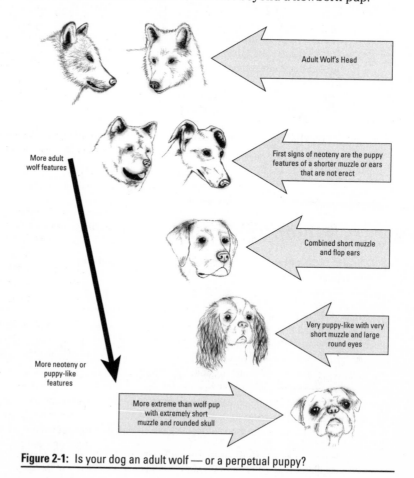

Figure 2-1: Is your dog an adult wolf — or a perpetual puppy?

In terms of relationships with dogs, however, the behavioral aspects of neoteny are most important. Dogs keep a number of puppylike behaviors that wolves lose as they mature. These puppy behaviors are what make dogs fine companions, while the adult canine behavior makes wolves so difficult to tame. Table 2-1 offers an interesting look at what the adult wolf characteristics are like compared to the wolf-puppy characteristics that you see in dogs.

Table 2-1   Dogs Act More Like Wolf Puppies Than Adults

Behavioral Trait or Characteristic	Adult Version Seen in Wolf	Puppylike Version Seen in Dog
Fear of strangers (xenophobia)	Common and not easily changed	Are usually friendly and approach strangers if the dog is brought up with adequate human contact
Acceptance of leadership	Often challenges for leadership and dominance	Usually accepts humans as leaders and challenges are rare
Dependence	Independent	Tend to look to humans or other dogs for guidance
Play behaviors	Very rare in adults and then only shown around puppies	Urge to play continues throughout life
Trainability	Minimal; obedience commands learned when young, often aren't responded to when adult	Much more trainable than wolves; furthermore, obedience training can occur throughout life, and trainability is retained through adulthood
Barking	Rare and brief — only in warning or surprise	Common in many settings, with variations serving as communication
Yelping	Absent except in pups	Common in many settings
Group howling	Common social activity	Less common in dogs, and much like pups, when it does occur, it includes barks and yelps
Muzzle biting and pinning canines to the ground	Common as part of the ritual display of dominance	Rare except in the most wolflike breeds (such as Malamutes)

(continued)

Table 2-1 *(continued)*		
Behavioral Trait or Characteristic	*Adult Version Seen in Wolf*	*Puppylike Version Seen in Dog*
Licking as a greeting	Occurs only occasionally and for short duration	Quite frequent, especially in the most puppylike breeds

Behavioral Traits Bred in the Bone

Though no one seriously worries that their pet dog will stalk, kill, or eat their neighbor, many dogs still get busted for stealing the roast off the countertop, chasing bicycles, or tipping over garbage cans. Case in point: Although dogs have been domesticated, their genetic heritage as hunting predators hasn't completely disappeared. It has, however, as with many other aspects of canine behavior, been modified in both strength and likelihood of occurrence. As in the case of neoteny, different breeds may show more or less of these behavior patterns (see Chapter 6).

In wolves and other wild canine predators, the hunting sequence is complete and balanced, with a fairly fixed sequence of behaviors that occur during a hunt:

1. **Searching**

2. **Stalking**

3. **Chasing**

4. **Biting**

5. **Grabbing**

6. **Killing**

During the process of domestication, and then later by selective breeding, humans have created specific breeds in which some or all of these six steps have been changed in their strength — either made stronger or weaker. Many of these dogs are so driven by their genetically specified hunting instinct that merely enacting the behavior is a sufficient reward in and of itself.

✔ The searching instinct in dogs used for narcotics detection or search-and-rescue work must be strong enough to keep these animals hunting for hours in the hope of finding their quarry. A dog with little searching instinct won't turn out to be a successful detection or search dog.

✔ Chasing is strongest in the sight hounds, such as the grey-hounds, and you can see the power of this instinct in a dog race.

✔ Herding dogs, such as Border Collies, use the stalking and chasing aspects of their hunting instinct to control the movement of sheep and other animals. However, they do not grab, bite, or kill their charges.

✔ Corgis carry the behavior a bit further, all the way up to the biting stage (Step 4) because they regularly nip at animals to get them moving. Again, grabbing and killing is forbidden.

✔ Retrievers are expected to search, chase, and grab prey to bring back to their human hunting companion. However, both the strength of the biting and their killing instincts must be toned down because the dogs must not damage the birds they retrieve.

✔ In scent hounds, such as Beagles or Bloodhounds, the searching component of their hunting instinct has been increased to ensure a dedication to the detection, tracking, and finding of quarry.

✔ Working terriers used to control rats or go after foxes have only a weak searching instinct, but their chasing, biting, and grabbing instincts are all present in full force.

✔ For some terriers, such as the Staffordshire Bull Terriers or the American Pit Bull Terriers, the grabbing instinct has been greatly amplified. These dogs were originally bred to be used in *bull baiting,* a blood sport where they were placed in a pit and required to restrain bulls by biting and hanging onto their noses to bring them to their knees. Obviously, searching or stalking was not needed in these animals, so those behaviors were weakened.

Very often, strong hunting instincts go hand in hand with high levels of energy and intensity in a dog. Lots of play with balls, Frisbees, Kongs, or other toys is a good way to use up that energy while at the same time activating your dog's natural instincts to chase, capture, or retrieve a moving object.

Curing the Dog with an Overdeveloped Chasing Instinct

In some dogs, the chase instinct is so strong that it becomes a problem. Such dogs chase everything: cars, bikes, skaters, joggers. Anything that moves seems like it may be prey and triggers the chasing component of the hunting instinct. Such behaviors aren't only annoying, but may be dangerous, such as when a dog chases a car down the street and gets hit by a car or chases a person on a bicycle, causing them to swerve and fall.

If your dog has a strong hunting instinct, you can take some common-sense precautions to help keep him out of trouble:

- ✔ Always leash your dog when he is walking through fields or yards containing livestock or near playgrounds with active kids. Also, keep your dog on his leash in places where swiftly moving vehicles, bikes, or skateboarders can instigate the chase instinct.

- ✔ Don't allow your dog to stray too far from you when out on walks.

- ✔ Never leave your dog alone with small pets, such as rabbits and hamsters, infants, toddlers, or small children.

 The most general solution to problem chasing behavior involves taking the dog's attention away from the situation producing the behavior and giving him a competing behavior that interferes with the chase. Initially, the dog must learn a command, such as "Stop it!", to halt the chase and turn his attention to you.

How strong is your dog's hunting instinct?

Are you living with a real predator? Here is a simple test that can help you judge the degree of your dog's hunting instinct.

Start by attracting your dog's attention to a favorite toy. Then toss the toy across the room and watch his reaction.

He ignores the toy. Don't bother looking for the wolf in this dog. His hunting instinct is virtually absent.

He runs after the toy, but does not pick it up. The chase instinct is present but little else, which indicates a low overall hunting instinct.

He picks up the toy and carries it all the way, or part of the way, back to you. Chase and grab are present, evidencing a moderate level of hunting instinct.

He pounces on the toy, shaking and chewing it. This reaction is a strong hunting instinct, with all the main behaviors present. Your dog is still a hunter!

Having a dog with a strong hunting instinct (sometimes called *prey drive*) is not necessarily a bad thing. Hunting instincts invade every part of a good working dog's training, whether tracking, obedience, or protection. Many dog sports, such as flyball or Frisbee, depend upon hunting behaviors and instincts.

The choice of the command to stop chasing is important. When a child or a cyclist is being chased by a dog, they naturally respond by shouting "Stop" or "Stop it!" When the dog hears those words from the person that he's distressing, he should understand that he's being told to break off the chase (without any need to teach anything to the person being chased).

1. **Start with the *chase recall.***

    For this training exercise, you need two people and at least two of your dog's favorite retrieving or chasing toys. It may help to start indoors where there are fewer distractions or in a quiet enclosed area outdoors.

2. **Start by having one person hold the dog and then throw the toy past the other person, who is standing about 15 feet away.**

3. **Randomly, say every third or fourth throw, the other person should catch the toy, hide it out of sight, and, as the dog starts to run toward him, the person hiding the toy shouts "Stop it!"**

    Normally, once your dog realizes the toy has disappeared, he looks back at you.

4. **As soon as that happens, show the dog the other toy, throw it in the opposite direction, and run in the direction that you tossed it to make it more likely that the dog will enthusiastically chase it.**

    What the dog is learning is that by responding to "Stop it," by breaking off the chase and looking at you, good things are apt to happen.

5. **Next put the dog on a long leash and take your dog to a place that contains things that he usually chases. When he starts to chase something, yell "Stop it!" and bring him back to you for some praise and an occasional treat.**

    The dog gradually learns to break off chasing on command.

When you can roll a ball away from your dog and he doesn't chase it when you command him not to, then you know that he's under control.

Understanding Your Dog's Sex Life

Dogs are a lot more sexually promiscuous than their wild cousins. Compared to wolves, for example, dogs tend to reach *puberty* (sexual maturity) between 7 and 10 months of age, while wolves are sexually immature until they're 22 to 24 months of age.

Smaller dogs tend to reach puberty earlier than larger dogs.

Dogs are also a lot more promiscuous than wolves. Generally speaking, wolves are relatively monogamous, with the leadership (or *alpha pair*) forming a sexual partnership with another wolf and sticking to that relationship fairly exclusively.

Dogs, on the other hand, are philandering Casanovas. They're polygamous and are willing to accept multiple sexual partners: an attribute deliberately selected during the domestication process, allowing them to breed more freely. (Needless to say, this trait was a good thing in the eyes of humans because it allowed chosen dogs to be readily mated with partners selected not by them but by their breeders.)

Another adjustment that came about through the process of domestication was a change in dogs' breeding cycles. Female wolves come into season and are sexually receptive and fertile only once per year. Female dogs, on the other hand, come into season and can be bred twice a year, with few exceptions — namely dogs that are very close to their "wild ancestors," such as the Basenji, which comes into heat only once a year.

Most people don't know that a male reproductive cycle, at least in wild canines, occurs. Male wolves are able to breed only during a short period each year. Between breeding seasons, the male wolf's testes actually shrink and become unable to produce sperm. Male dogs, however, seem to be randy all the time. They're fertile and willing to mate whenever a receptive female is available.

For the eight or nine days before ovulation and for the next nine days when the female dog is fertile, major hormonal changes occur. Females in heat become more playful around males in general, although they also become more aggressive toward males that they want to reject.

In dog matings, the choice is always up to the female! The most dominant male doesn't always get to mate with the female. If she wants to reject a dominant male, she simply rolls over on her back or side and refuses to stand for his attentions. Less dominant dogs who are rejected, however, get nipped and growled at. The female may also become more aggressive around other females at this time.

Domestic overpopulation crisis

In evolutionary terms, dogs are more than a thousand times more successful than wolves based on their numbers. It is estimated that more than 400 million dogs exist in the world (which is equivalent to the human populations of the United States, Canada, Great Britain, and France combined) compared to a worldwide total of only 400,000 wolves.

One reason for dogs' biological success has to do with their shortened breeding cycles. An average female dog can have her first litter of puppies when she is only 10 to 12 months of age. It takes 58 to 70 days to have the puppies. The average number of pups is usually between 6 and 10. Every female dog can have two batches of puppies each year. Now, if half of these puppies are female, they can also have pups when they grow up. That means that one female dog and her offspring can produce 4,372 puppies in just seven years!

The truth about spaying and neutering

When dogs are brought to veterinarians to be neutered, the scene usually involves a wife agreeing to the procedure while her husband sits with his legs crossed and appears uncomfortable. Though neutering is obviously done to prevent the birth of unwanted puppies, it also affects the behavior of dogs — and almost always for the better.

In male dogs, the dramatic reduction in hormones after neutering reduces their desire to mark their territory with urine, to be aggressive with other male dogs, and to wander from home following sexual scents.

In female dogs, the effects are mostly on the twice yearly changes that occur when she's in heat, such as protective urges for puppies, or puppy substitutes, such as toys. In female dogs, however, the reduction in the hormone progesterone, which normally has calming effects, can exaggerate dominance behaviors in an already dominant female.

The major benefits to society from spaying female dogs is that it reduces the overpopulation of unwanted dogs, who eventually end up living in the streets or euthanized by dog pounds. It also reduces the likelihood that every hopeful male dog in the neighborhood will show up at your doorstep or molest you on your walks when your furry girl goes into heat.

Neutering doesn't affect house guarding, fear biting, and predatory or territorial aggression.

Now or later? The best age to spay or neuter a dog

Science is quite clear that just before puberty is an excellent time to carry out this procedure. Neutering a dog before it reaches sexual maturity freezes its personality in its present puppylike form. If you like your dog's personality at 6 months of age and your veterinarian agrees, there is no reason not to neuter him or her at that age.

Neutering a dog too early (say, at 2 or 3 months) may affect the dog's growth patterns as well as his personality. It appears that certain levels of sex hormones are needed for the dog to grow to its full size and to allow it to develop some aspects of adult behavior. You see, Mom was wrong — it's not too much sex that stunts your growth, but too few sex hormones.

The scent of a female dog in heat can drift over a quarter of a mile and attract male dogs to her vicinity. The nearness of a sexually receptive female can make male dogs quite excited and aggressive toward other male dogs. It can also cause frustration within the confines of a house, causing otherwise sedentary dogs to wander well away from home.

Chapter 3

Communicating with Your Dog

*I*f your dog could talk as you do, she would have a lot to say, both good and bad. But alas, for better or worse, she cannot. Your dog's brain, not her determination or will, limits her ability to use and understand human dialect. However, your dog can, and will, communicate in her own unique language, which we call Doglish.

Doglish consists of many elements, the least of which is vocalization. Unlike people, dogs watch more than they verbalize. In this chapter, we reveal how dogs use their body language (and at times, their voice) to convey mood and meaning.

An English to Doglish Translation

Imagine being a foreigner in a country where you don't understand the language. Though you'd be eager to communicate, all your efforts would be thwarted by the language barrier. Now you know how your dog feels.

You can think of training your dog like teaching English as a second language: The better you know your dog's native tongue, or Doglish, the easier it is to understand her behavior. More physically expressive than verbal, your dog uses her entire body to convey emotion: from the top of her ears to the tip of her tail. The following sections help you translate — by simply observing all elements of her body language — your dog's mood, intentions, and desires.

Seeing Eye to Eye

Group interaction is the highlight of your dog's day, and your eye contact is a sure sign of acknowledgement. Because your dog can't comprehend frustration, your negative eye contact often gets interpreted as confrontational play. The result? Many negative situations are exacerbated.

For example, if jumping gets even a sideward glance, your dog will jump again to get your attention: a repeat performance is guaranteed. If stealing an object ensures a group chase, it will quickly become your household's favorite pastime, at least from your dog's perspective.

Fortunately, you can also use eye contact to encourage and discourage behavior after you realize how your dog processes your visual attention.

Here's what you're saying with your eyes, whether you realize it or not:

- ✔ **Engaging in excessive eye contact:** If you stare at your dog in adoration, frustration, or merely out of habit, you look like a follower. Leaders lead; followers watch. Though quiet time and playful interactions may call for a visual connection, avoid staring at your dog.

  The more you look at your dog, the less she'll look to you. Fortunately, the opposite is true, too: The less you look at your dog, the more she'll look at you. Be a leader, not a follower — give direction, don't take it!

- ✔ **Staring:** Staring conveys a social challenge, so you're best off avoiding this interaction altogether. Use the *brush-off technique:* If you've given her a direction, follow through by positioning her as you ignore her visually. If your dog is intent on this activity, see Chapters 4 and 12.

- ✔ **Staring while ignoring your direction:** One of two things is going on. Your dog may be trying to challenge your authority by staring at you as she deliberately ignores a direction. Don't take this move personally — it's just a test. Staring back, however, will bring you to her level. Instead, brush it off and position her.

  On the other hand, if your dog is young, new to your training routines, or simply insecure, she may stare at you in hopes for more direction. (You can tell the difference by her submissive posture: ears back, body curved down into a submissive pose.)

In this case, position her calmly and consider using the luring technique described in Chapter 12 to boost her confidence.

✔ **Ignoring your dog:** Often, you can extinguish behaviors by simply ignoring them. Because your dog repeats any behavior (negative or positive) that gets your attention, try the opposite: Block facial interaction by folding your arms over your face. Your dog jumps — close shop. She barks for attention — nobody home. This easy-to-replicate response is a sure signal that the behavior gets decidedly less attention, not more.

If your dog becomes persistent, it's a good sign that your efforts are having an affect. Accustomed to your normal reaction, she's determined to get your attention. Some professionals call this an *extinguish burst,* but we like to think of it as a sign of doggone determination!

Look at your dog when she's cooperating, not when you're giving her instruction. For example, when calling your dog, don't stare at her. Either look at the ground (she'll think you've found something interesting) or turn away as you call out her name. Your trailing voice will spark her curiosity.

Dogs, like people, use eye contact to assess and reinforce status and other communications (see Figure 3-1). Table 3-1 identifies your dog's thoughts.

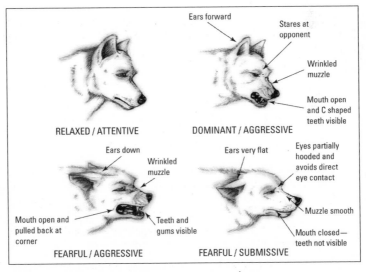

Figure 3-1: Dogs also use eye contact to communicate.

How your dog views your language

Are you convinced that your dog understands you — that she "knows" she's done something wrong? Though her posture may look like an assumption of guilt, most dogs are merely afraid when humans berate them.

Think about it. It's likely that dogs interpret human yelling as barking. When vocalization is loud and excessive, it sounds frantic and bespeaks lunacy, not direction.

Running at a dog is terrifying. Imagine some giant running at you for handling something you thought was the normal way of reacting. Your dog simply doesn't respect material value.

Hitting a dog? Anyone that hits a dog should be ashamed! Poor defenseless creature — the only lesson a hit dog will learn is aggression.

A young or uncivilized dog doesn't know right from wrong any more than a mole would know whether she dug in the wrong dirt pile. Fortunately, you can teach your dog what pleases you and how to contain specific impulses, but first you must learn to speak your dog's language and respect how she thinks.

Table 3-1	Eye Contact Translation	
Visual Eye Signal	*Translation*	*Condition/Emotions*
Direct eye-to-eye stare	"I challenge you!" "Stop that now!" "I'm boss around here, so back off!"	This active dominant/ aggressive signal is given by a confident dog who is having a social confrontation with another.
Eyes turned away to avoid direct eye contact	"I don't want any trouble!" "I accept the fact that you're boss around here."	This is a signal of submission, with some undertones of fear, or appeasement.
Blinking	"Okay, let's see whether we can avoid a challenge." "I'm not really threatening you."	Blinking adds a pacifying gesture to the threat stare and lowers the level of confrontation without giving up much status.

Though you may not have paid much attention to the size and shape of your dog's pupil in the past, this little disc communicates loads. The larger the pupil, the more intense your dog's emotional state and arousal. A widening eye and pronounced round shape heralds a dominant or threatened individual. On the flip side, a small eye or squinting brow signals passivity and submission. Please reference the other components of your dog's posture in this chapter for a more thorough examination of how body postures, eye expressions, and tail positions convey a dog's emotion.

Watch your dog's brow. Any action that you see in the forehead region conveys virtually the same emotional response as in a human's forehead.

Interpreting Vocal Tones and Intonations

Dogs can't process a great deal of chatter. They can't talk, but they can communicate and respond to spoken directions that are given properly. Table 3-2 outlines what our dogs hear when we speak to them.

Table 3-2	Vocalizations Interpreted	
Your Vocalization	*Your Intent*	*Dog Interprets As . . .*
The human yell	Expressing frustration; you're asking the dog to please stop doing what he's doing	Excessive barking, which encourages a bark-fest or instills aggression or fear.
Repeating direction	Wanting a response	Annoying, so dog learns to either ignore direction or only responds to multi-syllable directions.
Repeating direction loudly	Making sure that a dog heard the direction	Demands, so dog learns to listen only to a loud voice and ignores everything else.
Sweet tone	Being nice	Like submissive whining so that the dog automatically assumes that you're nonthreatening and approachable.
Clearly spoken one-word directions	Giving a command	Demanding focus and respect because it sounds like a clear short sound directional bark.

Humans learn primarily through auditory recognition: We listen to directions. Sight is secondary. On the other hand, dogs learn by watching each other instead of by listening or "talking." Teach your dog hand signals for every verbal direction ("Sit," "Wait," "Down," "Come," and so on). See Chapter 12 for a chart on corresponding hand signals.

Making the Most of What You Say

When training your dog, think of your efforts as teaching her the proper responses to each direction. Training doesn't give you license to order your dog about: like a child, your dog is an individual and makes her own decisions. If you're confident and supportive, she'll respect you and take direction with joy. If you frustrate easily and are demanding, she may tune you out and run from you at every opportunity.

Here are a few more tips for communicating with your dog through words:

- ✔ **Think of directions as though you were your dog's teacher or coach.** Say your directions as you would tell a player to move to the left or as though you were telling your class to have a seat or come to the blackboard. Nothing should be spoken in a tone too dramatized or placating.

- ✔ **Give directions once.** If your dog doesn't know the direction, simply position her as if she's not paying attention.

- ✔ **Don't yell at your dog.** If you're frustrated, you may speak sternly, but keep it short. The phrases "That's unacceptable" or "shame on you" spoken and properly timed convey your disapproval without fanfare or confusion.

- ✔ **Don't bother modifying your voice.** Speaking in a deep voice may not come naturally to you, and if you're faking it, you'll likely see your dog giving you the teenage version of an eye roll.

For basic training exercises, see Chapter 12.

Listen to Your Dog's Voice

Though your dog won't "talk" to you in English, you can interpret both her intentions and immediate desires if you know what to listen for. In Table 3-3, we outline the range of sounds dogs make, providing you with a human translation and the moods behind every utterance. Overall, a low pitch indicates a more dominant or threatening stance, whereas a high pitch conveys just the opposite — insecurity and fear.

A dog whose pitch or vocalization varies is emotionally conflicted. Unsure and unable to properly interpret a situation, this dog needs a lot of direction and interference to feel secure. (Refer to Chapters 12 and 14 for more information.)

Table 3-3	Barking Interpreted	
Sound Signal	*Translation*	*Condition/Emotions*
Rapid strings of three or four barks with pauses between (midrange pitch)	"Gather together. I suspect that there may be something that we should look into."	Alerting call suggesting more interest than alarm in the situation.
Rapid repetitive barking (midrange pitch)	"Call the pack!" "Someone is entering our territory!" "We may need to take some action soon."	Basic alarm bark. Dog is aroused, but not anxious. Initiated by nearing of a stranger or occurrence of an unforeseen event. More insistent than the broken bark.
Continuous barking (a bit slower and lower pitch)	"An intruder (or danger) is very close." "Get ready to defend yourself!"	A more worried form of the alarm bark, which senses imminent threat.
Long string of solitary barks with pauses between each one	"I'm lonely and need companionship." "Is there anybody there?"	Usually triggered by social isolation or confinement.
One or two sharp short barks (high or midrange pitch)	"Hello, there!" "I see you."	Typical greeting or acknowledgment signal. Initiated by arrival, or sight, of a familiar person.
Single sharp short bark (lower midrange pitch)	"Stop that!" "Back off!"	Annoyance bark when disturbed from sleep, hair is pulled, and so on.
Single sharp short bark (higher pitched)	"What's this?" "Huh?"	Sign of being surprised or startled.

(continued)

Table 3-3 *(continued)*

Sound Signal	Translation	Condition/Emotions
Single bark, more deliberate in delivery, and not as sharp or short as above (mid to upper midrange pitch)	"Come here!"	Often a learned communication, which tries to signal a human response, such as opening a door, giving food, and so on.
Stutter bark (for example, "ar-Ruff!")	"Let's play."	Usually given with front legs flat on the ground and rear held high as a play invitation.
Rising bark	"This is fun!" "Let's go!"	Excitement bark during play or in anticipation of play, as in the master throwing a ball.
Soft low-pitched bark (seems to come from the chest)	"Back off!" "Beware!"	From a dominant dog who is annoyed or is demanding that others should move away from her.
Growl-bark (low pitched "Grrrrr-Ruff")	"I'm upset, and if you push me, I will fight!" "Pack mates, rally round me for defense!"	A somewhat less dominant sign of annoyance, asking for help from pack members.
Growl-bark (higher midrange pitch)	"You frighten me, but I will defend myself if I have to!"	A worried threat from a dog who isn't confident but will use aggression is pressed.
Undulating growl (pitch rises and falls)	"I'm terrified!" "If you come at me I may fight, but I also may run."	This is the fearful-aggressive sound of a very unsure dog.
Yip-howl ("yip-yip-yip-howl, with the howl prolonged)	"I'm lonely." "Is there anybody there?"	Triggered by isolation from family and other dogs.
Howl (often sonorous and prolonged)	"I'm here!" "This is my territory!" "I hear your howls."	Dogs use this to announce their presence, socialize over a distance, and declare territory. Although it may sound sad to a human, the dog is quite content.

Sound Signal	Translation	Condition/Emotions
Bark-howl ("for example, "Ruff-Ruff-howl")	"I'm worried and alone." "Why doesn't somebody come to be with me?"	A mournful sound of a dog who is lonely and isolated, but fears that nobody will respond to its call.
Baying	"Follow me!" "All together now!" "I've got the scent, so keep close!"	A hunting call from a dog that has the scent, is tracking the quarry, and is assuring that his pack mates are alerted and near for assistance.
Whining that rises in pitch at the end of the sound (may sound like it is mixed with a bit of a yelp)	"I want . . ." "I need . . ."	A request or plea for something. Louder and more frequent means strong emotion behind the plea.
Whining that drops in pitch at the end of the sound or simply fades with no pitch change.	"Come on now! Let's go!"	Usually indicates excitement and anticipation, such as when waiting for food to be served or a ball to be thrown.
Soft whimpering	"I hurt." "I'm really frightened."	A fearful passive/submissive sound that occurs in adults as well as puppies.
Moan-Yodel (for example, "Yowel-wowel-owel-wowel") or Howl-yawn (for example, a breathy "Hooooooo-ah-hooooo")	"I'm excited! Let's do it!" "This is great!"	Pleasure and excitement signals when something the dog likes is about to happen. Each dog will settle on one of these sounds to express this emotion.
Single yelp (may sound like a very short high-pitched bark)	"Ouch!"	A response to sudden, unexpected pain.
Series of yelps	"I'm really scared!" "I'm hurting!" "I'm out of here!" "I surrender!"	An active response to fear and pain, usually given when the dog is running away from a fight or a painful encounter.

(continued)

Table 3-3 *(continued)*

Sound Signal	Translation	Condition/Emotions
Screaming (may sound like a child in pain combined with a prolonged yelp)	"Help! Help!" "I think I'm dying!"	A sign of pain and panic from a dog who is fearful for its life.
Panting	"I'm ready!" "When do we start?" "This is incredible!" "This is intense!" "Is everything okay?"	Simple sound of stress, excitement, or tense anticipation.
Sighs	"I'm content and am going to settle down here awhile." "I'll give up now and simply be depressed."	A simple emotional signal that terminates an action. If the action has been rewarding, it signals contentment. Otherwise, it signals an end of effort.

Reading Body Talk

Your dog is communicating a lot through her body postures and also tuning in to your body language more than you might imagine. Regulating how you hold your posture and recognizing your dog's body language can enable a fluent dialog between the two of you. Figures 3-2 and 3-3 illustrate common dog postures, and Table 3-4 highlights their translation.

Remember that if your dog is shrunk and low, she's feeling insecure or scared. If her weight is pitched forward, she's confident, on alert, or in defense mode. If her head is hung low, but her body is relaxed, the message is loud and clear: "I'm exhausted!"

General rules apply to body posture for both of our species. An alert upright posture conveys confidence. A sudden rise in stature often underscores a need to gain control or dominate others. A fully directed body is often used to issue a threat (although in young or submissive dogs, it's used to elicit play or pity). When normally socialized dogs meet in an open area, they approach at side angles, which is pacifying and conveys a willingness to greet one another and get along.

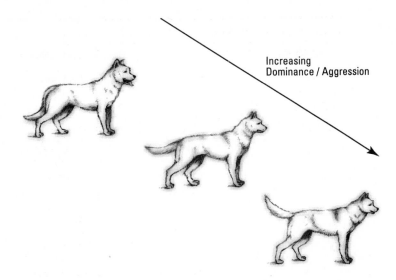

Figure 3-2: Common dog postures showing dominance and aggression.

Increasing
Dominance / Aggression

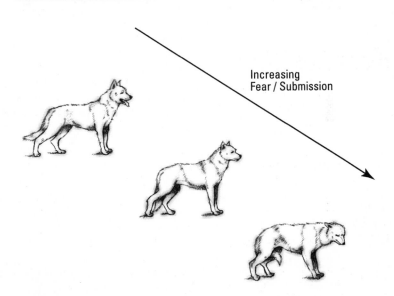

Figure 3-3: Common dog postures showing fear and submission.

Increasing
Fear / Submission

Professionally, we're often asked why an otherwise social dog becomes aggressive on a leash. When strained, the leash pitches an otherwise passive body into a defensive pose. To another dog, this positioning sends an alert and causes defenses to go up. If this dog is also held by leash in a strangle hold, the tension only escalates.

What is the solution? Dogs must be taught to walk on a loose lead behind their people. In this position, they naturally take direction and don't charge. (Chapter 12 covers leash etiquette.)

Table 3-4 can help you decode the meaning behind every posture.

Table 3-4	Posture in Translation	
Visual Signal	*Translation*	*Condition/Emotions*
Stiff-legged, upright, posture or slow stiff-legged movement forward	"I'm in charge around here!" "Are you challenging me?"	An active aggressive signal from a dominant dog that is willing to assert his leadership.
Body slightly sloped forward, feet braced	"I accept your challenge and am ready to fight!"	This signal is usually a response to a threat, or the response to another dog's failure to back down from a threat. It's a signal that active aggression is imminent.
Hair bristles on the shoulders and down the back	"I've had it with you! Take your pick, give it up now, fight or back off!	This is a sign of rising defensive feelings, either prompted by arousal, aggression, or extreme fear. In a confident, dominant dog, it may indicate that an attack may occur at any moment.
Hair bristles only on the shoulders	"You're making me nervous! Don't push me into a fight."	This is often the sign of fearful aggression from a dog that is threatened but feels that it may be forced to fight.
Dog lowers its body or cringes, while looking up	"Let's not argue." "I submit to you." "You can be in charge."	An active appeasement gesture that signals submission to a more dominant dog.
Muzzle-nudge	"You're my leader. Please acknowledge me." "I want . . ."	A request for social attention that can also be used to ask for things.

Visual Signal	Translation	Condition/Emotions
Dog sits when approached by another, allowing itself to be sniffed	"We're nearly equal in status, so let's be peaceful and civil around each other."	A small pacifying gesture by a usually dominant dog who is only slightly outranked by another.
Dog rolls on side or exposes underside and completely breaks off eye contact	"I am just a lowly beast that accepts your full authority and am no threat at all."	This is passive submission and is the dog equivalent of groveling.
Standing over another dog who may be lying down. Head over back or shoulders of another dog. Paw over or on another dog	"I am bigger, taller, stronger, and really the leader around here."	All are mild active assertions of social dominance and social status.
Shoulder bump	"I am dominant over you, and you'll give way to me when I come near."	A more vigorous assertion of relative social dominance. A milder version of this same signal is leaning.
Dog turns its back or side toward another animal	"I accept that you're more dominant than me, but I can still take care of myself."	This is a mild admission of slightly lower social rank by a confident dog, without any fear or distress. If a larger social gap exists, she may turn her hindquarters toward the dominant dog.
When threatened by another dog, dog sniffs the ground or digs at something; stares at horizon; or scratches itself	"I don't see you threatening me and am not going to respond to it, so calm down."	These are pacifying or calming signals based upon distraction. They signal an absence of hostility but no submission.
Dog sits with one front paw slightly raised	"I'm a bit anxious, uneasy, and concerned."	A sign of insecurity and mild stress.

(continued)

Table 3-4 *(continued)*

Visual Signal	Translation	Condition/Emotions
Dog rolls on its back and rubs its shoulders on the ground (sometimes associated with nose rubbing)	"I'm happy and all is well."	A ritual that often occurs after something pleasant has happened, hence sometimes called a *contentment roll.*
Dog crouches with front legs extended, rear body and tail up	"Let's play!" "Oops! I didn't mean to frighten you. This is all in fun!"	Standard play invitation, which may also be used to reassure another dog that rough or threatening behavior wasn't intended to be taken seriously.

The ups and downs of the ears

Focus on your dog's ears. Whether floppy or erect, their various poses provide insight into her focus and intention, especially when looked at in relation to other postures, positions, and vocalizations. Table 3-5 highlights the meaning behind the many ways dogs use their ears to communicate.

Table 3-5   Ear Signals

Visual Signal	Translation	Condition/Emotions
Ears erect or slightly forward	"What's that?"	Sign of attention.
Ears definitely forward (combined with bared teeth and wrinkled nose)	"Consider your next actions carefully —I'm ready to fight!"	This is the active aggressive challenge of a dominant and confident dog.
Ears pulled back flat against the head (combined with bared teeth and wrinkled forehead)	"I'm frightened, but I will protect myself if I you appear to be trying to hurt me."	This is a fearfully aggressive signal from a non-dominant dog who feels threatened.
Ears pulled back against the head (teeth not visible, forehead smooth, body held low)	"I accept you as my strong leader." "I know you won't hurt me because I'm no threat."	An active pacifying and submissive signal.

Visual Signal	Translation	Condition/Emotions
Ears pulled back against the head (tail held high, blinking eyes, and relaxed open mouth)	"Hello there. We can have fun together."	A friendly gesture which is often followed by mutual sniffing or an invitation to play.
Ears pulled slightly back to give the impression of a slightly splayed or sideward spread of the ears	"I'm suspicious about what's going on." "I don't like this and may fight or run."	A sign of tension or anxiety about the situation that is unfolding. This may quickly turn either into aggression or fear depending upon what happens.
Ears flickering, usually slightly forward and then a moment or so later slightly back or downward	"I'm just looking this situation over, so don't take offence."	A submissive and pacifying signal from a dog who is undecided and perhaps a bit apprehensive.

Facial signals

Though facial signals may vary slightly based on coinciding gestures or postures, Table 3-6 outlines the scope of emotions that can be predicted when the facial cues are watched.

As a general rule, the more teeth that show when a dog is growling, the greater the threat. When a dog's mouth is open, you should look at the shape of the opening: A "C" shape is dominant, whereas drawn lips, with the rear corners pulled back, gestures submission or fear.

Table 3-6	Reading a Dog's Face	
Visual Signal	Translation	Condition/Emotions
Mouth relaxed and slightly open (tongue may be visible or even slightly draped over the lower teeth)	"I'm happy and relaxed."	Closest dogs come to a human smile.
Mouth closed (no tongue or teeth visible, dog looks in a particular direction, leaning slightly forward)	"This is interesting." "I wonder what's going on."	Sign of attention or interest.

(continued)

Table 3-6 *(continued)*

Visual Signal	Translation	Condition/Emotions
Lips curled to expose some teeth (mouth still mostly closed)	"Go away! You're bothering me!"	First sign of annoyance, menace or threat. May be accompanied by a low, rumbling growl.
Lips curled up to show major teeth, some wrinkling of the area above the nose, mouth partly open	"If you press me, or do anything that I may interpret as a threat, I will fight."	Active aggressive response, which may be motivated either by a challenge to social dominance or by fear.
Lips curled up to expose all the teeth and the gums above the front teeth, visible wrinkles above the nose	"Back off now — or else!"	High level of active aggression, with a high likelihood that failure to give the dog additional space will result in an attack.
Yawns	"I'm a bit tense right now."	Simple sign of stress or anxiety. It may also be used to diffuse a threat.
Licking the face of a person or dog	"I am your servant and friend and recognize your authority." "I'm hungry. Do you have a snack?"	A pacifying gesture of active submissiveness, acknowledging the dominance of another. As a holdover from puppyhood, this is also a food request.
Licking the air	"I bow before your authority and hope you won't hurt me."	An extreme pacifying gesture showing fearful submissiveness.

Tail talk

When reading your dog's tail, you must interpret all motions based on her tail's normal resting pose. A Greyhound, for example, carries her tail low when she's relaxed, as compared to a Malamute, whose tail is upright and curled when she's calm. With that said, generally a higher tail indicates a dominant attitude, whereas a low tail communicates submission or fear (see Figure 3-4).

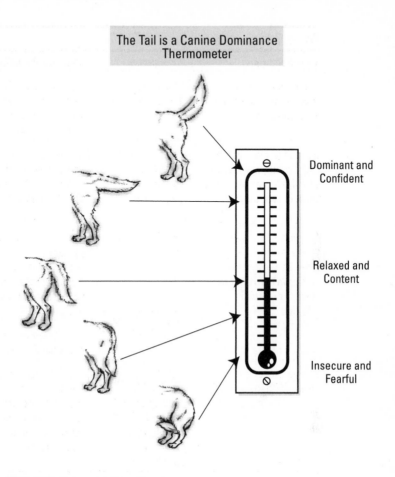

Figure 3-4: Common tail positions.

Also consider the rate of the wag, because faster motion evidences a higher level of arousal. The exception to this rule? A trembling tail, which actually looks as though it's vibrating. This tail isn't "wagging" so much as its signaling intense emotion and excitement.

A wagging tail doesn't always invite interaction, nor is it always a gesture of good will. Dogs use their tails (see Table 3-7) in combination with the many other body signals outlined in this chapter to convey various "moods," from pleasure to emotional agitation.

Table 3-7	Tail Talk	
Visual Signal	*Translation*	*Condition/Emotions*
Broad tail wag that doesn't involve the hips or a lowered body posture	"I like you." "Let's be friends."	A casual friendly gesture, not involving any social dominance. It may also be seen during play.
Broad tail wag with wide swings that actually pull the hips from side to side, perhaps with lowered hind quarters	"You're my pack leader, and I'll follow you anywhere!"	A sign of respect and mild submission for the person or dog to which it's directed. The dog doesn't feel threatened, but acknowledges its lower rank and its confidence that it will be accepted.
Slow tail wag with tail at a moderate to low position	"I don't quite understand this." "I'm trying to get the message."	A sign of indecision or confusion about what's going on or what is expected of her.
A crick or sharp bend in the tail	"If I have to, I will show you who is boss around here!"	Adds both dominance and imminent threat to any other tail signal or position.
Slight tail wag, each swing only of small size	"You like me, don't you?" "I'm here."	A somewhat tentative submissive signal, which can be added to most tail positions.

Chapter 4

Seeing Life from Your Dog's Perspective

*Y*our dog, regardless of his size or coat color, is hard-wired to act like . . . well, like a dog. He isn't a kitten, bunny, guinea pig, or child. His behavior is unique and predictable: He'll walk on four legs, sleep at night, and seek affection. These universal behaviors can give you a leg up in communicating with and training him.

Our goal in this chapter is to help you recognize your dog's behavior patterns, understand his communication style, and adjust your approach to teaching him how to behave. Here, you discover how to talk "dog" and look at your current situation from his point of view. This chapter also helps you get a handle on everyday life immediately, from civilizing your dog's manners to de-escalating mismanaged behaviors, such as hyperactivity, assertiveness, fear, and impulsivity.

Like Person, Like Dog (Similarities and Differences)

Dogs and people have many things in common. Both species define their positions based on social interactions, each likes to learn and know things, and both need to identify their surroundings in order to feel safe and in control.

Your dog also strives to mirror you; if you're going out for a walk, he wants to go. If food is being prepared, your dog wants a piece of that action as well. When someone visits, your dog needs a formal introduction. If your dog doesn't handle these situations well at this point, don't despair.

Although many similarities exist between dogs and people, differences occur, too — chiefly that children mature into adulthood, while dogs stay very puppy-like and devoted throughout their lives. Though a puppy matures during his first two years, he won't voluntarily leave the home or charge your credit card. A more realistic example is that most dogs never learn to share objects unless they're taught to do so, and many, in fact, guard possessions from even the most beloved family member (see Chapter 15). Though it's tempting for you to be angry at your dog for this and other "disobedient" behaviors, once you understand how he thinks, you'll have an enlightened view and be more open to performing the exercises necessary to remedy all of your frustrations.

Your Dog Needs Affection

Dogs like to be praised, and they need feedback and encouragement. Too many dogs live in homes where negative feedback is their bread and butter, a pattern that leaves many manic from confusion or reactionary out of sheer frustration. Poor dogs! Imagine a loved one berating you — "This meal is awful," "That was a bad toss," "You're a lousy spouse, parent, or child . . . ."

We'd love to have a nickel for every time we've heard the exclamation, "But he knows he's wrong!" Dogs simply can't perceive interaction in the way another human would. When a dog looks fearful, it's because he is, in fact, afraid. We want to offer you a better, more cheerful approach to both training your dog and problem solving, one that leaves you and your dog feeling exhilarated and connected, not drained.

Your dog needs a lot of organized structure and positive reinforcement in the form of rewards and incentives, which we discuss in this chapter and throughout the book. If the most common thing that you're saying to your dog is "No," your dog can't possibly understand what he can do to make you happy. In Chapter 15, we talk about the Family Cooperation System, also known as nothing in life is free. Each time you offer your dog praise, toys, or attention, simply ask him to sit. In essence, you're teaching him to say please.

If you're feeling a little guilty that you haven't been offering a lot of positive reinforcement these days, there's no better time than the present to change! Praise your dog every chance you get! "Good catch" (don't worry if he doesn't fetch quite yet), "Good boy" (when he's chewing his toy), "Nice dog" (when he's relaxing). Your positive outlook will motivate his cooperation.

Make an Encouragement Chart, shown in Table 4-1, and share it with family and friends. Teach your dog what he can do to please you, no matter how insignificant it may seem.

Table 4-1	Sample Encouragement Chart
Praise Your Dog for Anything He Does Right	
❏	Resting (not in a deep sleep)
❏	Chewing a bone
❏	Playing with a dog toy
❏	Not chasing the cat
❏	Eating
❏	Sitting instead of jumping
❏	Going potty
❏	Sitting on the first command
❏	Licking instead of biting
❏	*(Teach him things to earn your affection)*

Though it's hard to always act positively when you're at your wit's end, please fake it for awhile. Your dog would rather have positive attention for behaving well than negative attention for behaving poorly. If you don't highlight his strengths, however, he'll default to being naughty, because any attention is better than none at all.

Group identity

Dogs so completely identify with their group or "family," that few would even know how to cope if left on their own. Ask various breeds what they'd do if they were suddenly put out on the street and, although you may get different answers, none would much enjoy their independence:

✔ **Golden Retriever:** Would scramble about for the nearest ball or stick and drop it eagerly at the nearest foot

Pet status and isolation

Only recently have people had the expectation that dogs adjust to long periods of alone time. For most of the 20th century, no leash laws existed — hard to imagine, but true. Dogs were left out on the back porch during the day and often left to run free at night.

Long ago, most dogs weren't even considered pets. They were domesticated and bred to aid man in tasks that clearly advanced society, from herding sheep, to guarding property and towns, to hauling supplies in wagons or sleds.

The evolution of dogs as "pets" has come with the expectation that they put their working genes to rest (which isn't entirely possible), as well as a growing awareness of their psychological and emotional needs. For more information on breed-specific information, see Chapter 6.

- **Border Collie:** Would herd all the people within sight into a tight circle

- **Beagle:** Would sniff merrily through a crowd until someone started to follow

- **Jack Russell:** Would bark fanatically at a mysterious noise in the corner of a building until a crowd gathered

- **Cavalier King Charles Spaniel:** Would head for the nearest lap

- **Labrador Retriever:** Would race into the nearest restaurant, lie under the table, and wait eagerly for scraps to fall

In short, no dog — not yours, not anyone's — enjoys solitude. As a species, dogs glean their identity through interaction. Call them "groupies," or put it in more scientific terms, but either way, limit the amount of time your dog must spend alone.

Some breeds are more sedentary than others, while certain breeds are bred to work independently. If your schedule demands time away, see Chapter 6 to find out which breeds will be more apt to flow with periods of solitude and what you can do to ease their isolation.

Using reflection and praise to influence behavior

Imagine your dog's level of energy on a scale from 1–10, where 1 equals sleep and 10 is an excessively hyper, fearful, or aggressive response. Now, further split the scale into two zones: the contained happy zone (1–7) and the detached, chaotic zone (8–10). Your goal in understanding and training your dog is to help him learn to function with enough presence of mind to live with you predictably and comfortably — in other words, to operate in the 1–7 zone.

Do you suspect that your dog is operating in the 8–10 zone all too often — for example, when the doorbell rings, the kids come home, or just when you're sitting down to relax in front of the television?

Of course, you'd like your dog to simply reflect your energy level: that he rest when you're relaxed, accompany you when you go outside to walk or play with him, and otherwise entertain himself when you're occupied. Though this level of attention is asking a lot of an untrained dog, once educated, a dog naturally mirrors your timetable.

In Chapter 13, we discuss specific responses to discourage problem behavior, but for now, suffice it to say, whatever behaviors you pay attention to will tend to be repeated. If your dog responds to a direction or chews a toy and you praise him for that, he'll remember. If your dog's acting wild or repeating mischief and your frustration leaks out, he'll respond to negative attention just as easily and repeat the very behaviors that are driving you crazy.

How Hierarchy Differs from Democracy

Your dog looks to you and your family in much the same way he would seek inclusion in a group of dogs. This truth places dogs, on a whole, above other species in their loyalty and focus for our direction. Defining his life's orientation to your group activity, he focuses on his position within your family, and yet reflects his position in hierarchical terms, not as a democracy. This defining difference between our two species must be fully embraced. Democracy is an ineffective model when civilizing a dog.

Choose your role now! Either be the leader of the group and give your dog direction, or he will — out of his desire to keep the family or pack system working — take over the leadership role and train you.

In a group, someone must take charge and make the important decisions.

A hierarchal analogy, in human terms, is team play. At the top is a single captain or co-captains, and then below them is a hierarchy of players, which is based on their seniority, strength, and potential. The captain's role is to organize the space and activity of each player to highlight his talents. In turn, the players strive to get along and work together towards a collective goal.

It's in their genes

Most people wouldn't ignore a toddler who looked at them with a confused expression, but those same people may overlook a similar expression coming from their dog. Because dogs are genetically programmed, especially when young, to look for direction, the opportunity to capitalize on their devotion is in the human's hands. When ignored, a dog often repeats whatever behavior got him attention previously, creating a hard-to-break cycle.

Teach your dog three directions that you can use whenever he looks to you for direction:

- ✔ Get your ball.
- ✔ Let's find your bone!
- ✔ Sit/settle down.

If your dog hasn't learned these directions, look carefully at the upcoming "Giving direction" section and then direct him to the object or into position. Praise his cooperation, even as you're helping him respond appropriately.

When your dog stares at you, he is often looking for guidance.

Constant adoration makes your dog restless. Acting out soon follows, often in the form of house-soiling, destructive chewing, or stealing objects.

A better approach is to teach your dog the instructions in the upcoming "giving direction" section, so that you can give him guidance when he looks for it.

If your puppy has been assertive from the get-go, he's likely to have a more dominate, leadership-oriented personality. This puppy needs a consistent take-charge approach. If you feel that you're losing the training battle, practice the exercises in Chapter 12, getting a professional to help you, if required.

There is a leader born to every litter

In each litter of puppies, a leader is born — one who is easily identified by 8 weeks of age. This puppy is demanding at meal times, assertive when playing, and bossy. In a human family, this puppy exhibits this same attitude, quickly determining just who he can boss around. If you suspect that you may have a strong personality type under your roof, ask yourself the questions listed in the following table and check the appropriate response.

Behavior	From the moment I brought my puppy home	My dog developed these behaviors	This does not accurately describe my dog
Plays rough, actively; insistently pawing at or trying to climb on top of people			
Stands in the doorway; blocks the stairs			
Excitable around new people or reacts negatively to changes in normal routine			
Demands attention; won't share toys; guards objects or food dish			
When socializing with other dogs, continually tries to climb on their back or mount them			

If your dog developed these traits during his adolescence or later, he has taken the leadership role only because you did not. So you need to change your behaviors to regain your status, and although you need to be consistent, this dog will be grateful that you're taking over this demanding job. Being a leader is hard work!

Asserting benevolent authority

If you suspect that your dog is organizing your routines, you'll need to reorganize the hierarchy. Unless you want to be *dog trained,* the first step in the process is deciding that you want to do it and reassuring yourself that you can do it. Attitude is everything. If you feel yourself floundering, see whether you can find the answer to your issues by checking for help in this book's index or calling in a professional to help.

Your dog is pre-programmed to accept direction, so in many ways you're already ahead of the game.

Defining your space

Dogs define their role based on social and spatial definition. If you walk around, step over, or move out of your dog's way, your message is loud and clear: Your mindful avoidance communicates your respect for your dog's authority. Stop right there and try the following exercises:

- ✔ **Teach your dog "Excuse me."** Your dog identifies your relationship based on spatial deference: Either you move out of his way, or he moves out of yours. Teach him to respect your space immediately! If he's in your way, say "Excuse me" and nudge him gently with your foot until he moves. If he cuts in front of you, walk straight into him until he shifts out of your way. Is he leaning against you excessively or inappropriately? Say "Excuse me" and use your leg to push him off until he respects your personal space.

- ✔ **Condition your dog to lie on the sidelines.** Have you got a dog who always positions himself underfoot? Aside from being dangerous, his intrusion is a cry for attention. Provide him with a proper area in each room of your house and identify it with bedding and toys. If he's reluctant to stay there, check out the upcoming "Assign play stations in each room" section.

The two preceding exercises are important lessons in civility, and even more essential if you're living with a problem dog (see Part IV).

If you ask your dog to move and he growls at you, stop. This is a sign that it's time to refer to Chapter 15 on aggressive problems to see what you can do or to go to the phone immediately and call for professional help. Actively aggressive behaviors require expertise that may go beyond the scope of this book.

Don't be afraid to use a leash

We hear it all the time . . . .

"I want my dog to join me, but he's so unmanageable. We try, but after a short bit, we have no choice but to shut him away by himself again. If he'd learn to behave, he'd get a lot more freedom."

If the thought of letting your dog loose leaves you shaking in your shoes, you've probably gotten yourself caught in a vicious cycle. You may not realize that, ironically, it's the prolonged periods of isolation that result in your dog's impulsivity and mischief.

Here's one solution: Use your leash indoors. Find an appropriate training collar (see Chapter 11) and use a collar and leash ensemble to lead him through your home. Use the directions in this chapter to teach him his manners and socialize him to each room.

The leash is not a cruel devise; think of it as synonymous with holding a child's hand. What's cruel and confusing is forced isolation. Once your dog is cooperating, let him drag the leash behind him so that you can easily grab it if needed for additional control. When you're sure his manners have improved and he's acting civilly, you can dispense with the leash — but not before you're certain that it's no longer needed.

Encourage all your friends and family to take part in your efforts to civilize your dog. If your dog ignores any of them, step in to reinforce their directions. Your dog must learn to respect everyone.

Giving direction

Everyone knows that a small toddler needs lots of direction, interaction, and patience. Dogs do, too. The key difference is that children are programmed to communicate with words, whereas dogs are not, although they can learn to respond to sound cues and hand signals (see Figure 4-1). You need to teach your dog the proper response for a series of everyday directional cues. Here are six cues to get you and your dog started:

✔ **Name:** Help your dog create a positive association to his name. Call out your dog's name whenever you come home or to highlight a positive moment, such as when you're offering a treat, loving pats, or playtime with a favorite toy.

Don't call your dog for unpleasant activities, such as isolation or unwanted grooming. If you do, he just might hear "Come" and think run! If "Come" has a reverse effect, stop using it. Use a treat cup and also check out the other training techniques in Chapter 12. Of course, you could just keep your dog on leash.

Call your dog as you're walking away from him or when you're hidden from sight to peak his interest. Shake a cup of treats while saying his name to encourage his enthusiasm for listening and following you. Though initially he'll respond for the food, you'll eventually condition a positive cooperative habit. Ultimately, you can phase out food treats and replace them with praise and petting.

✔ **Ball and/or toy:** Often during the day, your dog may look to you for ideas. If you say nothing, his restlessness may lead to mischief. Instead, teach him these words. Each time you play with him or give him a chew, repeat a word like "Toy" or "Bone."

✔ **Sit, please:** A dog who sits politely is, in essence, saying please. Teach your dog to sit by either enticing him with a treat held near his nose and moved back over his head or by placing pressure on his waist muscles with your thumb and forefinger as you put gentle upward pressure under his chin.

Teach your dog that he must sit before rewards, food, or attention.

✔ **Wait/okay:** This direction tells your dog to freeze and wait for your next cue. Use it at thresholds and curbs or when entering or exiting your home, a building, or your car. To teach it, either control your dog on a leash or hold him steady, pulling back as you say "Wait," and then releasing him with "Okay."

✔ **Follow me:** This direction simply reminds your dog that you're the leader and will make all the directional decisions for both of you. More than a dominance gesture, your leadership efforts convey your willingness to be his guardian and protector. If your dog's taken this role, use a leash and a proper training collar to manage him (see Chapter 11). Also consider using treats, a treat cup, or a clicker to inspire his cooperation (see Chapter 11).

✔ **Settle down:** This direction encourages your dog to relax. As often as possible, direct your dog to a mat or comfortable rug/bed and provide him with a displacement activity, such as a bone or toy, which will distract him and keep him from idly wandering about. You can use it both in your home or when traveling about. Whether your dog is restless at your dinner hour or quiet time, or you're waiting your turn at the veterinarian, this familiar direction will give your dog a sense of calm.

Figure 4-1: Basic directions can help you organize your day. Encourage your dog to sit before giving him anything pleasant. Always lead your dog through the door. He should not leave the home "den" without your accompaniment. Teach your dog to follow your lead.

Establishing your social status

Your dog is programmed to accept you and your family as if they were other dogs. He depends on the social structure you create to make him feel connected and safe. If you communicate direction to him and provide for his needs with consistency, he will look to you to interpret other situations as well. If your dog is unclear as to what you want or you get frustrated with him often, he may perceive you as a moody adolescent dog instead of a leader. Even worse, your dog may decide that you're an unreliable or incompetent leader, which is bound to make him insecure and frustrate him. When this happens, later behavior problems are virtually guaranteed.

Was that out of spite?

Do you think your dog behaves poorly out of spite? Think again. Although the authors agree that dogs repeat behavior that get them attention (good or bad) and often act out of anxiety when left alone, dogs don't react out of spite.

Dogs aren't dishonest or mean. The conclusion that your dog is vengeful will do nothing for your relationship — such thoughts only result in bad energy in the home. Ask not what your dog is doing wrong, but what you may not be doing right.

Practice the exercises in the following sections to reestablish your social status.

Assign play stations in each room

Your home is nothing more then a big den to your dog. How you establish routines indoors affects your relationship more than any activities or training programs you're involved in.

Think of providing your dog with a play station like offering a guest in your home a chair. Your dog doesn't know where to go in your house until you tell him; when you do, he'll feel welcome, calm, and included. If you don't, he'll likely misbehave, which provokes your negative attention. Because your negative reaction can be interpreted as a controlled or restrained confrontation, your dog may think his freedom is an invitation to play!

Here's how to give your dog a play station:

1. **Decide the rooms your dog will be welcome in.**

   If you have to isolate him now but want him to share, say, the whole house or the downstairs area, take strides immediately toward this goal.

2. **Go into each room and select a spot on the floor (or a section of a chair/sofa) for your dog to call his own.**

   For our purposes, we call this area a *play station*.

3. **Identify that location with a rug, a flat mat, or bedding, and place a few of your dog's favorite bones or toys on it.**

4. **Introduce your dog to his special area.**

   Bring him into the room on a leash if he's too fidgety and say "Settle down" (see the earlier "Giving direction" section) as you lead him to his play station. Sit with him and encourage him to focus on his things. Give him lots of attention and feed him treats.

Bring your dog with you to these places often. If he won't stay at his play station, make sure that he's had a good romp and time to potty and then hold him still with a leash or secure a leash to something immovable.

Restraint at the door

From your dog's perspective, your main door is the mouth of his den. Whoever orchestrates comings and goings runs the show. If your dog barges through or reacts inappropriately when visitors arrive, he'll assume he's in charge.

In essence, you may be paying the mortgage or rent on a very elaborate dog house! Changing this situation is easy enough, but to do so, consistency is a must:

1. **Teach your dog to follow you in and out of the door.**

   Initially, manage him on a leash and teach him to properly respond to the directions "Wait" and then "Okay." (See the earlier "Giving direction" section.)

2. **Teach your dog a proper greeting ritual, remembering that good manners start at home.**

   Ignore your dog if he behaves in an overexcited or inappropriate manner when you or other family members arrive. (For more tips on responding to jumping or nipping, see Chapter 13.) If he's been confined alone in a crate, pen, or room, don't speak to him until he's calmed down or is chewing on a toy. After he's calmed down considerably, brace him as you greet him (see Figure 4-2), with your thumb clipped over the underside of his collar to prevent him from jumping up.

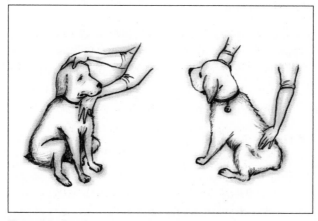

Figure 4-2: Bracing a dog during greetings.

To create a greeting station, choose a location 6–15 feet from the door. This location is the place where you'll send your dog before opening the door when company arrives. Teach your dog the term "Go back" ahead of time, leading him to the area and telling him to "Wait" while you open and shut the door.

If your dog doesn't stay put when no one is present, he won't sit still when they are. In this case, affix a leash on an immovable object. When you send him back from the door, secure him on the leash. Practice doing this when no one is there, then with your family, and each time someone calls. (If your dog is distractingly rowdy, aggressive, or fearful, please refer to Part IV.) Release your dog after you've welcomed the visitor and only when he's calmed down.

The goal is that your dog mirror and mimic your response to newcomers. Your dog isn't the leader, you are. You can shape his responses by establishing your authority in this way.

Reinforcing Good Manners

Teaching your dog new behavior shouldn't be an exercise confined to 15-minute periods throughout the day. As you teach your dog new words, implement them into your daily routine as soon as possible, and come up with a list of constants — directions that highlight everyday activities, such as going "Upstairs," to the "Car," or out for a "Walk."

Identifiable words add a punch of excitement to your dog's day, similar to being in a foreign country and finding an individual who speaks your language. Good manners flow from calm, consistent directions.

To reinforce good manners, don't forget to

- ✔ **Follow through.** If you give a direction, reinforce it. Praise your dog for cooperating or position him if he ignores you.

- ✔ **Give directions once.** If you repeat yourself, your dog will catch on and will not respond immediately.

- ✔ **Keep your expectations in check.** Just because your dog behaves well with you doesn't mean he'll mind his manners when the doorbell rings or you visit family. Keep a leash on your dog if necessary and/or reinforce all your directions immediately.

Part II

Embracing Your Dog's Identity

"Like a lot of Beagles, he's pretty domesticated, but there's still some of the hunter in him."

In this part . . .

*B*eyond your simple communication and empathetic effort lies something that you can't touch: your dog's instinctive, and innate, personality encoded at birth. Once her temperament — whether shy, comic, or bold — is defined (at 7 weeks of age), you can modify it, but not extinguish it. In this part, we help you gauge your expectations and modify your mannerisms to improve your daily interactions, providing handy worksheets and visual identification charts to help you recognize what your dog is trying to say or do, and to give you the means to modify your dog's behavior.

Chapter 5

Identifying Your Dog's Individuality

*L*ike snowflakes and paw prints, every dog is unique. Their actions and responses are what make up their personality. Broken down, a dog's personality is made up of three components that blend together to create the individual: genetic drives and instinctive traits, emotional responses, and behavioral tendencies.

As you teach your dog and expose her to various settings and situations, you can predict her responses based on her personality. For example, if you have a shy dog, you don't need a crystal ball to foresee her response when a stranger comes to call. On the other hand, if your dog is assertive and outgoing, you can easily anticipate her reaction if you were to bring her to a picnic. Identifying your dog's personality can help you in your training endeavors, from the directions you teach to how you can extinguish undesirable behaviors.

Pet dogs don't exist alone, nor can they just "pick up" information from human language naturally. The first step in any humane endeavor to live happily with your dog must be to identify her personality and then create a training regimen that empathizes with her learning style and abilities.

Identifying Your Dog's Personality

The various kennel clubs around the world divide their recognized dog breeds into groups. The American Kennel Club has seven such divisions, which group dogs according to function. The Hound group, for example, links dogs who are designed to hunt prey. Though you can reference more information on each breed in Chapter 6, simply being aware of the various tasks your dog was bred to fulfill provides invaluable information about his genetic drives and instinctive traits.

Although breed characteristics are a matter of genetics, individual dogs within any given breed can have vastly different personality traits, from shy to laid-back to bossy. For example, if you're observing a litter of cairn terriers, you can predict that each puppy would be alert to sounds and love to dig. However, the shy puppy would be more responsive to your interference than would the self-assured one.

Spaniels are from Venus, and terriers are from Mars

At the end of the day, the real foundation for your dog's personality is encoded in his genes. In essence, his personality won't vary much over his lifetime. This knowledge can give you a pretty good idea of how your dog will act in many different situations and does allow you greater flexibility to influence his behavior. For example, if you have an active dog that is overstimulated in social settings, simply hoping he'll calm down is not an effective training technique. Exercising him a few hours before the event, teaching him to fetch, and arriving with a favorite toy, however, are effective ways to encourage a high-energy dog's cooperation.

As far as breed-specific tendencies go, recognizing the passions and limitations of your dog's breed or mix of breeds also helps you select appropriate games, displacement activities to distract him so that he stops an unwanted behavior (which may include offering chew toys and such), and training exercises patterned to be consistent with his predispositions.

Compare two breeds: a golden retriever and a German Shepherd. Retrievers are a highly sociable breed, with few serious thoughts save, "Could you please just toss the ball one more time — pleeaaassse." German Shepherds, on the other hand, are dignified, territorially proud, and mindful of other's social intent. Mix these two breeds, and you'll notice their difference immediately. Whereas the German Shepherd will be reserved and spatially respectful, the retriever will throw herself on everyone just to be acknowledged.

The Puppy Personality Test

The following personality form is a generic test generally offered to puppies between the ages of 7 weeks and 6 months of age. You can also apply the test to older dogs, with appropriate modifications, to take into account the dog's size or potential for being snappish or fidgety.

Each part of the test focuses on specific issues that, when examined as a whole, outline personality characteristics that make a certain breed or individual puppy ideal for a particular person's interest. For example, the traits that make a good guard or protection dog aren't those that would make for a good pet in a house full of young children.

Puppy personality tests were developed to predetermine appropriate candidates for service work — for example, Guide Dogs for the blind — as an economic necessity because no one wanted to spend time and money training dogs that wouldn't successfully finish the course and fulfill the work requirements. Over time, behaviorists modified these tests for the general public; William Campbell and Joachim and Wendy Volhard are names to be recognized in this effort.

Preparing for the test

The test is ideally administered by someone unfamiliar to the dog in an unfamiliar environment because you're interested in the dog's initial reactions to someone he doesn't know. If you're meeting the puppy for the first time, and you're confident in your ability, simply ask the breeder or facility to grant you access to a private room to employ the following series of exercises.

If you're familiar with the dog or puppy, ask a friend or a professional to give the test. If you'd like to observe, please do so from a window or distant area in the room so as not to influence the dog's reaction to the tester.

Gather these materials for the personality test:

- A stopwatch or a clock with a second hand
- A crumpled ball of paper, a bit smaller than a tennis ball
- A metal pot and spoon
- A leash and collar
- A towel or a rag with a long piece of string attached like a leash

✔ An umbrella, preferably one that opens using a spring-release mechanism

✔ A small amount of attractive food in a dog bowl

✔ A writing instrument and the scoring form (see Table 5-1)

Table 5-1	Puppy Personality Test Score Sheet			
	S	**N**	**I**	**A**
Test	**Sociable-Adaptable**	**Nervous-Shy**	**Independent-Stubborn**	**Aggressive-Dominant**
1) Social attraction (approaching)				
2) Social attraction (following)				
3) Social dominance (restraint)				
4) Forgiveness				
5) Social dominance (loss of control)				
6) Willingness to work (retrieving)				
7) Touch sensitivity				
8) Sound reaction				
9) Reaction to novel stimuli				
10) Stability (reaction to threatening stimuli)				
11) Food guarding				
12) Reaction to outside				

Can you modify your dog's personality?

While you can't change your dog's genetic makeup and the predispositions that make up his personality, you can certainly influence many of his *behaviors*. A dog that is naturally dominant and aggressive can learn to control those behaviors in many circumstances; a dog that is naturally shy and fearful can learn to deal with frequently occurring events that initially frightened him.

In Chapter 11, we provide tools and techniques that can be effective in shaping behaviors, and in Chapters 8 and 12, we outline specific socialization, training, and problem-solving exercises to help you positively influence your dog's personality.

Giving the test

This test generally takes 10–15 minutes and should be administered when the dog is relaxed, such as after a nap, but before mealtime. (Please check the shelter's time schedule and make the appointment ahead of time.) Limit the noise and visual distractions when testing the dog or puppy.

Test 1: This exercise measures the dog's social attraction to humans. The tester kneels on the floor to be level with the puppy to appear less threatening (see Figure 5-1). The assistant carries the puppy into the room and places her about 3 or 4 feet from the tester, facing him or her. As soon as the dog is on the floor, the tester calls her. However, don't use the dog's name or the word "Come." The tester should attract the dog by using a sing-song or playful "Puppy, puppy, puppy" perhaps assisted by lightly clapping his hands.

If the pup comes to the tester, put a check mark in column S. If she acts anxious, runs and hides, or stays and whimpers, put a check in column N. If she ignores the tester or wanders off on her own agenda, mark column I. If she comes readily but then jumps up on the tester or mouths or nips his hands, or if she doesn't come at all but growls, check column A.

Test 2: This exercise, which looks at the pup's attention and willingness to follow or stay with a person, is also a test of social attraction. The tester stands and verbally encourages the dog to follow by saying "Puppy, puppy, puppy" (not the dog's name) as the tester walks forward and pats her leg (see Figure 5-2).

If you're testing an older dog, avoid using familiar terms, such as "Heel," "Come," or "Let's go."

Figure 5-1: Test 1 for social attraction involving approaching a person.

If the dog follows readily, check S. If the dog runs away or doesn't move while acting anxiously or whimpering, check N. If she doesn't follow at all or wanders off without any signs of nervousness, check I. If she follows immediately, but gets underfoot while mouthing or nipping at the tester's feet, check A.

Tests 3 through 5 measure the balance of dominant and submissive traits and a puppy/dog's willingness to accept human leadership when socially or physically forced to submit or comply.

Using these tests on a mature dog that has a history of aggression is both unwise and unsafe. If you're testing an older dog, conduct these tests carefully. Immediately terminate any test in which the dog growls or snarls, entering a check in the A column and moving on to the next test, or terminating the test session if you feel the least bit threatened.

Test 3: This exercise involves kneeling on the floor and gently rolling the pup onto its back so that his legs are pointing up, as in Figure 5-3. The assistant starts the stopwatch while the tester's hand exerts just enough pressure on the dog's chest to keep her on her back. The tester should look directly at the dog with a nonsmiling but nonthreatening expression. If the dog looks away, don't force eye contact. When the assistant indicates that 30 seconds have passed, the test is over, and the puppy should be released immediately.

If the pup initially struggles but then settles down or gives up, check S. If the pup doesn't struggle and tries to avoid eye contact, whimpers, or dribbles urine, check N. If the dog struggles a bit on and off throughout the time period and doesn't seem to be settling down, check I. If the dog struggles fiercely throughout the 30 seconds, or if the dog tries to bite or growls at any point, check A.

Figure 5-2: Test 2 for social attraction involving following a person.

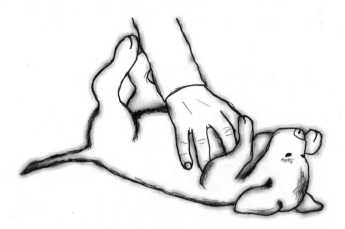

Figure 5-3: Test 3 for social dominance when the puppy is restrained.

Test 4: This next test measures a dog's forgiveness, so it must be done immediately after Test 3, because the dog has just been physically restrained and may hold a grudge for that. It begins with the tester kneeling down and placing the puppy in a sitting position in front of him, as shown in Figure 5-4. The dog should face the tester, not directly, but at an angle of about 45 degrees. Now the tester should begin to stroke the pup slowly and gently with one hand starting at the head and continuing down to the tail. All the while, the tester should talk quietly to the dog, while leaning with his face close enough for the puppy to lick it if she wants to.

If the dog snuggles closer to the tester and tries to lick his face or squirms a bit and licks the tester's hands, check the S column. If the dog rolls over and then licks the tester's hands or tries to move away, check N. If the pup growls, mouths, or nips, check A. If the dog seems unresponsive, neither approaching nor moving away, and seems unconcerned and uninterested, check I.

Test 5: This social dominance test measures a dog's response when she's placed in a vulnerable position. The evaluator bends over the puppy, who is facing in the opposite direction, and lifts her so that her legs are just off of the ground (see Figure 5-5). An assistant can time 30 seconds before the pup is returned to the ground. (Obviously you can't easily do this test with larger dogs.)

If the pup is relaxed and doesn't struggle, or if she struggles briefly and then settles down, check S. If the pup doesn't struggle but whimpers or runs away when placed back on the ground, check N. If the pup struggles fiercely for most of the interval, runs away when placed back on the ground, or growls, nips, mouths, or barks while being held or when returned to the ground, check A. If the dog seems unresponsive and simply wanders away as if nothing happened when returned to the ground, check I.

Figure 5-4: Test 4 for social forgiveness.

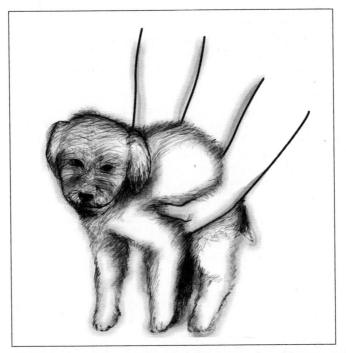

Figure 5-5: Test 5 for social dominance when puppy doesn't have control.

Test 6: This test involves retrieving, which shows a dog's willingness to work with people. The evaluator kneels, placing the puppy just in front of his knees, as shown in Figure 5-6. Dangle a crumpled-up ball of paper (slightly smaller than a tennis ball) in front of the puppy's face — tease the dog, as well as verbally bait her: "Do you want it?" The moment the puppy shows any interest, toss the ball 3 feet in front of her. If the puppy sets out to retrieve it, the evaluator should back up a few feet and cheer the puppy back to his side.

If the puppy returns (even part way) with the paper or if she drops the paper but still comes back to the tester, check S. If the pup chases the paper ball and then stands over it and doesn't return, or if she starts to chase the paper and then loses interest, check I. If the pup fails to chase the paper at all, moves away from the tester (and the paper), or seems simply uninterested and doesn't move toward the paper ball, check I. If the pup chases the paper, picks it up, and then runs away, check A.

What does retrieving have to do with personality?

Clarence Pfaffenberger developed a puppy evaluation test to determine the probable success of puppies chosen to guide the blind. Until the mid-1940s, when he first became involved in Guide Dog selection and training, only 9 percent of the dogs successfully finished the training program. When Pfaffenberger started a testing program, he found that the best single indicator of whether a dog would successfully complete the program was whether she would retrieve as a puppy. Pfaffenberger believed that retrieving at this age was really a test of willingness to work for and with humans.

Figure 5-6: Test 6 for willingness to retrieve.

Test 7: This exercise focuses on a puppy's touch sensitivity, noting that a dog who is too touch sensitive is often hard to handle. It involves pinching the pup's ear flap three times, starting with medium force, with the next pinch being medium hard, and the last very hard. The tester should practice beforehand on himself (not the pup) by squeezing the forefinger of one hand between the thumb and forefinger.

Make sure that the squeeze doesn't involve gouging with fingernails.

The tester should grasp the flap of the dog's ear between his thumb and forefinger and give the first pinch, followed by the second and third separated by about two seconds (see Figure 5-7). If the pup responds to the first or second pinch by whimpering or yelping, stop the test immediately and check column N. If at any point the pup growls, mouths, or nips, stop immediately and check A. If, on the second or third pinch, the pup tries to pull her head or body away, or turns to look at your face without any other response, check S. If the pup seems unresponsive or uncaring during the whole test, check column I.

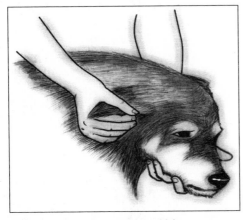

Figure 5-7: Test 7 for touch sensitivity.

Test 8: This exercise focuses on a puppy's threshold of excitement as it relates to unfamiliar sounds. When applying this test, the puppy should face away from the direction of the sound and not interact with the evaluator until the exercise is finished. An assistant hidden from view should give three sharp raps of a metal spoon against a metal pot and should then freeze in position, avoiding eye contact with the dog (see Figure 5-8).

If the dog acts interested and moves toward the sound or obviously listens and orients her head curiously in the direction of the sound, even if she seems startled at first, check S. If the pup barks in the direction of the sound or growls or mouths the assistant, check column A. If the pup cringes, backs off, or tries to hide, check N. If the pup locates the sound but stays in place and barks, enter a check mark in column S. If the pup ignores the sound completely or only gives a quick flick of its head in the direction of the sound and then looks away, check I.

Test 9: This test measures a pup's reaction to unusual, but nonthreatening, events. Initially, an assistant stands off to the side, holding on to the end of a string tied to the end of a towel. The assistant then jerks the towel in regular intervals toward himself (see Figure 5-9).

If the dog looks at the test object, displays curiosity by approaching, or tries to investigate it, check S. If the dog ignores the test object, check I. If the dog lunges, stands fast and barks at the towel, growls, or attacks it, check A. If the pup shies away or hides from the towel, check N.

Figure 5-8: Test 8 for sound sensitivity.

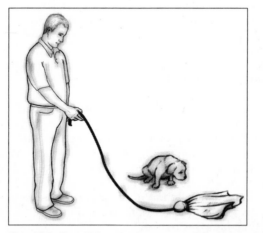

Figure 5-9: Test 10 for reaction to potentially threatening events.

Test 10: This exercise tests a puppy's reaction to a perceived threat. The assistant should position himself about 6 feet from the dog, quietly holding an umbrella (one that opens on a spring release is best). Now the evaluator should turn the pup so that she's facing in between the assistant and the tester, as shown in Figure 5-10). When the puppy is looking toward the assistant, she should open the umbrella quickly, quietly setting it on the floor without looking or addressing the puppy.

If the dog reacts but regains its composure within a moment and then approaches to investigate the umbrella, check S. If the dog stands and barks, or approaches and growls or snaps at the umbrella, check A. If the dog tries to run or hide, check N. If the dog shows little or no interest in the umbrella, check I.

Test 11: The next test measures possessiveness.

If the puppy you're testing has many checks in the "A" column, be mindful of her reaction. An aggressive puppy may bite if her growls aren't met with an immediate withdrawal. If the puppy/dog growls, consider this candidate seriously: She'll require mindful and consistent training and isn't suitable for a family with any exposure to young children.

Place a bowl on the floor and add kibbles to it. When the pup has started to eat, use a long stick, broom handle, or baseball bat to pull the bowl away from her, as shown in Figure 5-11. If the pup looks at you and wags her tail expectantly, put a check in the S column. If she runs away or acts as if she is now too upset to eat, check N. If she growls, barks, bites the stick, or jumps on you to get the food back, check A. If she acts as if she's uninterested in the food after all, check I.

Figure 5-10: Test 9 for reaction to novel events.

Test 12: If the puppy you're evaluating is comfortable on a leash and collar, lead her to an unfamiliar room or, if inoculated, outside. Observe your candidate's behavior as you walk around the block or circle the house. Try to find birds, cats, squirrels, or people for the puppy to encounter. If the pup stays close to you even though she's showing a curious interest in things going on around her, check S. If the pup acts nervous and scared and tries to run from any encounter, check N. If the pup barks and lunges at everything, check A. If the pup acts uninterested in anything that you try to point out to her and shows interest in only occasional things that she finds for herself, check I.

Figure 5-11: Test 11 for social dominance and guarding of possessions.

Evaluating Your Adult Dog

If you've shared life with a dog for some time, you already know a lot about her personality. If you haven't given it much thought, we encourage you to use the following questionnaire to determine your dog's personality. This test is designed to measure the personality of an adult dog (actually, any dog older than 6 months) who has lived with you for at least one month.

Of course, as every parent knows (whether your child walks on two legs or four), you may have a bit of bias. As you ponder these behavioral adjectives, check with a family member or friend. The purpose of this test is for *you* to learn the real nature of your dog's personality.

This test is made up of a set of words or short phrases, which are descriptions that can apply to a dog. For each one, your task is to consider whether that description applies to your dog. If it does, then simply put a check mark next to it. If not, leave that word blank and go on to the next. Check all items that describe your dog.

❏ afraid[4]

❏ aloof[3]

❏ anxious[4]

❏ approachable[1]

❏ assertive[2]

❏ barks at people and dogs[2]

❏ bashful[4]

❏ bites at leash[2]

❏ bold[2]

❏ bossy[2]

❏ cautious[4]

❏ cool[3]

❏ cordial[1]

❏ detached[3]

❏ disconnected[3]

❏ disinterested[3]

❏ distant[3]

❏ easy[1]

❏ fearful[4]

❏ fidgety[4]

❏ forceful[2]

❏ gentle[1]

❏ good-natured[1]

❏ hesitant[4]

❏ high-strung[4]

❏ independent[3]

❏ indifferent[3]

❏ irritable[2]

❏ loner[3]

❏ loud[2]

❏ lovable[1]

❏ mellow[1]

❏ mouthy[2]

❏ neighborly[1]

❏ nervous[4]

❏ outgoing[1]

❏ playful[1]

❏ pleasant[1]

❏ pleasure-seeking[1]

❏ possessive[2]

❏ pushy[2]

❏ reserved[3]

❏ self-assertive[2]

❏ sensitive[4]

❏ shy[4]

❏ skittish[4]

❏ snappish[2]

❏ sociable[1]

❏ solitary[3]

❏ sometimes growls[2]

❏ standoffish[3]

❏ suspicious[2]

❏ sweet-tempered[1]

❏ thick-skinned[3]

❏ timid[4]

❏ touchable[1]

❏ uneasy[4]

❏ unimpressed[3]

❏ unresponsive[3]

❏ uptight

Scoring the personality tests

Both the puppy and adult personality tests use the same final score sheet and general interpretation scheme. For the puppy personality test, the scoring is quite simple. Using the score sheet in Table 5-2, simply count the number of check marks in the column marked S, and enter that total on the line marked S below. Count the check marks in columns N, A, and I, and enter their totals, respectively, in the score sheet, and you're now ready for interpretation.

Table 5-2	Personality Score Totals	
	Interpretation	*Enter Total*
S	Sociable, responsive, adaptable, and people-oriented	
N	Nervous, shy, or unsure	
A	Dominant, aggressive, or controlling	
I	Independent, indifferent, and uninvolved	

For the adult personality test, look back at the list of items. Notice that each item has a little number superscripted just behind it. These numbers are your scoring codes. First go through the list and count all the items you checked that have the number 1 code. (Remember, you're counting the total number of checks, not adding the scores.) That total is entered on the line marked S in the score sheet. Next count all the items you checked with the number 2 code, and this total is entered in the line marked A. The total number of items that you checked with the number 3 code goes on the line marked I, and the total with the number 4 code goes on the line marked N.

Interpreting the personality tests

For each of the tests, you can look at the total scores and get a general overview of the dog's personality. The category that has the largest total score shows what kind of a dog you're dealing with and allows you to generally predict what you may expect from her.

For the puppy test, the general personality classification is the kind of dog the pup will mostly grow up to be. However, because the dog is still young, its personality can still be somewhat shaped and modified by how you treat it and the kinds of experiences that it has in the future and as it matures.

For the adult test scores, we're looking at a broader range of behaviors so that we can be a bit subtler in our description of the dog. In essence, the adult has had more time and experience in the world, which has molded her behavior so that we can pick up on some nuances and shadings.

Some interesting combinations

At times, the adult personality scale allows a greater range of interpretation because each dimension can go up to a score of 15, and a score on one dimension doesn't affect the scores on the others. A score of 11 to 15 is considered high. A score of 5 or less is low, while scores between 6 and 10 are midrange. Here are a few special combinations:

High Sociability, High Dominance, Low Nervousness, and Low Independence: These dogs enjoy working, have a strong sense of themselves, and aren't easily stressed. Highly motivated, these dogs require a delicate balance of firmness and structured inclusion to bring out the best in them.

Medium Sociability and Dominance with Low Nervousness and Low Independence: These are easily trained dogs who are easy to get along with and aren't easily flustered or distracted. This combination makes good all-around dogs.

High Sociability, Low Dominance, Low Nervousness, and Low Independence: These dogs are laid-back and loving, seldom, if ever, frantic or hyper, and an ideal pet for families or novice dog owners.

Assertive/Aggressive: Two combinations of personality scores may be difficult to deal with in the wrong environment. The first is the dog with High Dominance and High Nervousness with Low Sociability and Low Independence. This dog is highly reactive when startled, and, when fearful, may snap out at anyone — friend, family, or stranger. This dog may also show displaced aggression when overstimulated, striking out at anyone if she's unable to attack the source of her frustration.

The second troublesome personality combination is the dog with High Dominance and High Independence with Low Sociability and Low Nervousness. This dog is often more focused on her own needs than on the collective dynamics of her group. Unless coached with persistence, this dog may use aggression to modify others and as a means to get his way.

We're measuring four basic dimensions:

- ✔ **Sociability** (scale S) is really more than its name suggests. An important aspect of this personality dimension is friendliness and a desire to interact with others — what some researchers may call a *pack drive*.

    Dogs that score high on this dimension bond well with people, and because they look to humans (or other dogs) for guidance and feedback, they're extremely adaptable. These dogs are probably best for first-time owners and people who want a low threat, low hassle, and friendly family pet.

✔ **Nervous/Shy** (scale N) is a measure of both how submissive and how reactive a dog is. A high score indicates a puppy/dog who is notably reactive to change or stimulation. Common adjectives include "shy," "timid," and "skittish." Common complaints include "easily frightened," "afraid of men with hats (or beards or glasses)," "frightened by the sound of trucks (or vacuums, thunder, or crowds)," "uneasy around children (or large dogs or flickering lights)," and so on.

Unless extensively socialized, these dogs are unpredictable and react to any fluctuation in their schedule or unexpected events. Though not a family dog candidate, this dog can flourish with a steady trainer and predictable environment, as found with single people, an adult couple, or older persons without grandchildren. In these settings, these dogs are often affectionate and needy: a good match for the right person.

The greater the score in the N range, the more unsteady the dog will be when interrupted or stressed. This dog necessitates more patience and support and isn't recommended for families or social people who intend to bring their dog along with them wherever they go.

✔ High scores in the **Aggressive/Dominant** (scale A) area indicate dogs that are active and pushy and who may not hesitate to use aggression to get or keep what they want. Common adjectives include "dominant," "pushy," and "snappish." Common complaints are "suspicious of men in raincoats (or dark-skinned men, or men smoking)," "aggressive toward children (or puppies or any other dogs)," "snatches treats," "barks at strangers," "jumps assertively," and "watches strangers in the home."

Dogs in this category require careful watching and a lot of training to put them under control. Untrained or mismanaged, these dogs may assert themselves over whomever they can: children and other pets decidedly not excluded. In the right home, however, these dogs can be managed, trained, and appreciated. A high score in this area indicates a high-intensity performance drive. Active, curious, and driven, these dogs excel at specific activities, such as agility or flyball, or service tasks, such as tracking or bomb detection. Though not dogs for the average family or novice handler, they can make good reliable companions who will devote themselves to a handler that is just a little more dominant than they are.

If your dog has bitten you or anyone else, please get professional help. Active aggression is beyond the scope of this book.

✔ Dogs with high scores in the **Independent** (scale I) dimension can be standoffish, stubborn, and uncooperative, committing to family affairs on their terms alone. Comfortable with their own agenda, these dogs relate to people when prompted by a positive source, such as food or a favorite activity. Many of the instinctive breeds (from the Terrier or Hound groups, for example) score high on this scale, as they weren't bred to work with man, but rather on their own, tracking or hunting game. Lest anyone discard this group of dogs altogether, they're ideal for many situations, such as living with people who are busy or away from home for regular stretches.

Dogs that score high on the independence range are often more distractible, prioritizing their environment over human direction.

Chapter 6

Interpreting Your Dog's Breed-Specific Traits

*I*n this chapter, we take the word *breed* and look at its value in helping you understand your dog. If you've ever watched a dog show, you've probably noticed a lot of different types of dogs prancing around the ring all prim and proper, some with little bows, others with their fur sculpted like ornamental hedges. In case you have the idea that a breed is nothing more than a fashion statement, we'll take the time to educate you on the psychological, emotional, and physical needs and differences between each and every dog breed you see.

What Are Dog Breeds?

The essence of creating specific breeds of dogs was to guarantee that useful characteristics were passed on from one generation to the next. Careful breeding records were kept for each puppy, tracing its genetic lineage and establishing a group of dogs that were *purebred*.

The job of kennel clubs is to file and organize all the breeding records of each dog, and to record every mating to ensure that there has been no *outbreeding,* which is simply defined as mixed matings between dogs of different recognized breeds. Kennel clubs also establish the *standard of the breed,* which is simply a description of what the ideal dog of a particular breed should look like, what its distinctive natural behaviors are, and what its personality or temperament should be like.

Checking out the top dog shows

Westminster Kennel Club and Crufts are two world-renowned dog shows that high-light the top dogs in each breed recognized in their kennel club roster. Crufts, the largest dog exhibition event in the world (attracting more than 20,000 entries each year), began in England in 1886. The Westminster Dog Show (whose winners are considered to be the top dogs in North America) is held at Madison Square Gardens in New York and began its competitions in 1877. Check them out on television or in person if you're able.

The American Kennel Club (AKC) recognizes around 160 breeds of dogs categorized into seven groups: sporting dogs, hounds, working dogs, terriers, toy dogs, nonsporting dogs, and herding dogs. The AKC is sort of the Microsoft of dog clubs and serves as the standard around the world, so we refer to its listing throughout the book.

The AKC also has a Miscellaneous Class for breeds recognized in other countries or by other kennel clubs, but that aren't yet recognized by the kennel club. Nearly every year, one or more breeds are recognized and moved from the Miscellaneous Class to one of the other groups, and additional new breeds are added to the Miscellaneous Class.

Several breeds of dogs were created based on their aesthetic appearance alone. The Cairn Terrier and West Highland White Terriers, for example, started out as the same breed. In each litter, some dogs were white, and some weren't. Because the whites produced other white-colored dogs when interbred, they were separated into two distinct breeds. Structurally and behaviorally, the two breeds remain virtually identical. The Norfolk and the Norwich Terriers are another example of breeds that only differ in the shape of their ears (Norwich has pricked ears and Norfolk floppy ears).

This division of dogs based solely on appearance is a distortion of what breeds are all about. Dogs were originally domesticated because they had skills and behavioral traits that made them useful. What makes this important for understanding the psychology of dogs is that creating a breed was originally an attempt to create lines of dogs that had predictable behaviors and temperaments.

A New Breed of Dog Classification

In the interests of presenting breeds according to their behavior and psychology, we divide the AKC's seven groupings into subgroups. Each group is based on a dog's breed's individual behavioral characteristics.

For example, we divide the dogs in the herding group into *drovers* (who work more independently and move flocks over great distances) and *herd minders* (who move flocks about the farm, generally under the guidance of a shepherd). Behaviorally speaking, drovers are more independent and likely to roam, where as herders are intensely focused and stay centered about their flock.

Sporting dogs

Sporting dogs are bred to help man hunt. Though blasting a defenseless duck from the sky likely isn't necessary for survival, don't tell your dog. He still views his purpose with high regard. Fortunately, you don't have to take up hunting to keep one of these dogs happy: a tennis ball or Frisbee works just fine. However, knowing specifically what your dog was bred to hunt can help you better understand your dog's behavior.

The Labrador and Golden Retrievers are among the most commonly used service dogs, assisting blind or handicapped people, and also detecting drugs or explosives and assisting in search-and-rescue tasks.

Go to England, and you'll find the hunting dogs under the title Gun Dogs. In America, they're referred to as *sporting dogs*.

The sporting group actually contains five different types of dog, each of which has somewhat different purposes and thus may be expected to have different behavior patterns:

- ✔ **Retrievers:** Dogs in this group are bred to retrieve fallen game, which turns out, in family life, to be a dog who is alert, has a good memory, and is eager to participate and please. Because their intended purpose demanded close human contact and direction, retrievers are sociable and attentive. *Chesapeake Bay Retriever, Curly Coat Retriever, Flat Coat Retriever, Golden Retriever, Labrador Retriever, Miniature Poodle, Nova Scotia Duck Tolling Retriever, Standard Poodle.*

- ✔ Pointers: These scouts of the dog world have an attentive eye and nose for game. Though they work more independently than a retriever, and certainly have been bred to expend more energy in the pursuit of quarry, the pointers are patient — originally so patient they would hold a pointing pose until the hunter got into position and (finally) released. Brittany Spaniel, English Pointer, German Shorthaired Pointer, German Wirehaired Pointer, Pointer, Wirehaired Pointing Griffon.

When a pointer finds game, it exhibits a behavior that contradicts evolution. Instead of rushing forward to capture its quarry, a pointer freezes in position with its head pointing to where it believes the quarry is hiding.

✔ **Setters:** Pointers and setters have a lot in common. Think of setters as being faster and more exuberant versions of pointers. Their name comes from an old English alternative for the word *sitter*. Like pointers, their job was to find the game and then indicate its position to the hunter by sitting or crouching down and looking directly at it. They then had to hold that position until the hunters had time to drop a net over the covey of birds. *English Setter, Gordon Setter, Irish Setter.*

✔ **Spaniels:** These are high-energy hunting dogs that have been bred to quarter the field to find and flush game. When they're working, they dash around searching for scents. However, when they find their quarry, they don't wait for the hunter, but simply charge at the birds to cause them to take flight so that the hunter can take his shot. When their hunting genes are no longer in high demand, exercise and interaction will be! *American Water Spaniel, Clumber Spaniel, Cocker Spaniel, English Cocker Spaniel, English Springer Spaniel, Field Spaniel, Irish Water Spaniel, Sussex Spaniel, Welsh Springer Spaniel.*

The name spaniel was given to them because of their friendly, loving nature. The *span* in spaniel is for Spain, which at the time was considered to be the nation of lovers.

✔ **Multipurpose hunting dogs:** Some hunters set their sights on creating an all-around, multipurpose hunting dog who would do all the main functions, such as pointing, flushing, and retrieving game. These stunning adaptations, basically mixing other dogs from the preceding groups, have all the general demands of a sporting dog, yet all the benefits, too. *Portuguese Water Dog, Vizsla, Weimaraner.*

These manipulations of dogs continue today, and there is now a line of Pointing Labrador Retrievers, which, as the name indicates, not only retrieve but point as well and they may someday be a separate breed.

Hounds

"You ain't nothing but a hound dog" doesn't actually reflect favorably on these loving, though independent, dogs. Hounds are also hunting dogs, but were designed to work without human guidance or intervention. The human hunter is only needed if the game finds refuge in a den, burrow, or tree or is too large and dangerous for the dogs to kill. In all other cases, these hounds are supposed to be able to dispatch their target when they catch it, without any human help. How does this play out in today's society? These dogs are still motivated chiefly by their passions, though they're often amiable and happy-go-lucky.

Hounds naturally fall into two clear groupings:

- ✔ **Scent hounds:** These dogs are supposed to track their quarry by the faint odor they leave as they move over the landscape. Their noses are highly developed for this purpose. *American and English Foxhounds, Basset, Beagle, Black and Tan Coonhound, Bloodhound, Harrier, Otterhound.*

- ✔ **Sight hounds:** These dogs have keen eyesight and tremendous speed. Their task is to visually locate their quarry in the distance and run it down. *Afghan Hound, Basenji, Borzoi, Greyhound, Irish Wolfhound, Saluki, Scottish Deerhound, Whippet.*

Though we don't depend on hounds for our sustenance, their instinct to hunt is still very much intact. Let a scent hound (such as a beagle) loose, and he's likely to disappear, whatever the terrain, as he follows some interesting smells. Unharnessed, a sight hound won't be able to resist the temptation of chasing after a mobile tidbit, which may be a neighbor's cat or a kid on a skateboard. Best to keep these dogs leashed in open areas at all times.

The fastest animal in the world?

When creating special-purpose dogs, humans developed some breeds that can run much faster than wolves or other wild animals. The fastest of these are the sight hounds, and the greyhound is the gold medalist. While the average dog can run about 19 miles per hour, greyhounds can run at speeds of 35 to 40 miles per hour.

You may have heard that the cheetah is the fastest animal in the world, because it can dash at speeds around 65 mph. However, this speed is reached only for short runs that may last a few seconds and seldom covers more than an eighth of a mile. Greyhounds, however, can run at their top speed for distances as great as 7 miles. That means that although the cheetah can win the short sprint race, in any long race, the greyhound will leave him way behind, panting in the dust. So who really is the fastest animal in the world?

Working dogs

Working dogs like to . . . work. They're a task-oriented group that feels most fulfilled when they have a job. Though each dog in this group shares a practical function, the behaviors and temperaments needed for varying tasks can be quite varied and different:

- ✔ **Guard dogs:** These dogs were originally designed to protect livestock or territories without any human direction. Though a person may not desire such a devoted guardian in their home today, this point needs to be driven home. Both then and now, a human didn't have to be home to trigger defensive reactions. *Bullmastiff, Dalmatian, Great Dane, Great Pyrenees, Komondor, Kuvasz, Mastiff, Rottweiler.*

- ✔ **Personal-protection dogs:** Although these dogs are also guard dogs, they differ in that they're supposed to work intimately with people, under direct human control. Think of it this way: A guard dog is like an automated security system, while a personal-protection dog is more like a human body guard. *Boxer, Doberman Pinscher, Giant Schnauzer, Rhodesian Ridgeback, Standard Schnauzer.*

- ✔ **Draft dogs:** These dogs were bred to pull carts and carry packs. Most people have difficulty recognizing how important dogs were for transportation prior to the invention of motor vehicles. Dog-drawn carts were perfect for old cities where streets were often too narrow for a horse cart to negotiate. Furthermore a working man could keep his dog in his house with his family, with no need to have a stable and outbuildings. *Bernese Mountain Dog, Newfoundland, Saint Bernard.*

The Rottweiler actually began as draft dog, pulling butchers' carts and then guarding it while the butcher was inside making deliveries. After awhile, however, its guarding functions became more important so we now classify its breed as a guard dog instead of a draft dog.

- ✔ **Spitz-type dogs:** These northern dogs are bred to withstand cold temperatures, and many were intended to pull sleds. These dogs have pricked ears, sharp muzzles, a flowing tail that curls high over their backs, and often dense insulating coats. That tail carried high may be all that distinguishes some of these dogs from arctic wolves, and their temperament often reflects this upbringing as well because they're frequently suspicious of strangers and are very concerned about dominance and status in their social life. *Akita, Alaskan Malamute, Chow Chow, Keeshond, Norwegian Elkhound, Samoyed, Schipperke, Siberian Husky*

Terriers

Terriers may be big, small, and every size in-between. These tenacious, spirited dogs add punch to the word "zing." Bred originally to keep homes and farms vermin-free, they bring their original feistiness and heart into the 21st century. As history progressed, certain breeds were streamlined, and the "fight" was accentuated in certain breeds that were ultimately changed into fighters for the amusement of humans. Though this "sport" still continues in underground circles, the current breeders of the fighting terriers have been mindful to diminish this impulse by selective breeding.

Terriers fall into two main groups:

✔ **Vermin hunters:** The majority of terriers were purchased and bred to rid homes and farmland of all sorts of pests — from a lowly mouse to foxes, badgers, and other poultry-killing vermin. Many of the breeds were deliberately kept small and agile to meet the task of digging underground, or wriggling their way into burrows or dens to find their targets. The coats of the terrier also played into their design because their rough, hard, or wiry coats can protect them against abrasion from rocks and rough ground and also provide a kind of armor against the teeth of their quarry.

The size differential also gives a clue into the exercise requirements of the individual breed, as short-legged terriers were carried in a basket on horseback during hunts, whereas larger terriers were designed to run with horses and hounds on the hunt. *Airedale Terrier, Australian Terrier, Bedlington Terrier, Border Terrier, Boston Terrier, Cairn Terrier, Dachshund, Dandi Dinmont Terrier, Irish Terrier, Kerry Blue Terrier, Lakeland Terrier, Manchester Terrier, Miniature Schnauzer, Norfolk Terrier, Norwich Terrier, Parson Jack Russell Terrier, Scottish Terrier, Sealyham Terrier, Soft Coated Wheaten Terrier, Silky Terrier, Skye Terrier, Smooth Fox Terrier, Welsh Terrier, Wire Fox Terrier, West Highland White Terrier.*

✔ **Fighting dogs:** Some dogs were bred specifically to participate in blood sports. They were put into arenas (called *pits*) and forced to fight bulls, bears, or other dogs. The natural scrappiness of the terrier was enhanced to make these dogs tough and willing to fight. *American Staffordshire Bull Terrier, Bull Terrier, Staffordshire Bull Terrier.*

WARNING! Expecting a terrier not to bark may be the definition of asking too much. Specifically, all terriers were bred to bark, and barking is part of the definition of a terrier's behavior. Though the necessity to alert a hunter to the location of the quarry by barking isn't often sought after by terrier owners, it comes with the package. Though you may be able to curb the tenacity (see Chapter 13), the urge to be heard will never go away completely.

Toy dogs

Though decidedly not toys, each of the dogs in this group were bred for one purpose and one purpose alone: to be cuddled. Though they are quintessential companions and require less exercise than larger dogs, these breeds still have the heart and mind equivalent to that found in much bigger dogs. Though the urge to baby these dogs may be overwhelming, hold off spoiling them until you have some structure in place. Otherwise, as they say, you'll pay the price. *Affenpinscher, Bichon Frise, Brussels Griffon, Bulldog, Cavalier King Charles Spaniel, Chihuahua, English Toy Spaniel, French Bulldog, Italian Greyhound, Japanese Chin, Lhasa Apso, Maltese, Miniature Pinscher, Papillion, Pekingese, Pomeranian, Pug, Shih Tzu, Tibetan Spaniel, Tibetan Terrier, Toy Poodle, Yorkshire Terrier.*

Herding dogs

The herding dog group contains dogs that were used, at least originally, to herd, drive, and protect livestock. Though those traits aren't often necessary, don't tell a herding dog. Task-oriented and driven, they'll find something to herd or protect — and watch out. If you don't provide a proper outlet, the one they may be herding or protecting just might be you! There are actually two types of herding dogs:

- **Drovers:** These hardy dogs were bred to drive sheep and cattle over long distances, often with minimal or no direction from humans for long periods of time. *Australian Cattle Dog, Bouvier Des Flandres, Briard, Cardigan Corgi, Pembroke Corgi.*

- **Herd minders:** These dogs were indispensable to shepherds because of their ability to keep herds of animals together and to move them short distances. They work closely with, and under the direction of, a human shepherd. At home, this turns into a dog who will either look to you and your family as a sheep or a shepherd. In short, you better train, or be trained. *Australian Shepherd, Bearded Collie, Belgian Malinois, Belgian Shepherd, Belgian Tervuren, Border Collie, Collie, German Shepherd Dog, Old English Sheepdog, Puli, Shetland Sheepdog.*

Mixed breed dogs — the "love child"

If knowing a dog's breed allows you to predict a dog's behavior, how can you assess the behavior of a mixed breed dog?

Fortunately, based on research from the Jackson Laboratories in Bar Harbour, Maine, indicators suggest that form predicts function. It seems that data shows that a mixed breed dog is *most likely to act like the breed that it most looks like*. Thus, if a Labrador Retriever/Poodle cross looks much like a Labrador Retriever, it will probably act much like a Labrador Retriever. If it looks more like a Poodle, its behavior will be very Poodle-like.

The more of a blend that the dog's physical appearance seems to be, the more likely that the dog's behavior will be a blend of the two parent breeds.

Nonsporting dogs

The American Kennel Club originally had only two groups of dogs, *sporting dogs* and *nonsporting dogs*. The current AKC classification is much broader in scope. However, it still keeps this group as a sort of catchall for breeds it has problems classifying.

In our manuscript, we've chosen to eliminate this classification and sort these breeds into the preceding groups.

Predicting Behavior from Breed

Using the preceding 16 group classifications of dog breeds, we apply some scientific research out of the University of British Columbia that estimates that one half of the genetic makeup of any dog is genetically based.

In that study, 98 dog experts were surveyed and asked to rate the breeds on 22 aspects of their behavior. After much statistical analysis, it was found that, in reality, five important behavior dimensions existed, and systematic differences occurred among the various breed groups on these dimensions. The following sections look at these ratings to see how the different dog breeds stack up.

Intelligence and learning ability

The first important dimension is a measure of how easily a dog learns and solves problems, which is generally what people mean by intelligence. It also indicates how easy it will be to teach the dog obedience commands and to perform service activities, which some dog experts refer to as *trainability*.

The experts list herding dogs and retrievers at the top of the list in intelligence, which probably explains why the top-ten lists of dogs in obedience competitions tend to be dominated by Border Collies, Shetland Sheepdogs, and Labrador and Golden Retrievers (see Table 6-1). It also probably explains why German Shepherds, Labrador Retrievers, and Golden Retrievers are frequently the preferred breeds for service dogs, guide dogs for the blind, and other complex tasks.

Table 6-1	Dogs Ranked by Intelligence and Learning Ability		
High	**Moderately High**	**Moderately Low**	**Low**
Herd minders	Draft dogs	Vermin hunters	Fighting dogs
Retrievers	Pointers	Setters	Guard dogs
Drovers	Spaniels	Spitz type	Sight hounds
Personal-protection dogs	Multipurpose sporting dogs	Companion dogs	Scent hounds

Though having a really smart dog may sound dreamy, it's not. These dogs do best in highly structured, dog-savvy homes.

Dominance and territoriality

Think of this area as a measure of how "hard" or "soft" your dog is in its personality. It's actually a measure of how assertive and possessive a dog is. The dogs that are high on this trait make good watch dogs and guard dogs (see Table 6-2). However, they may also be demanding, possessive, and pushy. They may guard their possessions, such as food and toys, vigorously. They're also willing to use aggression against people and animals if it suits their purposes. Dogs low on this trait are unchallenging and nonthreatening.

Table 6-2	Dogs Ranked by Dominance and Territoriality		
High	*Moderately High*	*Moderately Low*	*Low*
Fighting dogs	Pointers	Multipurpose sporting dogs	Scent hounds
Personal-protection dogs	Vermin hunters	Spaniels	Sight hounds
Guard dogs	Drovers	Herd minders	Draft dogs
Spitz type	Setters	Retrievers	Companion dogs

Sociability

This area refers to how friendly and agreeable a dog is. It reflects how much a dog seeks out companionship. A dog high on this trait happily greets any new person with its tail wagging (see Table 6-3). A dog low on this trait may appear shy and aloof and may frequently prefer to be alone rather than with people.

Table 6-3	Dogs Ranked by Sociability		
High	*Moderately High*	*Moderately Low*	*Low*
Setters	Multipurpose sporting dogs	Herd minders	Drovers
Scent hounds	Draft dogs	Vermin hunters	Personal-protection dogs
Retrievers	Pointers	Guard dogs	Fighting dogs
Spaniels	Spitz type	Companion dogs	Sight hounds

Emotional reactivity

This trait refers to the dog's emotional state in the sense of how quickly its mood may change (see Table 6-4). Dogs high on this dimension are easy to excite but also calm down easily — their moods may rapidly fluctuate from confident to cautious and so on. A dog that is low on this trait may be much more difficult to excite, but once excited, it takes much longer to calm down.

Table 6-4	Dogs Ranked by Emotional Reactivity		
High	*Moderately High*	*Moderately Low*	*Low*
Pointers	Retrievers	Spaniels	Companion dogs
Setters	Sight hounds	Scent hounds	Guard dogs
Multipurpose sporting dogs	Personal-protection dogs	Vermin hunters	Fighting dogs
Herd minders	Spitz type	Drovers	Draft dogs

Energy level

This trait is actually a multifaceted measure that includes both indoor and outdoor activity level and the amount of force and energy the dog brings to common activities (see Table 6-5). A dog high on energy not only races around, but also may tug strongly on the leash or quickly and forcefully grab a treat from its owner's hand.

Because experts feel that all breeds are capable of periods of high energy, even the lowest rankings aren't truly inactive dogs.

Table 6-5	Dogs Ranked by Energy Level		
High	*Moderately High*	*Moderately Low*	*Low*
Pointers	Fighting dogs	Multipurpose sporting dogs	Guard dogs
Drovers	Personal-protection dogs	Companion dogs	Sight hounds
Vermin hunters	Setters	Spaniels	Scent hounds
Herd minders	Spitz type	Retrievers	Draft dogs

Chapter 7

Sensory Perceptions

· ·

· ·

*A*ll animals interpret their environment through a complex mingling of information filtered through their five senses: sight, hearing, smell, touch, and taste. What separates one species from another is the degree to which each of these senses is used. Humans, for example, depend primarily on sight to interpret their environment; a dog, on the other hand, relies heavily on her sense of smell. To fully comprehend a dog's life experience, a person must be willing to look at their environment and daily sensory stimulation from their dog's perspective.

Sight, Psychology, and Survival

The human eye is built around the same general design as the dog's eye: Both contain cornea, pupil, lens, and retina. Still, major differences between them affect how images are perceived. People rely on their visual sense to interpret incoming information about the world, and our brains use more space and more neurons to process visual information than they do for any other sense. Dogs do not process images this way; for them the world is more of an off-colored and blurred landscape.

A dog's primary use of sight is to process motion, a skill vital to their ancestors' survival. Dependent on the sustenance of hunted game, their eyes evolved into sharp motion detectors. You're most likely to see this skill activated when a dog follows the trajectory of a toy or chases other animals.

Hand shy?

Though some dogs are hand shy as a result of being hit, many dogs veer away from the hand for another reason, namely their evolutionary instinct to avoid sudden approach or attack. The sight of a human approaching straight on, tone high pitched, eyes wide open and glaring, often sets a dog's reactionary impulses in motion. Even a hand suddenly reaching to pat a dog may spell hesitation or withdrawal.

When you first approach a dog, she'll be unable to reason your intentions. Speak to the person at the end of her leash first, and if she says that the dog's friendly, kneel down and extend your hand at her nose level. If she turns her head away, respect her and back off. If she sniffs it, you may pet her from the side or just beneath her line of vision.

If your dog is suffering hand shyness, offer her a spoonful of a lickable reward or canned food with one hand as you reach repetitively with your other hand to pat her head.

Do you have a small dog that backs away from your approach? Do not keep following her: You'll look like a predator! Shake a treat cup or toy as you kneel down and encourage her to come to you.

And please, no matter how frustrated you may feel with your dog's behavior, don't run after your dog to catch her. She will run, not out of disrespect, but out of sheer panic. The light of her life, the one she turns to for reason, is now the one hunting her. Flip to Part IV to discover a healthier approach to problem solving.

If you'd like to speed up your dog's learning process, add signals with a broad motion component to your verbal directions (see Chapter 12). These hand cues increase your dog's visual attention to you and align with her species-engrained impulse to watch a leader figure for instruction.

Are dogs colorblind?

One of the things that people seem to be most curious about when it comes to what their dog can see is whether their pup can see colors. The simple answer that scientists give, namely that dogs are colorblind, is usually misinterpreted as meaning that dogs see no color but only shades of gray. This assumption is wrong.

Colorblindness, to the scientist, means that at least one of the three color receptors found in the normal eye (we have red, green, and blue receiving cones) isn't working. Thus, with only two functioning color systems, an individual can still see colors, but the range is limited, and he confuses certain colors that a normal person can perceive as distinct. This situation is the same with dogs. They do see colors, and they see them well enough to help guide their behaviors. However, the colors they see are neither as rich nor as many as those seen by humans.

Figure 7-1 shows what a human sees when looking at a rainbow or a color spectrum and also what a dog sees. Instead of seeing the rainbow as violet, blue, blue-green, green, yellow, orange, and red, a dog would see it as dark blue, light blue, gray, light yellow, darker yellow (sort of brown), and very dark gray. To put it simply, in addition to gray, black, and white, dogs see the colors of the world as basically yellow and blue. They see violet, blue, and a cool blue-green as blue; greenish hues as gray; warm yellow-green, yellow, and orange as yellow; and red as shades of gray.

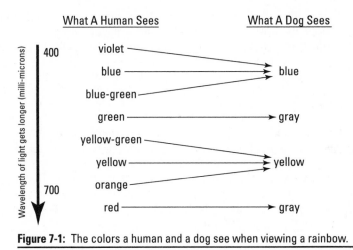

Figure 7-1: The colors a human and a dog see when viewing a rainbow.

Do dogs have night vision?

Three attributes of the canine eye allow for clear vision after dark. The most recognizable is the dog's pupil, which is much larger than a human's. Because the *pupil* is the opening that lets light into the eye, the big pupil gives the dog better light-gathering ability. Still, this skill doesn't come without a cost. The wide pupil prevents clear focusing on images and objects, and depending upon their distance, they may appear blurry: A smaller pupil is needed to have good *depth of field.*

Which way did it go?

Walk into any pet store, and you may be immediately drawn to a vibrant orange-colored object. These brightly colored toys (the color of a utility cone) are becoming increasing popular, although for reasons you may not have imagined. You see, unless a dog watches the trajectory of the thrown toy, he may run right by it, and though he may find it by using his nose, he is often puzzled why he can't see it.

The reason is quite simple. For the dog, the bright orange color of the toy is seen as nearly the same grayish color as the green grass on which the toy landed. In other words, it becomes virtually invisible to your pup! The designers of these toys are clearly concerned about whether the dog's owner can find the toy easily in the store, rather than whether the dog can see it clearly on the grass!

The other aspect of a dog's eye that allows for a wide field of vision depends upon optics. The dog has a bigger *cornea* (the clear part of the eye that bulges out), which allows the collection of more light. The dog also has a larger lens, which gathers the light from the cornea and focuses the images that enter the eye. Together these optical components collect more light and allow better night vision than is found in the human eye.

Ever wondered why your dog's eyes reflect in the night, especially when flashed by oncoming headlights or when spotted by a flashlight? The effect comes from a component of the eye called the *reflecting tapetum*. This mirrorlike surface is located behind the retina, reflects light not yet absorbed by the light receptor cells, and gives the light-collecting cells in the retina a second chance at responding to faint images.

Try this little experiment to discover how different life looks from the eyes of your dog. Smear a face-sized piece of cellophane with a light coating of petroleum jelly and look around. Although you can still make out the general outlines of objects, a lot of the smaller details are blurred and perhaps even lost.

What about vision on the move?

Dogs have one visual advantage over humans: They can see moving objects better and faster than we can. This particular skill is obviously an evolutionary advantage for a hunter who has to detect his prey and run it down. One study of 14 police dogs found that the dogs could recognize an object when it was moving even at a distance of over a half a mile, but if that same object was stationary and much closer, they had much more difficulty identifying it.

A dog's heightened sensitivity to motion explains why some dogs like to watch TV. The motion elicits their predatory instincts and causes many dogs (especially hounds and terriers) to jump up and respond any time a vehicle or animal races across the screen.

Hearing the World

Your dog's sense of hearing is actually more important to her than her eyesight. Though she relies on sight for locating and allowing the grabbing of a moving object, she determines the identity and relative location of objects by sounds coming from them.

Wild canines with pricked ears can move them to help determine the location and direction of sounds. Meanwhile, the changes in sound qualities traveling through the air and deflecting around the ear flap can help precisely determine the distance away of their prey or other pack members.

Hearing capacities in comparison

A person's and dog's hearing capacities are quite different. While most people believe that dogs have better hearing than humans, it's not the case for all sounds. Rather, the dog's advantage is in her capacity to respond to a far broader range of auditory experiences.

To fully grasp the difference in auditory perceptions, it's helpful to understand how a noise is recognized by the brain. The noises that enter the ear can be described as waves: The lower the pitch of the sound, the lower the frequency of the sound pressure peaks that hit the ear; the higher the pitch, the greater the frequency of the wave's undulations.

The pitch of a sound (high versus low notes) is indicated in a measurement known in professional circles as a *Hertz,* or Hz, and it's really nothing more than the number of sound pressure peaks that hit the ear in a second. Sounds that are important for understanding human speech range from about 500 to 4,000 Hz, and humans have ears with their peak sensitivity in that range. Dogs' hearing isn't any better than humans for these sounds. The highest notes that a human can hear are around 20,000 Hz.

Freeze

Many of the animals that were hunted by the dog's wild ancestors evolved a set of behaviors to take advantage of their visual limitation. Specifically, when being pursued, the prey animals would simply freeze in place. Because of a canine's lack of visual acuity, when something is motionless, it becomes virtually invisible. Try this one out on your dog. Stand very still at a distance of around 20 feet and see whether your dog responds to you. Remember, the moment you move, the game is over.

Dogs, on the other hand, evolved from a species that hunted for survival. Thus, their hearing had to be sensitive to the high-pitched sounds of animals rustling in the leaves and brush and emitting scrabbling noises in hidden spaces. For this reason, the hearing range of dogs extends to much higher frequencies than our own, to between 47,000 Hz and 60,000 Hz, depending on the breed and the conformation of a given dog's ears. It's not that dogs have better hearing sensitivity than humans do; it's simply that they can hear higher frequency sounds than people can, which gives them a much broader range of hearing.

Recently, an accurate measure of a dog's hearing capacity was made possible by the development of a hearing test known as Brainstem Auditory Evoked Response (BAER). BAER measures the electrical activity in the inner ear and in the neural pathways that send sound information to the brain. With small electrodes attached to a dog's head, short bursts of sound were put into her ear, and her brain's response was recorded by a computer.

Calling all cat lovers. This mighty hunter, whose entire sustenance may depend upon small rodents that make squeaky sounds, can hear sounds that are 5,000 to 10,000 Hertz higher than can dogs.

Breeds, genetics, and deafness

Some dogs are born with a predisposition toward poor hearing or deafness. Research done at Louisiana State University in Baton Rouge involving nearly 17,000 dogs showed that it's the dog's coat color that is associated with congenital deafness. The genetic defect that produces deafness is closely linked with the genes that produce coats that are white, *roan* (a dark color coat that has been liberally sprinkled with white), and *piebald* (spotty, especially black and white) colors in dogs.

Eyes and ears

Just as coat color makes a difference, eye color also can indicate the likelihood of deafness in some breeds. Dogs with blue eyes are more likely to be susceptible to congenital deafness. For example, in Dalmatians with blue eyes, the rates of deafness can run up to 50 percent. For this reason, some kennel clubs (such as those in Canada) try to discourage the breeding of blue-eyed Dalmatians by barring them from the dog show ring.

The classic example of a piebald dog is the Dalmatian. In this breed, 22 percent are deaf in one ear, and 8 percent are deaf in both ears, amounting to an amazing 30 percent born with some form of hearing deficit. In some breeds of dogs, the white, roan, or piebald genes are found in certain individuals, but not others. For example, a Bull Terrier can be either white or have prominent color patches. Among those Bull Terriers who are white, the rate of congenital deafness is 20 percent, while for those with color patches, it's only around 1 percent.

Table 7-1 shows common breeds of dogs that are likely to have congenital deafness either in one or both ears. The problem usually becomes apparent in the first month or two of the dog's life.

Table 7-1	**Dogs Born Deaf**
Breed	*Percentage Deaf in One or Both Ears*
Dalmatian	30
Bull Terrier (white)	20
Jack Russell Terrier	16
Australian Cattle Dog	15
English Setter	8
English Cocker Spaniel	7

Odd as it seems, deafness in a dog can often go unnoticed by its owner. One of the authors of this book had a Cavalier King Charles Spaniel named Wiz who had become quite deaf, yet visitors seldom noticed because he was always present to greet arriving people and always showed up when the other dogs in the house were called for a treat. The trick was that he was living with two other dogs who bustled around actively. Seeing and feeling their movements gave him enough information to know what was going on without his actually being able to hear human sounds.

Often the first sign of hearing impairment in a dog is subtle — it shows up as an inability to locate sounds accurately. For example, your dog may act confused when you call her, and she can't see you. She may look around uncertainly and come to you only when she finally lays eyes on you. Or you may notice that when a loud noise occurs, she swings her head first to the wrong side, away from the direction that the sound occurred, or acts confused as to where the sound came from. Sometimes, this loss of ability to locate sounds is an indication that your dog has lost hearing in only one ear, and that her other is still functioning. However, it may indicate a more general loss of hearing.

To test your dog's hearing accuracy, stand behind her and out of sight and then either squeak a toy, whistle, or bang two pots. (Make sure that you're out of sight and that your dog is unaware of your presence.) A normal dog pricks its ears or turns its head or body toward the source of the sound.

A newborn puppy is unable to process sound and, in fact, relies on touch and heat sensors to locate its mother. At three weeks of age, a puppy's ears open, although nearly another month is needed for her to develop mature auditory sensors. When testing for diminished auditory perception, delay any hearing tests until the pup is at least six weeks of age for the sake of accuracy.

Noise pollution

The reason why dogs (and humans) tend to lose their hearing with increasing age is due to prolonged exposure to loud sounds. Deep in the inner ear, in a structure called the cochlea, tiny hair cells flex to register the arrival of sounds. Unfortunately, exposure to loud sounds can cause these hairs to break. Once damaged, a hair cell doesn't grow back, so for each hair cell lost, an animal's hearing ability is diminished.

Some breeds seem to be more predisposed to the deafness associated with aging than others, particularly hunting dogs, such as retrievers. Though a sensible hunter wears ear protection to prevent the damaging sounds of gun shots to his own ears, the same isn't provided for the dog, and we now know that the sounds of gunshots can contribute to the late-life loss of hearing in working hunting dogs.

What a Dog's Nose Knows

A dog's nose not only dominates her face, but her brain, as well. In fact, a dog relies on her sense of smell to interpret her world, in much the same way as people depend on their sight. Although this contrasting world view may be hard to imagine, know that your dog interprets as much information as you do. However, she does much of this by smelling an object or animal, not by staring at it.

Born to sniff

To gain more respect for your dog's olfactory ability, compare it to a person's nose. Inside the nose of both species are bony scroll-shaped plates, called *turbinates*, over which air passes. A microscopic view of this organ reveals a thick, spongy membrane that contains most of the scent-detecting cells, as well as the nerves that transport information to the brain. In humans, the area containing these odor analyzers is about one square inch, or the size of a postage stamp. If you could unfold this area in a dog, on the other hand, it may be as large as 60 square inches, or just under the size of a piece of typing paper.

Though the size of this surface varies with the size and length of the dog's nose, even flat-nosed breeds can detect smells far better than people. Table 7-2 shows the number of scent receptors in people and several dog breeds.

A dog's brain is also specialized for identifying scents. The percentage of the dog's brain that is devoted to analyzing smells is actually 40 times larger than that of a human! It's been estimated that dogs can identify smells somewhere between 1,000 to 10,000 times better than nasally challenged humans can.

Table 7-2	Scent-Detecting Cells in People and Dog Breeds
Species	*Number of Scent Receptors*
Humans	5 million
Dachshund	125 million
Fox Terrier	147 million
Beagle	225 million
German Shepherd	225 million
Bloodhound	300 million

Nose work

Human beings have taken advantage of the dog's wonderful sense of smell to perform many important jobs. Some of the better and less well known of these jobs include

✓ Detecting drugs, explosives, and weapons

✓ Tracking lost individuals and fleeing criminals

✓ Searching for survivors (and dead bodies) after a natural disaster, accident, or manmade calamity

✓ Finding termite infestations in homes

✓ Searching for smuggled food products

✓ Searching for hydrocarbons (like gasoline or other flammable fluids) that may have been used in cases of arson

✓ Finding mold and spores that may cause disease in residences and other buildings

✓ Detecting oil and gas pipeline leaks, even if the leak is in a pipe buried 30 feet underground

✓ Telling by scent when an animal has ovulated, which is useful for dairy farmers because cows have such a short period in which they're fertile and can breed.

Recent evidence shows that dogs can detect cancer by scent. Dogs have been reliably trained to find melanoma-type cancers and are able to do so much earlier than other methods can diagnose it. Current research is being done to see whether bladder and prostate cancer can be detected by having the dogs sniff urine samples, and whether lung cancer can be detected by having dogs sniff a person's exhaled air.

Finally, some dogs are very sensitive to human moods and can be trained to pick up the scent changes associated with human emotions. This skill allows them to be very good at assisting psychotherapists and to assist police in detecting when a person is lying. Research on this issue is continuing, but there is a suggestion that dogs may actually be more reliable lie-detectors than the commonly used electronic apparatus.

Your dog's unique nose

Your dog's nose has a pattern of ridges and dimples that, in combination with the outline of its nostril openings, make up a *nose print* believed to be as individual and unique as a human being's fingerprints. Companies even register nose prints as a way of identifying and helping to locate lost or stolen dogs, a system that is now being used by kennel clubs around the world.

If you want to take a nose print from your dog just for fun, it's quite simple: Wipe your dog's nose with a towel to dry its surface. Pour food coloring onto a paper towel and lightly coat your pet's nose with it. Then hold a pad of paper to her nose, making sure to let the pad's sides curve around to pick up impressions from the sides of the nose, as well. You may have to try a couple of times until you get the right amount of food coloring and the right amount of pressure to produce a print in which the little patterns on the nose are clear.

The food coloring is nontoxic and is easily removed. Never use ink or paint, or you may have to explain to your friends why your dog has a green or blue nose.

Chapter 8

Meeting the Needs of Your Growing Puppy

In This Chapter

▶ Recognizing how your puppy's needs affect his behavior

▶ Teaching your puppy his first lessons

▶ Understanding your puppy's emotional development

▶ Knowing how to socialize your puppy from the start

*T*his chapter helps you understand the needs of your growing puppy. Here, you find all the information on how she thinks and how best to gauge your expectations at each developmental stage. During your puppy's early months, the best investment of time is to socialize her to all life's nuances. Advanced obedience lessons can wait, but you have a short window of opportunity to ensure that she's comfortable with the world around her.

Puppies are like developing children in many ways. Your puppy's neediness must be your priority, as you help to shape her impulse control and communication skills. For now, her love and attachment to you is directly reflective on your daily interactions. Do it once and do it right.

If this chapter leaves you wanting a little auxiliary help, consider *Puppies For Dummies* (Wiley), written by one of the authors, Sarah Hodgson.

Creating a Lifelong Bond

Everyone who gets a puppy envisions an idealized relationship — a lifelong bond that fulfills all the reasons the puppy was adopted in the first place: to be a buddy for the children, a protection dog, a simple companion, and so on. This fantasy isn't unusual or even unhealthy, but it is a fantasy. The truth of the matter is that puppies mature gradually, and their adult behavior is directly influenced by daily interactions and experiences. A lot of time, patience, and understanding go into raising a puppy. The more you can learn about your individual puppy's needs and learning patterns, the greater your chance for mutual respect.

Is the experience of adopting a puppy already leaving you feeling overwhelmed and enslaved to your newest family member? It may help to know that most people feel this way at some point. Your only mistake may be in setting your expectations beyond your puppy's capacity. Organize both your schedule and your surroundings to prevent mishaps to ensure that you can both meet your puppy's needs and have time for yourself, too.

An alternative is adopting an older dog, or at least one that is past the puppy stage. The advantage is that someone else will have put in the hard work of living through the puppy stage. The disadvantage is that you don't have the opportunity to shape your pet's behavior exactly as you want, from the beginning.

Initially, your attention will encourage any behavior, so use this fact to your advantage and give your puppy every opportunity to behave well. Puppy-proof your home, leaving appropriate toys out to encourage good chewing habits; brace your puppy (see Chapter 4) to condition four-footed greeting manners; and use treat cups and other gadgets to motivate good behavior (see Chapter 10).

If you have a young puppy, please spend more time encouraging her, rather than discouraging her, using the simple games and tricks mentioned throughout this chapter.

Meeting your puppy's needs

A puppy has the same survival needs as a young baby — and the same dependency on others to provide for them. Each day, she needs to eat, drink, sleep, go to the bathroom, and play. All her needs are equal: If one is overlooked, you pay a high price. Babies cry when they need something. For puppies, the signs that they're in need can include restlessness, whimpering, or even nipping.

Meeting your puppy's needs goes a long way in the bonding process. The person who is most consistently there to take care of a puppy's needs will be revered. Try to read your puppy's signals so that you can address her needs before they become intrusive. Good observation on your part can teach you your pup's "native language," and many of those signals will persist throughout life. Once you know them, you can understand what your pet is feeling and avoid problems that may arise if his needs aren't met.

Puppies need a lot of sleep. If a puppy is overtired, she'll display all the signs of a colossal meltdown: random motions, wild nipping, even snapping at the hands that hold her. If you suspect that your puppy is reacting out of exhaustion, don't correct her. Calmly escort her to a quiet area, leaving her with a chew toy.

Providing early lessons

Puppies are eager to know things and are naturally conditioned to look to a leader for direction. Though you may be unaware, you carry a lot of weight in your puppy's eyes: Be the leader or puppy parent that you would hope for.

Puppies have a short attention span: Keep lessons short and weave them into your daily interaction with them versus setting specific times aside, especially in the early months. Choose a word a week, such as "Sit" or "Give," saying it to your puppy interactively as discussed throughout this book.

Refer to Chapter 10 for a thorough description of positive training tools, such as treat cups, snack packs, and clickers. These items are equivalent to the candy and toys of our fondest childhood memories.

The detrimental effect of discipline

Many of the most common frustrations with puppies (especially young puppies) are created by over-disciplining. Although this mistake is quite innocent, shouting "No" at a puppy under the age of 5 to 6 months is equivalent to yelling at a 1-year-old baby. The very person the puppy turns to protect her and interpret her new world has turned on her. The result is either panic, which people mistake as understanding, or a defensive stance that instills confrontation, not cooperation.

Are you wondering how you can teach your puppy right from wrong? The short answer is that a very young puppy can't grasp these concepts: Life is simply too new. Simply reward the behaviors that you like and ignore the others for now.

Conditioning

Conditioning is the process of pairing a behavior to a word cue, until your puppy connects the two. For example, if you say "Get busy" as your puppy is eliminating, eventually this phrase prompts her to potty. Sound too good to be true? You can teach many behaviors and lessons this way! Just catch the action that you want while it's in progress, attach a label to it, and then reward the pup.

You may use treats to reward your puppy's behavior initially, but phase off treating every time within a few weeks. Directions aren't really learned until they can be prompted without food.

Leash training

Even if you don't foresee using the leash often, your puppy should feel comfortable with it, as many situations require it (visiting the veterinarian, vacationing, and so on). Begin conditioning early!

- Initially supervise your puppy wearing a collar and then attach a leash and let her drag it for short, 10-minute periods. She may play with or carry it; don't interfere.

- When your puppy no longer reacts to the leash or collar, pick up the leash and follow her about. Tug on it gently to introduce the feeling of pressure.

- Using treats and enthusiasm, coach her to follow you. When your puppy cooperates, say "Let's go" and reward her.

Ringing bells and other housetraining signals

Often puppies understand the concept of going outside, but are unclear how to signal their people's attention at the door. As you go to the door, say "Outside," using the same door whenever possible. Secure a bell at your puppy's nose level and tap it with your finger, or encourage a "Let me out" signal, such as barking just before opening the door.

Stairs

Many puppies are initially afraid of going up or down the stairs due to their physical awkwardness and a fear of the heights involved due to depth perception. At first, carry the pup up the stairs, and place him on the next to the last step, and encourage him up by patting the floor on the step ahead and giving treats. The same goes for going downstairs. Carry the pup to the next to the last step and encourage him to complete the short journey down. When he's comfortable with two steps, go to three, and so on until he's confident walking the entire staircase — up or down!

Word association

The best way to introduce directions to your puppy is by associating them with positive games and experiences. Here are some fun and cheerful conditioning games:

- ✔ **Name game:** Place several treat cups about the house or use a positive alerting signal like clapping or a whistle. Call your pup's name after a short separation, kneeling down to bring yourself to her eye level. If she stops short, run away from her and clap your hands and repeat her name — she'll follow out of curiosity! If other people want to join you, offer them a treat cup — and call your puppy from person to person.

  If you repeat your puppy's name when you want to isolate or groom her, you may notice that she stops getting excited when you call out to her. Stop in your tracks! Only call her by name for positive interactions.

- ✔ **Sit, please:** Teach your puppy to sit whenever she wants attention, toys, food, and so on.

  Don't demand her response — simply position her as you direct her: Gently squeeze her waist muscles just below her ribs as you lift up her chin.

- ✔ **Proper greeting:** Puppies jump up to get closer to your face. Help your puppy learn a more acceptable greeting ritual. Whenever you greet your puppy or are introducing her to someone new, *brace her* by looping your thumb over the bottom of her collar and holding her waist to prevent jumping as you repeat the direction, "Say, hello." Another option is the *reverse yo-yo,* as illustrated in Figure 8-1. Leave a 4-foot leash on your puppy and step on it before greeting your company. If your puppy does jump, he'll be brought down: Introduce him when he's calmer. (For more insights, see Chapter 13.)

- ✔ **Natural come:** Say your dog's name and "Come" when you and your puppy reunite. Place treats in your pocket or wear a snack pack and reward your puppy when she chooses to check in with you. As you hand her a reward, say "Come." Within weeks she'll be conditioned that "Come" means you're close, and she, herself, will race over to close the gap.

  The biggest mistake puppy people make is to teach this command when they're standing apart from their puppy. A puppy then learns that "Come" highlights separation, not togetherness.

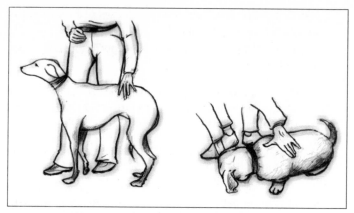

Figure 8-1: Using the reverse yo-yo technique during greeting.

You may give your puppy freedom in a fully enclosed area. If you're playing in an open field or yard, leave a long line (see Chapter 10) on her to supervise her wanderings.

Preventing Problems

You've probably seen an aggressive, hyper, or fearful dog. Though each may look different to you, each dog is showing signs of stress experienced in puppyhood.

Watch for signals of your puppy's confusion or stress, such as hyperactivity, excessive barking, jumping, or nipping. Intervention will help your puppy mature into a well-mannered family member.

For more thorough discussions about problem behaviors and their solutions, refer to Chapter 13.

Aggressive puppy

An assertive puppy can either develop into a protective family member or into a dog who will use aggression to make a point. The choice is up to you. If you think your puppy has this potential, ask yourself:

- ✔ Does she bait you to play tug-of-war?
- ✔ Is she relentless in her demand for attention?

✔ Does she refuse to relinquish toys or food and growl or snap if you try to take them?

✔ Will she grab you with her mouth to prove a point or bark back when you correct her?

Though her earliest attempts at being the boss (in her puppy litter) may have been successful, show her that she is not the leader under your roof:

✔ Use a head halter, such as a Halti or Gentle Leader, to better control her.

✔ Consider using *time-outs* (see Chapter 13) whenever the pup gets uppity. Direct him by voice or collar and simply say, "Time-out" while you place him into his kennel crate or a safe but uninteresting room such as the bathroom.

✔ Teach her other manners, such as sitting when she wants a toy or treat and lying down quietly with a bone when you're preoccupied.

✔ Only attend to your puppy when she's respectful of you.

If your puppy threatens or snaps at anyone, seek professional help. Although we can help control aggression (see Chapter 15), a full-blown aggressive response that threatens injury to someone requires instant attention and is beyond the scope of this book.

Hyper puppy

If your puppy has trouble with impulse control, you may mistakenly diagnose her as having an attention disorder. It's not unheard of for a dog to suffer from this affliction, although it's rare. Most hyperactivity results from inadvertent interactions given to a smart, energetic puppy. Eager to please, these puppies interpret any attention as positive and often note that wild behavior gets the biggest rise from those whom they love the most. If mania works, then mania it will be . . . in spades.

To avoid developing a manic puppy and a frustrated owner, simply place your dog in a time-out. The duration of time-out is determined by how long it takes him to calm down. Usually 3 to 5 minutes are all that's needed.

Timid puppy

Is there a more pitiful sight in the world than a frightened puppy? Of course, the immediate human reaction is to smother this puppy with love and affection. That, however, isn't an effective reaction. Puppies interpret our intention by how we look and not by what we're saying: A lowered posture communicates fear, direct focus is questioning, and high-pitched tones are a clear sign of panic. To your puppy, you look scared, too.

What a frightened puppy needs is a confident leader, so play the part: Stand tall and act cool.

Brace your puppy by kneeling down and holding her in a sit position or by holding her on a leash.

Whenever possible, step back from the stimulus to the point where your puppy is comfortable and be an example of confidence.

Use the socialization steps in this chapter to expose her to all that life has to offer, turning your "don't-wanna-do-it" puppy into a can-do dog.

Socializing Your Puppy

Your first priority is to socialize your pup. You'll have plenty of time to "train" her later, but only a small window of opportunity to familiarize her with life's nuances. If you miss out on experiences during this *impressionable period* (from birth to 14 weeks of age), many common situations and events will be unfamiliar to your puppy. What is unknown may provoke a whole host of undesirable responses, ranging from fear to aggression. During the socialization process, your puppy fills her memory bank with people and places that they successfully and safely encountered, and this will allow her to remain stable and confident. This section explains how to make socializing your puppy a positive experience for both of you.

Your puppy's brain is still developing even though she's 12 weeks or more of age. Though she will sleep a lot, her waking hours are spent absorbing experiences like a young child absorbs language.

It is possible to begin introducing your puppy to new experiences as early as 4 weeks of age. After 14 weeks of age, your puppy will be more rigid in her associations and less impressed by your example. Use Table 8-1 to monitor your socialization program.

Developmental stages

Puppies mature a lot like children, going through similar stages of development that are prompted by both self-awareness and hormonal release. Though certain stages can drag on, they won't last forever, and believe it or not, some day these puppyhood gripes will be a distant memory.

Infant (8–12 weeks): Also known as the angelic stage, most puppies sleep a lot and are relatively calm and observant when interacting. Though you can "train" your puppy at this age, her reactions are less learned than quick responses to get your attention. This phase is the ideal time to get your puppy to focus on lifelong routines, such as where to potty, what to chew, and where her resting areas are in each room.

Terrible Twos (13–18 weeks): This stage heralds an immediate fall from grace as your puppy develops a growing awareness of both herself and the world around her. Though your puppy may seem sassy and defiant, don't give up on her just yet: These are all signs of normal development and are often her way of dealing with her own emotional stress.

Learn creative ways to direct her impulsivity and then let time and maturity take its course. Focus on play training and basic manners like sitting for rewards and alerting to her name. Lastly, don't set yourself up for disappointment: Keep your home puppy-proofed and her schedule consistent.

Budding adolescent (4 1/2 months–8 months): For some puppies, this stage is the most trying. Old puppyhood problems re-emerge with a new twist: control. This stage is when your puppy is determining her place in your household: Does she watch you or direct you?

Now is the time to introduce the concept of "No" (see Chapters 3 and 12) and structured lesson time. All directions should be reinforced throughout the day so that your budding adolescent can learn that your directions aren't debatable.

Puberty (8 months–11 months): Puberty is a nightmare for any species. Remember that your puppy is on an endless hormonal rollercoaster. You'll have to endure this time. If you lose your patience, it will set you back, as your puppy is looking to you for a steady reaction. Repetitive lessons, a well-organized exercise plan, and containment around heavy distractions (for example, fenced area or leash) are musts.

Young adult (11 months–18 months): If you've kept up with your puppy's lessons, you'll clearly note that the end is in sight. Some days your puppy behaves like a well-mannered dog. Your role now is to follow through when your puppy ignores you, position her if she chooses to go her own way, bring her into unfamiliar environments often to highlight your worldliness and leadership skills, and stay on top of her lessons.

Table 8-1	Sample Socialization Chart		
When Introduced to Particular People	**1st Reaction**	**2nd Reaction**	**3rd Response**
Baby	Held back, sniffed air	Licked air, wagged tail	Licked baby's hand
Toddler	Stared, slightly lower tail, backed up	Went to sound of treat cup, reached forward to take treat	Approached slowly with tail wagging, looking to treat cup for reward
Adolescent child	Chased and jumped on	Responded to treat cup and direction to "sit" though somewhat hesitant	Didn't chase on skateboard when leashed, was calmer when petted, and followed children when led on leash
Older person	Hesitant, tail low but wagging	Approached too eagerly, jumped in response to offered treat	A far more accepting response, calmer, sat when given instruction, took treat gently

Don't take your puppy out on the town until she's gotten her inoculations and a thumbs-up from her veterinarian. Many airborne viruses can cause serious illness and even death.

Table 8-2 provides a list of things to socialize your puppy with.

Table 8-2	Itemized Socialization List
People	**Objects**
All sizes	Construction equipment
Ethnicities	Umbrella
Different ages	Stroller
Both sexes	Grates

Places	Sounds
City/town/suburbs	Appliances
Beaches	Vacuum
Busy parking lot	Siren
Stores/offices	Train whistle
Animals	**Surfaces**
Other dogs	Wood floor
Cats	Linoleum/tile
Rodents	Grass
Birds	Gravel
Farm animals	Wet/snow/ice

Creating a positive association

Take a cheerful attitude along when you're socializing your puppy, as your example will help her feel comfortable in the world around her. Use treats, toys, and patience — whatever it takes to keep your puppy's attention centered on you, as many new distractions can be frightening at first. Routine exposure will calm her reaction, and the time will be well spent: Your puppy will develop confidence in your worldliness and direction. Keep these things in mind as you socialize her:

- ✔ **Use the right leash and collar.** When you're out and about, condition your puppy to the direction "Let's go." Find an effective collar (for rambunctious puppies consider a head collar, such as a Halti or Gentle Leader) or a no-pull harness (see Chapter 10), as they guide your puppy without putting undo strain on her developing neck or back, and use a 4- to 6-foot leash.

  Avoid using long retractable leashes when socializing your puppy. This long lead gives your puppy far too much slack and endangers her safety near roadways. Such leashes are, however, useful when exercising your puppy in a field or on a beach instead.

- ✔ **Focus on their curiosity.** Most puppies stop in their tracks from time to time, refusing to move or freaking out when presented with a new situation. If you focus on your puppy at this time, you'll cement her fear. Instead, relax your body and look inquisitive by approaching the person/object when possible. Focus your attention on your puppy only when she warms to a situation, even if it takes several exposures.

✔ **Try coaxing gadgets.** Using favorite treats and toys while you socialize your puppy is a given, but you may want to consider other gadgets, such as treat cups, clickers, and targeting wands (see Chapter 10). You can use these associations to lure your puppy closer to a distraction that makes her wary and to reward her when she exhibits confidence.

✔ **Repeat exposures.** Some puppies are hard headed: If they don't like something, they stand firm. These pups need repeated exposures and positive modeling before they'll relax their guard. Consider a street grate, for example. The image confuses their depth perception and arrests the motions of even the most confident puppy. If your puppy refuses to go near one, don't avoid it. Create a can-do puppy by seeking out a grate each day and sitting by or on it as you lure your puppy closer with treats. Repeated exposure will do the trick — soon, your puppy will "catch your confidence" and approach with curiosity, not fear.

Does the thought of spending time socializing your puppy away from home seem like too much bother to you? If you're fortunate enough to live within a private enclosure, and you don't take the time to expose your puppy to other places, objects, and people, she may run the risk of territorial aggression or *outside world phobias* (growing wary of anything not found at her home base). If you ever want your dog to meet people and go to other places, you must do it or else spend the rest of the dog's life dealing with fears and aggression.

Exploring places

Dogs are more home loving than people are and are truly content to spend all of their lives in the same locale. Though your dog may be content to never stray beyond the boundaries of your home, neighborhood, and surrounding area, for her to do so is unrealistic. You're certain to take your dog out if only to the veterinarian or to the kennel during your holiday, although most people enjoy socializing with their dog elsewhere, too.

The surest way to guarantee your puppy's easy transition from one environment to another is by taking her with you often. If you live in the country, go to the city. If you're an urban dweller, go find some clean fresh air. Take your puppy to town, beaches, and in any dog-friendly building or store. Use the following directions to lead her about, always playing the role of the social director. (Go to Chapter 3 for more instruction on how to teach your puppy these directions.)

- ✔ **"Follow" or "Let's go":** This direction says, "I'm the leader, protector, and guardian — follow me!" When your puppy is walking behind you or standing behind you, she'll feel safe and protected.

- ✔ **"Wait" and "Okay":** Use this duo at all curbs, stairs, car doors, and thresholds, telling your puppy to stop at your side and look up to you before proceeding. These directions also communicate your reliability, saying, "Let me look ahead to make sure that we're safe."

- ✔ **"Sit":** When you're around distractions, your living-room champion may suddenly forget basic directions like "Sit." Don't despair — she's just distracted. Position your puppy, teaching her to focus on your directions.

- ✔ **"Stay":** This direction instructs your puppy to be still. If she's unable to cooperate (for example, during a greeting), either brace her or stand on the leash. If you're relaxing or eating, encourage stillness by sitting on the leash.

- ✔ **"Under":** Say this direction when you're sitting on a chair or bench, luring your puppy underneath your feet or the table leg with a toy or treat. This covered space helps your puppy feel protected and safe, and she will, in turn, be calmer.

- ✔ **"Back":** If your puppy pulls to walk in front of you, say, "Back" as you direct her behind you. If this direction proves too difficult to master, review the proper handling of the leash and your collar choice (see Chapter 10). Make the appropriate changes.

Use these foundation words for all your socializing experiences. Familiar words instill focus and trust.

Meeting other people

Whether you desire a friendly dog or hope that your puppy develops protection skills, socialization is critically important. A well-socialized dog has a broad horizon, having met all sorts of people, and isn't easily derailed by new experiences. This dog has learned to trust her people's responses and can easily identify those persons who have bad intentions.

If your puppy hasn't met children by the time she's a few months old, you'll notice her alarming reaction when she's confronted by them. Children smell different and look and move differently, too. Though each dog's response is unique, many will act defensively or aggressively or exhibit active fear of children. Once they've passed the impressionable stage (up to 14 weeks old), you'll have far less ability to positively influence their behavior.

Exposing to sounds

Your puppy is more acutely aware of sounds than you can imagine. We encourage you to expose your puppy to many different sounds.

If a certain sound startles your puppy, kneel down and brace her by holding her chest and back. Repeat "Stay" in a calm voice if she's familiar with the direction; if your puppy is unable to relax, step back a comfortable distance, outside of her *red zone* — the distance away from the object at which she feels comfortable (see Figure 8-2). If possible, modify the sound or mute it and engage your dog in welcomed activities, such as treat-based lessons and games.

Most puppies are startled when experiencing their first thunderstorm. Your initial reaction to your puppy's fear is critically important. If you coddle her, she'll grow fearful, as your posture and tone conveys the equivalent of fear and confusion. A better approach is to act completely unbothered, standing tall and moving about as if nothing were going on. If your puppy doesn't adopt your attitude, move into a small room, read, or chat on the phone. Above all else, stay calm. When she's less stressed, praise, play, and reward her to encourage more outward focus than inward fear.

Surfaces

Imagine life without shoes. Your dog walks on bare paws every day: New and unfamiliar surfaces will always give her reason to pause. Expose your puppy to as many surfaces as possible.

If your puppy acts confused or startled when you walk onto a new surface, don't drag her across it. Stop and sit a short distance from her and urge her to you with treats or a toy. When she gets to you, reward her for a few seconds, then place her back on the floor, and move a few feet away. Repeat the process several days in a row — spreading treats on the floor to override her trepidation.

Figure 8-2: Recognizing your dog's red zone.

 Introduce your puppy to as many indoor and outdoor sounds as possible. A vacuum cleaner can be as alarming as a siren if your puppy is unfamiliar with it. Use treats to measure her comfort zone: If she doesn't take them, she's in panic mode, so move back.

Introducing objects

The gift of socializing your puppy is the mutual benefit of being familiar with and relaxed around all life has to offer. Always remember that your puppy sees new objects differently than you do. For her to feel comfortable with anything, she must sniff it; her nose works like your eyes. For example, if you see a leaf bag blowing in the wind, you can interpret the sight from afar. Your puppy, on the other hand, can't. If it's a first encounter, he may act startled or even defensive until he's willing to come close enough to sniff it.

The goal in early socialization is to build up your puppy's bank of experiences so that throughout her life, she'll be less surprised by the variety of things that life will throw at her. Refer to Table 8-2 or create your own list of objects that you're likely to come across in your daily adventures. Introduce your puppy to these objects one at a time, always keeping in mind the following:

- ✔ If your puppy is startled, discover her red zone.

- ✔ Give her direction and treats at this distance. If she's still unable to focus on you or the food, back away until she can.

- ✔ When you're able, investigate the object yourself. Kneel down and pretend to sniff it — your puppy will trust in your bravery.

- ✔ As your puppy gets more familiar with the object, walk by it swiftly saying, "Let's go." Look straight ahead — your puppy will focus on your confidence.

Avoid the temptation to soothe your puppy if she's fearful. She'll interpret your soothing as submissive fear or confusion; instead of soothing her, it will underscore her concern.

Meeting other animals

No one wants a dog who's either afraid of other animals or dangerously aggressive with them. To an undersocialized dog, however, the "unfamiliar" is always a potential danger, which can prompt a host of unpredictable behaviors.

Ask friends, neighbors, and other family members to bring over a variety of pets to meet and handle your puppy while still on a leash to allow you full control. Stay calm, modeling behavior that you want your puppy to emulate.

If you can visit a farm or walk along a horse path or fence, do so. The more animals your puppy sees during this socialization time, the less they will worry him throughout your lives together.

Chapter 9

Reading and Communicating as Your Dog Ages

*A*s your dog ages, he'll adapt and change because of his own life experience. However, as time takes its toll, he'll process this information less efficiently. In this chapter, we lead you through your dog's aging process, helping you gain insight into age-related changes in your dog's mind and behavior. Simple awareness can instill empathy leading you to modify your environment and communicate in a manner befitting the dignity of an older dog.

Discovering Your Dog's True Age

The rate at which a dog ages depends a lot upon his size. Large dogs age more slowly when they're young and take longer to lose their impish ways and achieve sexual and social maturity. However, by the time they're around 3 years old, they've caught up with smaller breeds, and from then on, they age significantly faster. It's this pattern of aging that ultimately results in smaller dogs having a much longer life span than larger dogs. At the behavioral level, this faster aging process also means that large dogs will start to act like senior citizens much earlier.

Table 9-1 combines results from a number of different studies to allow you to convert your dog's actual age to its human equivalent in years. To find your dog's equivalent age in human years, simply find its actual age and then check under the column corresponding to its weight in pounds.

The old-fashioned folksy way of estimating a dog's age, suggesting that every 1 year of a dog's life is equivalent to 7 years of a human life, was really just a rough guess based on the fact that the average life span of a dog was estimated at that time to be around 10 years and the average life span of a human was around 70 years.

Table 9-1	Your Dog's True Age			
Dog's Actual Age (Years)	_Dog's Weight in Pounds_			
	0–20	21–50	51–120	Over 120
1	15	15	14	13
2	23	24	22	21
3	28	29	31	31
4	32	34	38	41
5	36	39	45	50
6	40	44	52	59
7	44	49	59	68
8	48	54	66	77
9	52	59	73	86
10	56	64	80	95
11	60	69	87	-
12	65	74	94	-
13	70	79	-	-
14	76	84	-	-
15	82	89	-	-
16	88	95	-	-
17	94	-	-	-

Other factors seem to affect aging, too. The shape of a dog's face is one such example: Dogs with sharp, pointed faces that look like wolves generally have longer lives and seem to age more slowly. Dogs with very flat faces, such as bulldogs and pugs, often have shorter lives and age more quickly. Of course, a dog who is well cared for can often live much longer than average for its size, shape, and breed.

Not only can your dog's age predict her life span, it can do the same for her behavior as well. The numbers in Table 9-1 give you an estimate of the mental age of a dog in human years, allowing you to judge how a dog may behave in certain situations or under particular stress.

Human thought processes slow down sharply at around 55 years of age. The giant breeds, such as the Saint Bernard, start showing the kinds of thought patterns, problem-solving changes, and learning problems that we associate with humans who are that age when the dog is somewhere between 5 and 7 years of age. Other big dogs (not quite as large as the giant breeds), such as the Alaskan Malamute, start thinking like seniors between 6 and 8 years of age. The medium breeds, such as the Cocker Spaniel, won't start acting like seniors until 7 to 9 years of age, while the smaller breeds, such as a Yorkshire Terrier, won't act like seniors until they're 9 to 11 years of age.

Of course, there can be a wide variety in the abilities and behaviors of dogs the same age, even within a single breed. Certain individual dogs seem to age more rapidly, while others go many years past when we may expect. Like people who remain active and engaged, dogs who use their brain and mind seem more vital as they progress into their golden years.

Battling an Aging Body

Dogs and humans age similarly both psychologically and physically, though with dogs, the process is accelerated. As the body matures, it stiffens and grows progressively weaker. Aging dogs move less quickly and are less agile as the process of growing older limits their flexibility and coordination. No less loving, an older dog grows more dependent on the care and affection of his family to stay connected to life.

When Stan's old dog Wizard lost his ability to jump up onto the bed where he had slept next to his master all of his life, Stan simply built a set of carpeted stairs that he placed next to the bottom of the bed. This adjustment allowed Wizard to hobble up and rest next to his companion's feet as he'd always done.

Older dogs are more prone to diseases and other conditions related to their overall decline. Because any discomfort will result in changes in behavior, it becomes increasingly critical for older dogs' guardians to nurture their existence. Detecting distress in an older dog isn't always easy, as he doesn't show the same symptoms that humans do.

As a species, dogs generally have a higher tolerance for discomfort than people do, leading many people to falsely assume that their dog is fine when he's not. Although people are quick to communicate the slightest distress, encouraging social support and medical help, dogs are more likely to adopt behaviors that hide their pain from plain view.

In essence, your dog hides his pain to appear to be more in control of the situation, thus making it difficult for you to recognize when your dog is hurting.

Many observable physical cues indicate pain. Though an obvious yelp or whimper would seem the first signal, if your dog is crying out, then the pain has reached a level of intensity that has broken through his protective barriers and his normal reserve. This is a dog that is hurting so badly that he doesn't care who knows it. In most cases, however, the signs are less obvious:

- ✔ Excessive panting and rapid breathing occur, even when the dog is at rest and not heat-stressed.

- ✔ The dog may shiver or tremble.

- ✔ Sometimes, the dog may appear to be extremely restless and change positions frequently while lying down or sitting. At the other extreme, he may appear extremely reluctant to change body positions.

- ✔ The dog may pull away when being touched, may appear to be guarding one part of his body, and may even show uncharacteristic aggression, growling or threatening when touched or even approached.

- ✔ Licking or chewing at painful areas is also common.

- ✔ You may see body cues, such as twitching, limping, or a frozen appearance.

- ✔ Dogs in pain often lose their appetite.

More subtle signs include rapid heart rate, dilated pupils, and a rise in body temperature.

If your dog is showing any of these signs, see your veterinarian immediately.

Diminishing Awareness

The effects of age are much the same on dogs and humans: joints wear out, systems break down from overuse, and faculties lose their functionality over time. Though the affects of time are universal, diminished sight and hearing can have a major effect on the human-animal bond. Fortunately, you can easily modify your environment and communication style to prevent this possible source of stress and ensure that he lives out his golden years happily.

One simple method is to always train your dog using both hand signals and voice commands at the same time. That way if age weakens his hearing he can still respond to your signals, and if his sight dims he can still respond to your voice.

When hearing fades

Hearing loss is commonly a result of physical wear and tear. In the inner ear (the *cochlea*), tiny hairlike cells bend to register the arrival of sounds. Unfortunately, this repeated bending and flexing over the years of a dog's life can cause a weakness in the material and the hair can break, just like a wire coat hanger that has been bent in the same place many times. Once these hairs are damaged, they don't grow back, so for each hair cell that is damaged, the dog loses a bit of his hearing ability.

Of course, age isn't the only reason why the hair cells that register sounds break. Hair cell damage is often the result of exposure to loud sounds and is more common in dogs who have been exposed to gun-shot noises in hunting or who have lived in cities and been exposed to high levels of urban noise. In addition, chemicals can play a role, particularly exposure to various common solvents (cleaning fluids, paint thinners, and plastic solvents), which can accelerate damage to the cells in the ear. A lifetime of minor stresses explains why most dogs in the 12- to 15-year-old range show some evidence of hearing loss.

Knowing the signs of hearing loss

Simple observation of your aging dog can usually tell you whether his hearing is failing:

- ✔ Your dog seems to ignore your calls, especially when out of sight or distracted.
- ✔ Your dog sleeps more soundly than he used to, instead of bolting awake at a loud noise.

- Your dog awakens with a growl or a snap if touched while sleeping.

- Outdoors, your dog may appear to be oblivious to the sound of approaching cars.

- Personality changes may occur, such as the dog appearing to be more fearful, dependent, lethargic, edgy, or snappish.

Living with a hearing-impaired dog

Your dog's world will change drastically as his hearing fades, although you can take some relatively simple steps to ease this transition:

- Most dogs rely on hearing to locate family members, so a hearing loss often leads to a sense of isolation, which can give a formerly confident dog bouts of separation anxiety and perhaps even bring on episodes of panic.

- For an easy solution, wear perfumed body lotion, scented perfume, or aftershave. Because your dog's sense of smell is his most robust sensory system and suffers least from the aging process, the scent you wear makes you a lot easier to track down. Furthermore, because scents tend to persist in the air and cling to surfaces, your dog will recognize that you've been nearby recently, and feeling your presence in the vicinity will comfort him even if he can't hear you.

- To wake a deaf dog without startling him, use your dog's sense of smell to avoid startling him from a sleep. When you approach your sleeping dog, hold your hand near his nose for a few seconds. Your scent will penetrate his sleeping brain, and he'll awaken when he recognizes your scent. Reach out to pet him only after he has roused naturally.

You can get a deaf dog's attention in several ways, although shouting at increasing decibels is not one of them:

- Thump on the floor with your foot or slap a wall or some solid furniture, which causes vibrations that the dog can sense.

- Wave your arms vigorously, because dogs' eyes are sensitive to movement.

- Wear a small flashlight or a laser pointer on a lanyard around your neck. A bright moving light quickly causes the dog to turn to you.

- If your dog is outside (enclosed) at night and you want to call him in, turning your porch light off and on serves as a good signal.

✔ Obviously, if you're close to your dog, you can always touch him. However, it's important to always touch him in the same place so that he recognizes that it is a signal and not a potential threat. The shoulder or top of the head are ideal.

Always leash a hearing-impaired dog when walking him in an unenclosed area, such as the park. In these areas, a long or retractable leash is ideal because it still allows the dog to run and play but gives his owner control over him. Buy a dog tag that states, "Help me home. I'm deaf," and includes an updated phone number, should he mistakenly get loose.

Other sources of hearing loss

In some cases, what appears to be age-related hearing loss may actually be due to other factors that can be remedied. The dog's ear canal is much longer than that of humans, and it takes a right angle turn as it reaches the eardrum. This shape, unfortunately, is ideal for collection of debris. Wax, dirt, and hair build up in the canal and create a plug that keeps the sound from reaching the eardrum. This same debris can also attract ear mites, which in turn can cause ear infections (called *otitis*). All these factors can result in swelling and fluid accumulation that can effectively block much of the sound from reaching the middle ear.

Dogs that spend a lot of time in the water (especially pond or lake water that may not be clean) are most susceptible to these problems. Furthermore, those long floppy ears that look so appealing on dogs like hounds and spaniels also tend to trap moisture and limit air circulation, which can turn the ear into a good breeding ground for infections.

As in most cases, visible signs and symptoms usually suggest a problem with a dog's ears:

✔ The dog frequently shakes its head or scratches its ears.

✔ Touching the dog's ears causes him to pull away or whimper.

✔ You can smell a putrid ear odor when you sniff.

✔ The dog walks with her head uncomfortably cocked to the side.

Lift the flap of the dog's ear or check closely on a dog with pricked ears. You're looking for normal ears that are pink with a small amount of amber wax. (The wax actually helps to protect the ear canal.) Warning signs include any discharge, blood blisters, excess reddening, or crumbly material.

These symptoms should prompt a call to your dog's veterinarian. It is often the case that a good ear cleaning and perhaps a course of antibiotics may well clear up hearing difficulties.

Why deaf dogs bark so much

A common problem with deaf dogs is excessive barking. While they obviously can't hear their own barks well, they still recognize the sensation barking creates and a human's reaction to their behavior. If their barking is effective in attracting attention, they'll continue to bark, and often bark louder in an attempt to hear themselves as they once could. Though the root cause of hearing-loss barking is often a feeling of confusion or social isolation, a human comforting the deaf dog that is barking noisily actually makes him more anxious about his predicament.

A much more effective strategy is to put the dog in a small room or his kennel until the barking stops. Wait for a pause in the barking of 30 seconds or more and then let him out and reward his now quiet behavior.

Put a bell on your dog. Though the bell is useless to a deaf dog, it allows you to hear your dog when he's on the move. This sound allows you to find him more easily because he clearly can't hear you when you call.

When vision fades

Vision often fails in older dogs, although for more varied reasons than the mechanical wear and tear most common in hearing loss:

- **Chemical changes:** As a dog ages, changes occur in the proteins that make up the lens of his eye. These chemical modifications create inflexibility that limits the eyes' focusing ability. Even under the best of conditions, a dog's vision for near details is poor, but when the composition of the lens protein shifts, he becomes even more farsighted. Though some focusing ability may remain, it may take more time for the dog to recognize objects and people.

- **Aperture dysfunction:** Another visual impairment occurs when the pupil of the eye (through which light passes) loses its ability to open and close efficiently. The inability to adjust the size of the pupil in relation to given light conditions degrades the quality of the visual image.

- **Nuclear sclerosis:** For most owners, the most visible change in the dog's eye is a haziness that appears on the lens of an older dog's eyes, called *nuclear sclerosis*. On the bright side, this condition doesn't affect sight much, unless this cloudiness becomes dense (when it appears to be almost white). An inexperienced viewer may mistake this cloudiness for the condition known as cataracts.

Cataracts are the single leading cause of blindness in older dogs; please seek a professional's opinion if you suspect your dog is suffering. You do have medical options.

✔ **Cataracts:** A cataract in a dog's eye results when cells within the lens of his eye become dark and opaque over time. Cataracts are often the result of events occurring in the dog's life. They can be the result of diabetes, nutritional deficiencies, exposure to certain toxins, or injuries to the eye. In addition, simple exposure to the ultraviolet light in bright sunshine can trigger cataracts. Hereditary factors are also involved, and several dog breeds, such as Cocker Spaniels, Poodles, and Lhasa Apsos, have a predisposition toward cataracts.

Veterinary science has recently developed effective surgical treatments and can implant a prosthetic device similar to the one used to restore human vision. These treatments are effective, though costly.

✔ **Glaucoma:** The second major condition that causes blindness in dogs is *glaucoma.* It is caused by an increase in fluid pressure, which then damages the neural tissues in the eye that are responsible for registering light. Normally, fluid is drained away at the same rate it enters the eye, but in glaucoma, the outlet for the fluid is narrowed or closed. Aging dogs with high blood pressure are most susceptible to this condition.

If the glaucoma is detected early, drugs and surgery can often hold off any loss of vision for quite a while, although the long-term success is disappointingly low. In glaucoma, as in cataracts, heredity is also a factor. Some dog breeds, including Cocker Spaniels, Siberian Huskies, Basset Hounds, and Beagles, appear to be especially susceptible to these problems.

Detecting failing vision

People often mistakenly think that their dog's loss of vision was a sudden occurrence. However, most dogs lose their sight gradually. Though some people don't recognize their dog's failing sense until it's virtually too late to affect change, you can often detect several signs that signal a loss of vision as your dog ages:

✔ Loss of interest in or the ability to retrieve or chase balls

✔ More cautious when climbing steps

✔ Hesitancy when jumping onto or off of furniture

✔ Going up or down curbs is accompanied by a cautious or high-stepping gait

✔ The dog may stop running and resort to walking nearly everywhere

✔ Personality changes, including increased fearfulness, increased dependency on the owner, increased lethargy, decreased playfulness, and sometimes more snappish or aggressive behavior

If you notice any changes in your dog's behavior or visual awareness, please make an appointment to see his veterinarian. Many treatable conditions affect vision.

Living with a blind dog

Blind dogs can live comfortably. Some take quite a while to even recognize the full limitations of their handicap, since sight usually diminishes progressively and isn't a dog's primary sense.

To help your blind dog live happily, take these steps to provide a new map of her living space. You will become like Annie to Helen Keller:

✔ Attach short directional word or phrases to daily routines. Verbal cues reassure your dog and help him feel connected to your daily interactions. Your voice will both guide and reassure him (see Chapters 3 and 12).

✔ Create landmarks for your dog, keeping daily objects, such as dog bowls and bedding, in the same place. In addition, avoid relocating furniture, TVs, or radios to prevent any disorientation that may result when the dog's mental map is disrupted.

✔ Use carpet runners to create a "road" to familiar rooms.

✔ Use different scents to map out locations or forbidden areas. For example, you can use scented oils or powders to cue your dog to avoid ledges or locate important places in a room. When you travel, these same scents can comfort and guide him in an otherwise unknown environment.

✔ If your dog is distressed at not being able to find you, wear a familiar scent or clip a small bell to your wrist or belt loop.

✔ Return objects to where they belong. Things that are left out are opportunities for collisions that may disorient your dog and lead to anxiety or fearfulness.

✔ If your dog is an outdoor pet, don't plan major landscape projects.

✔ If your dog is disoriented, lead him to a favorite anchoring spot, such as a familiar bed, and pet him calmly until he's settled down.

✔ Going up and down stairs is difficult for blind dogs. Install carpeting and chaperone your dog until he feels confident: Hold his midsection gently as you support his weight and/or lead him up each step by luring him with a favorite treat (see Chapter 12).

The most important tool in dealing with a blind dog is the leash. Think of the leash as giving you the ability to hold your dog's hand. Your dog will feel more secure because he knows where you are. Leashing the dog can be helpful even in the house until he gets adjusted. The dog should certainly be walked on the leash because his owner is now his eyes.

Feeling socially isolated is a problem with blind dogs just as it is with deaf dogs. Most dogs seem reassured if they know where their owners are. A dog that has been free to roam the house may have to be confined at night. Securing your dog next to your bed at night or using a crate is an ideal solution.

Once the dog gets used to the routine and has a mental map of his world, he'll do fine. Many dogs happily go around their homes and live a happy life despite their blindness. In fact, many do it so well that visitors don't even notice that the dog is blind.

Remembering the Aging Mind

Your dog's personality and behavior will change as she grows older, and although some dogs may lose the zest for life, it's not a necessary or even normal part of dogs growing older.

In today's society, where dogs are nurtured as never before, they're, living longer. Better nutrition and medical services ensure that dogs are often making it well into their senior years, and because of that we're seeing more of the degenerative conditions equated with aging, including arthritis, heart disease, cancer, diabetes, and even dementia.

Alzheimer's disease in dogs?

A medical condition known as *Canine Cognitive Dysfunction* (CCD) causes the same kind of disorientation, physiological brain alteration, confusion, memory loss, and personality changes that humans face with Alzheimer's disease. CCD is sometimes referred to as *old dog syndrome, brain aging, doggie dementia,* or *senility.*

The symptoms of this age-related mental problem are usually quite clear to a dog owner. The dog

- ✔ Stops responding to his name or other known directions
- ✔ Stares blankly into space or at walls
- ✔ May repeat behaviors, such as dragging a toy from room to room, or pacing or wandering aimlessly but using the same route or pattern around tables and chairs
- ✔ May get stuck in corners, or around furniture, needing assistance to get out
- ✔ May sometimes appear lost or confused, even in familiar surroundings, or when put out to relieve himself may seem to forget why he was there
- ✔ May experience changes in social behavior, such as no longer trying to get attention, no longer caring about being petted, or walking away when receiving affection
- ✔ May have changes in sleep patterns, including sleeping more during the day and wandering around at night instead of sleeping
- ✔ May sometimes forget his housetraining, even to the point of having accidents indoors immediately after coming inside
- ✔ May be easily agitated and begin vigorously barking for no apparent reason

Seldom does a dog show all these symptoms, but any dog that shows two or more of them may well be developing CCD.

Solutions for a fading mind

Several behavioral interventions can keep mental decline at bay even as your dog ages.

- ✔ *Pattern training* and repetition is reassuring to an older dog. Once a dog has established a regular routine, he'll hold to that pattern through his older years. Familiar directions encourage your dog's participation in daily activities and give him security and comfort.

  Old dogs can still learn, and they love the attention and the opportunity to please you and earn rewards. Though it may take more time and patience, recent research shows that older dogs are eager to learn new routines.

Older dogs have a hard time unlearning learned behavior patterns, such as jumping on guests or not barking at strange noises. Those lessons are better addressed while the mind is still impressionable.

✔ Perhaps the most exciting work about the aging mind is the finding that our day-to-day experiences affect the very structure of our brains and may allow us to counteract the effects of age on our brains. Researchers at the University of Toronto studied a group of aging Beagles in order to see how changing the day-to-day experiences of older dogs would affect their minds. Provided with a *cognitive enrichment program,* the dogs were challenged with learning tasks and puzzles, such as finding hidden food rewards, five to six days a week.

This stimulation went on for a year, at which point each dog was tested for mental awareness and new skill learning capacities. The dogs in this group universally showed better performance in learning and problem solving tasks than did their littermates who had not had these additional experiences.

Dealing with your dog at home is simple. From the earliest days of living with your dog, you should stimulate him by giving him things to learn, problems to solve, and new experiences. However, when your dog grows older, you should make an effort to increase, rather than decrease, your dog's activities:

✔ Provide mental stimulation in as many ways as you can.

✔ Play with your dog.

✔ Go for short walks, especially in new places.

✔ Talk to your dog.

✔ Pet your dog and socially interact with her.

✔ Try to teach your dog something new each week.

If you're willing to put up with a bit of controlled destruction, create problems to solve by putting kibbles or treats inside an old towel, rag, or crumpled plastic jug and allow the dog to tear the item apart to get to the food inside. The cardboard rolls that toilet paper and paper towels come on are great for this activity. Put some kibble in them, crumple the ends, and let the old dog tear apart the "toy" to get to the food.

Turning your dog's meals into searches can also be useful. Divide the dog's meal into small portions, each in a plastic container, and hide them around the house to keep your dog actively searching for a while. If you can put up with the potential mess, simply toss some nonmessy bits of food around a room or yard and encourage the dog to find them.

Part III
Doggie Delinquency

The 5th Wave   By Rich Tennant

"Okay, let's get into something a little more theoretical."

In this part . . .

There is so much more to training dogs these days, and you may need more than a standard chain and a six-foot leash! If your goal is to have a dog who not only listens to you, but enthusiastically *chooses* to respond to your directions rather than to his natural impulses, this part points the way. You can use many tools, techniques, and tricks to shape your dog's learning experience. Born with an innate desire to please those he respects, your dog will focus on your direction if your lessons are inspirational and supportive.

Chapter 10

Inspiring Behavior with Motivational Techniques

In This Chapter

▶ Sorting out training tools, from treat cups to clicker training

▶ Discovering what motivates your dog to respond

▶ Speeding up your dog's *behavioral memory*

▶ Understanding the role of a perfectly timed response

*I*f you've ever ogled over a seemingly perfectly trained or well-mannered dog, the first thing to know is that the dog's behavior wasn't developed overnight. Happy, sociable, well-mannered dogs aren't born that way — their demeanor reflects patient, consistent training techniques. The good news is that this process is within your reach and can be a lot of fun. With the right approach, attitude, and training tools, raising a puppy or training an adult dog can be a fascinating learning experience.

In this chapter, we introduce you to training tools and techniques that put a positive spin on everything from potty training to obedience lessons so that your dog will not just learn, but learn joyfully. (For actual commands and training exercises, see Chapter 12.)

If a dog impresses you and the handler seems approachable, compliment them and ask how they ended up with such a lovely companion. Dog lovers cherish their bragging rights; if they live in your area, you might discover a good school, technique, or trainer to help you.

Choosing Training Tools and Gadgets

When we began our careers, you didn't see much variety in training tools beyond a metal chain collar and 6-foot leash. Nowadays, shopping for your dog is as much fun as taking a child to the candy store. The toys are colorful, noisy, and creative. In the collar and leash section, lengths, style, and colors abound. Most excitedly, training sections contain gadgets, devices, and equipment to aid everyone and any dog, regardless of age, personality, or learning capacity.

The joy of new-age training tools and gadgets is that many of them assist your dog's learning ability, thus considerably shortening the time it takes your dog to learn a new behavior. It may take weeks for a puppy to associate sitting with your repeated direction, although it will take only minutes to associate a clicker sound with a tasty reward (see Figure 10-1).

Figure 10-1: Use the clicker to highlight moments when your dog is relating to you. Always follow the sound of a click with a food reward.

Collars

Different pieces of training equipment affect your dog's learning
and can shape how she relates to and associates with your direction. For example, a proper teaching collar is meant to condition
cooperative behavior or to discourage incorrect responses. Table
10-1 helps you choose the collar most appropriate for your dog's
personality, size, and temperament.

Table 10-1	Finding the Best Collar for Your Dog	
Collar Type	*Description*	*Best For . . .*
Buckle collar	A flat collar that encircles the head and buckles or snaps into place.	Ideal for tags, and,, when effective to get a dog's attention, can be used for training as well.
Head halter	Lays over the nose and wraps behind the ear of a dog like a halter fitted to a horse. When the leash is secured to a chin ring, the dog can be easily led by anyone. This collar conditions good behavior by guiding a dog through various exercises without resistance or tension. The positioning of the collar also has a subduing effect: A band rests over the dog's nose and behind her head, which are two acupressure points that condition calmness.	Ideal for young developing puppies, ardent pullers, dominant dogs (head collars calm these dogs by passively conditioning greater respect), and timid dogs whose confidence is bolstered by its gentle pressure and guidance.
No-pull harness	Secures to your dog's midsection in such a way that it reduces your dog's capacity to pull, thus conditioning cooperative walking skills without a battle. As with head halters, these harnesses are a conditioning tool.	A fine choice for developing puppies or insistent pullers.

(continued)

Table 10-1 *(continued)*

Collar Type	Description	Best For . . .
Good Dog collar	A plastic and decidedly more muted form of a prong collar. A good training tool, it provides your dog with feedback by giving him the equivalent of a scruff shake when he reacts impulsively. Used mindfully and never held taut, this collar can provide clear direction to a dog who may be otherwise difficult to walk or influence. This correction collar can also be used to discourage problem behaviors, including jumping and nipping.	Ideal for powerful, insistent, and headstrong dogs. Also useful when the size or natural strength of a dog can easily overpower the person holding the leash.
Martingale	Has two sections: a flat piece and a slip section made of either a soft material or chain that serves to issue a tug correction. With the chain version, it's the sound of the chain snapping, not the restraint, that teaches a dog; the tug of a cloth collar can be an adequate deterrent for dogs without the possibility of injuring the dog.	Originally designed for sight hounds or other long-necked breed. A popular training and everyday collar.

Leashes

Just like collars, many types of leashes are available, relating their use to both how they can accommodate you and what each communicates to your dog. Table 10-2 outlines popular options.

Table 10-2	Choosing a Leash for Your Dog	
Collar Type	*Description*	*Pros/Cons*
Standard 6-foot walking leash	Ideal for walks, especially in public areas or near roadways. The goal is to teach your dog to walk at your side, rather than to strain in front in a vigilant attempt to break free.	Ideal for trafficked areas and quick potty walks. The draw back when used exclusively, especially with impulsive puppies (under 6 months of age), is that their constant pulling strains their collar, putting undue pressure on their trachea and instilling the message that walking near you is asphyxiating.
Teaching lead	A hands-free walking system (see Figure 10-2). This beltlike leash (patented by author Sarah Hodgson) can be held or secured around the waist to expedite cooperative walking skills. Can also be used to station your dog to an immovable object for close observation or to prevent mischief.	Ideal training leash because it encourages togetherness and direction. Used mindfully, you can quickly condition your dog's cooperative responses while discourag ing mischief immediately. For some, the biggest downside is having their dog at their side throughout the day.
Station lead	A short 2- to 3-foot lead. Can be used to tether a dog to an immovable object to condition resting around household distractions and to teach a dog the direction "Stay."	Allows far greater household freedom while teaching your dog good containment skills. Not meant to be used to isolate your dog or to hold down without supervision.
Drag lead	Can be used to supervise your dog inside or out. Once attached, the lead can be stepped on or lifted to issue a discouraging tug or gentle reminder.	See indoor drag lead.

(continued)

Table 10-2 *(continued)*

Collar Type	Description	Pros/Cons
Indoor drag lead	This 4- to 6-foot lead is attached to your dog's buckle collar or a head collar when you're supervising her freedom indoors. Allows you to react calmly to any situation, from a knock on the door to an attempt to steal an otherwise forbidden object.	On the plus side, serves as an emotional reminder to behave and an easy tool for you to gain quick control over impulsive reactions. The downside: Unsupervised, your dog can easily get stuck; if bored, your dog may use it as a chew toy
Outdoor drag lead	Ideal for puppies and older dogs who can't be trusted to respond when called. Use a light 25- to 50-foot line to allow your dog the freedom to drag it about as she investigates her surroundings. Play games to encourage her interaction with you and offer plenty of rewards when she returns to your side.	Your dog will be able to act naturally in her environment while you can reinforce her natural response to check in with you with food and praise. Watch the line, however, as it can easily tangle in obstacles. And watch those ankles — rope burn if you're not quick enough.
Hand lead	A short 8- to 12-foot leash. Can be attached to your dog's buckle collar to allow easy interference and calm guidance. Ideal for small children who are eager to take part but may lose interest quickly (outside a regular leash can be affixed simultaneously to allow adult control).	Though spectacular for quick interference or guidance, your dog must be supervised when left on this lead as the loop can get caught or serve as a handy chew.
A retractable leash	Helpful training tools when used appropriately: in an open field or beach for exercise; to work on the directions "Come," "Stay," and distance downs; or to allow an untrained leash dog to interact with other off-lead-trained dogs.	A manageable leash extension ideal for use in open area, such as beaches and fields. Because it tangles easily, don't use around people or other dogs. Avoid using near roadsides; mechanical failure can lead to disaster.

Who is leading whom?

The average daily walk is an excellent example of how things get misunderstood between our species. When an uneducated dog pulls a person by her leash, the person often mistakenly assumes that the dog is stupid; otherwise, she wouldn't choke herself.

The dog (rarely dumb) is learning a very different lesson, however: that being near their person is asphyxiating. The more she pulls to get away, the greater the restraint and the more determined she is to break free. If this dog should escape, she'll have little to no incentive to return. Use this chapter to discover an effective training collar and Chapter 3 or 12 to discover more appropriate techniques to teach your dog to follow your lead.

 Retractable leads can cause incidents when used near roadways or in crowded situations. Less controllable than a standard leash, a retractable lead can malfunction, leaving the handler out of control.

 If your dog chews through cloth or leather leashes, you can use a chain leash to eliminate the habit. Once your dog is unsuccessful in chewing through the chain, her determination to chew any restraint should be cured. However, chain leashes are heavy and can cut your hands if you're trying to restrain a very active dog with one.

Figure 10-2: On a teaching lead and a head collar, this dog is a much more cooperative and cheerful companion.

Clicker-happy training

The *clicker* is a small handheld device that, when depressed, issues a sharp clicking sound much like a louder version of the sound of a shutter camera. When this sound is paired with a food reward, an association occurs, causing the sound itself to become rewarding. When highlighting desired behaviors, the clicker speeds up your dog's learning and amplifies her enthusiasm for the training process.

Why is the clicker such an effective training tool? The sound is sharp and distinct — different from any other sound heard during a normal day and meant just to signal a reward. Purposely tied to a treat, this sharp sound highlights what is to come when it's perfectly timed to reinforce a specific behavior. Once your dog learns the behavior, she'll achieve what every dog dreams of: the power to control you. But this time, she'll be controlling you with perfect, praiseworthy routines.

Clicker training is most effective for those dogs who are food motivated and for people who are organized enough to apply the technique either throughout the day, on an outing, or during organized lesson times. Though the ideal is to use the click-treat association all day every day while conditioning learned associations, few people have that presence of mind. Still, the clicker is an effective tool, even if used with only periodic regularity.

You can use the clicker to shape every behavior from simple directions, such as "Sit" and "Wait," to complex routines like housetraining and tricks. When using the clicker, pair each individual click with a food reward, timing each click to the moment your dog hits a position or finishes a sequence or behavior. Table 10-3 lists several ways to use the clicker-reward system.

Table 10-3	Clicker-Reward System
Command	*Action*
Sit	Holding the clicker in one hand and a treat in the other, lure your dog into the sit position by raising the treat above her head. As your dog shifts into position, say "Sit," click, and reward her.
Down	From a sitting position, take the treat hand and lure your dog into position by dropping your hand from her nose to between her front paws. As she shifts, say "Down," click, and treat.

Command	Action
Follow or Let's go	Tie a leash around your waist, positioning your dog on a consistent side — say to your left. Hold the clicker in your left hand, treats in your right, and your right arm over your left thigh to lure your dog into the proper following position. Say "Follow" or "Let's go," click, and reward her position at your heel.
Come	Come is the classic disconnection-reconnection sequence. When your dog is apart from you, the goal is to have a word cue to induce your dog to come close to you. When out in an enclosure or on a drag lead, click and reward the instant your dog chooses to check in with you. If you have a dog who seems oblivious to your presence, instigate her interest, not by badgering her, but by snooping in the grass or playing with her favorite toy or by giving another pet attention. When she saunters over, say "Come" as you click and reward her.

The purpose of the clicker is to highlight the moment your dog responds correctly, not as a command to actually trigger a behavior. For example, if your goal is to have your dog come when you call, click and reward when she's at your side, not when she's a distance from you. Though she may come initially in response to your click, she'll lose interest over time.

You can also use the click-reward system to highlight good behavior, such as good chewing, greeting, or housetraining habits. To do so, either keep a clicker and treats with you at all times (wearing a fanny pack is a good idea because it saves on soggy-treats-in-the-laundry mishaps) or place several cups around the house with ready clickers and treats. Each time your dog is chewing an appropriate toy, behaving well with children or other pets, greeting others respectfully, or eliminating in the right location, click and treat her.

Although nothing is as exhilarating as seeing your dog make a quick clicker connection, it's important to orchestrate its disappearance lest you or your dog become clicker dependent.

If you think of your dog's brain as a blank CD, you'll note that your interactions create behavioral memories that are replayed again and again. The use of the clicker simply speeds up your dog's association and memory for chosen words and/or signal cues. Once this process is completed, however, you need to phase off both the sound of the clicker and the reward so that you'll be able to call up these responses simply by word or visual prompting.

The best approach is two weeks on, two weeks to phase out. During the first two weeks, use your clicker to highlight a chosen behavior or behaviors, such as housetraining or teaching your dog to "Sit." Each time she successfully responds, click and reward her. After two weeks of focused reactions, begin to phase out the click-treat response intermittently: Click-treat every other time, then every third repetition, and back to one for one so that your dog doesn't know when she'll be rewarded with a click-treat response. Continually reward your dog with verbal praise, petting, or playful interaction to ensure her continued enthusiasm. During this two-week period, begin to eliminate the clicker response entirely so that you're able to direct her without food or a sound reward.

Targeting

Targeting uses an object as a pointer to direct your dog to a specified spot or in a certain direction. Targeting techniques help teach your dog basic training sequences and more advanced moves, as well as help you improve her behavior and social skills.

Targeting applies the behavior-reward system by using an object to guide a dog's focus:

✓ **Target disc:** Though commercial discs do exist, a discarded container lid is adequate. For this intended purpose, a dog is taught to step on or nose the lid and is rewarded each time she does. Once the association is clear, you can use the lid to enable a variety of learned behavior:

- Promote good household manners or confidence with unfamiliar people or settings, chiefly by teaching the dog where to stand or sit during meals, quiet times, and doorbell greetings.

- Aid advanced obedience lessons, agility exercises, and household manners by placing the disc at greater distances from the handler.

- If the dog is taught to nose the disc, it may be hung on furnishings or attached to persons to teach behaviors such as closing an open cabinet, approaching a person, or nosing a ball.

✔ **Target stick:** A target stick is basically a sort of baton or pointer. Like a disc, you can purchase a commercial stick, although you can use other objects (such as the end of a long spoon or child's toy) as well. With this tool, you can teach a dog to move toward or follow the stick with her nose, a process that most often involves the reward of food. You can then maneuver the stick to

- Encourage a dog's response to basic directions, such as "Sit," "Down," or "Follow."

- Aid a dog in more complex training sequences, such as those associated with agility.

- Help a dog overcome fears or phobias, as experienced with people or objects (street grates, unusual objects).

✔ **Point training:** Like targeting, this technique applies a stationary lure to help a dog move to where the handler wants him, thus the dog can be used to indicate a specific person or a particular location that the dog should approach. Initially paired with a food reward, a dog is taught the pointer can ultimately be replaced by her handler's index finger. Although the reach of the finger may be shorter than a target stick, it's always handy and can be used to signal basic training exercises.

Magical learning tools

We find two teaching tools indispensable: treat cups and snack packs. You can use them to condition cooperative behavior, reward good manners, and encourage your friends and family to take part in your dog's education:

✔ **Treat cup:** Take a cup or empty plastic container. Fill the container half full with bits of a chosen food reward. Shake the cup and reward your dog until he associates the sound with treats. (Cut a hole in the lid for easy distribution.) Use the treat cup as described throughout this book, but especially to condition a quick sitting response, appropriate greeting manners, and a cheerful "Come."

✔ **Snack packs:** Use a fanny pack or an otherwise designated pouch. Fill it with treats and a clicker if you're utilizing one. Use it as described throughout this book, but especially to condition your dog to interact politely. If your dog barks, jumps, or paws at you for a reward, ignore her. Only reward good manners, such as sitting calmly in front of you or chewing on a toy or bone.

Where does your dog's heart lie?

To discover which reward holds top billing with your dog, do the following test:

Ask two friends (whom your dog knows) to stand 10 feet apart. Give one a cup of treats and the other a favorite toy. Bring your dog into the room and have them simultaneously try to lure and then reward her. Repeat this exercise three times.

Take the chosen reward from the last exercise and now ask the other person to simply kneel down and call to your dog sweetly, rewarding her with affection when she responds. Repeat this several times.

Prioritize your rewards, using the most attractive one for difficult sequences, but using the others intermittingly or when applicable to mix it up.

Using a Reward System

Dogs, like people, love rewards; however, different things motivate each dog. Some dogs will do back flips for a flake of cereal, while others demand chopped liver. Some love a toy above all else, while others (though rare) are justly satisfied with quality attention.

Treats and toys

If you're on the fence about using treats to condition your dog's good behavior and responsiveness, it may help to know that you'll not be using treats forever. Food is initially offered to help your dog understand your direction. Think of it less like a bribe and more like a positive reward to highlight good behavior, or perhaps simply pay for a job well done.

Once a particular direction is understood, you can phase out treats and replace them with petting and verbal praise.

Rank toys and treats. If your dog will sit happily for a Cheerio but does back flips for dried liver, set aside this high-ranking snack for more difficult behaviors, such as coming outside or ignoring a temptation (for example, another dog). Rank toys with the same focus on finding one that trumps all others.

If you're averse to using treats or your dog simply doesn't like them, you're not alone. There are many theories of dog training, and the first thing to note is that they all work to some extent and also reflect the attitudes and beliefs of the trainers. If you'd like to use praise or toys to motivate your dog's cooperation instead of treats, then do it with gusto, selecting a word to highlight the moment your dog cooperates. However, the psychological research is quite clear, suggesting that food works faster and is easier for inexperienced trainers to use.

Step 1: The treat connection

Your dog doesn't have to mind you. She'll choose whether to listen, especially when she's off leash. Using treats motivates learning, and, once the behavior is conditioned, a verbal direction is sufficient to encourage a response. To flow seamlessly from using treats to relying on verbal directions and praise, follow this pattern:

- ✔ **Introduce your dog to one new word or sequence at a time.** Say the direction as you lure your dog into position with a treat or toy. If your dog is confused, stop saying the direction and simply concentrate on luring him into place. After he moves into position reliably, say the word the moment he cooperates.

- ✔ **In addition, say the direction anytime you see your dog moving into the position naturally.** For example, if you're working on "Down," say it anytime you see your dog lying down naturally. Praise her verbally or with loving attention.

- ✔ **Show family members and friends how to give your dog direction and prompt good manners,** providing everyone with treats and toys, so that your message transfers.

Step 2: Phasing out treats

As your dog show signs of learning a command — for example, moving into the down position quickly and without pause or confrontation — over-exaggerate a hand signal that will enable you to direct your dog visually as well as verbally. Phase out treat-dependence as you stagger your rewards so that they come every other response, and eventually in an irregular pattern. Keep up the praise and verbal appreciation.

 If you're using a clicker, pair each click with a food reward. After a behavior is learned, you may phase out the clicker by using it only intermittently. Though you can use food without a clicker, don't click without a food reward, lest the sound lose its dramatic influence.

 Once your dog has learned a direction, reward her intermittently. This system keeps her attention sharp, while highlighting the verbal direction over the reward.

Timing your treat

The timing of your reaction can help or hinder your dog's learning capacity. To understand this concept, ask someone to toss a ball into the air. Mark the moment the ball reaches its highest mark by saying "Yes" or by depressing a clicker. Repeat this exercise until your timing is perfect.

Now relate this exercise to your dog's capacity to understand your desire: If you're trying to teach your dog to sit versus jump, you'll want to mark or click the second her bottom hits the floor. Your reward will guarantee a repeat performance. On the other hand, if you mark the moment she jumps, she'll just as willingly repeat that behavior instead.

Meals

At times, we recommend using a dog's regular feeding to encourage good behavior by dispensing food one bit at a time for good behavior. In these situations, a person can elevate his or her social standing while conditioning civility. Note that practice sessions with the dog/puppy must be coordinated to your regularly scheduled mealtimes. Use a dog's meal when you want to

- Calm an assertive puppy/dog's personality
- Bond with a stressed shelter/abused dog
- Encourage a timid puppy/dog's confidence
- Associate the direction "Come" positively

A few other training tools, namely the clicker and the snack pack, are especially useful in this process and can accelerate your dog's behavioral memory. (See the section "Choosing Training Tools and Gadgets," earlier in this chapter.) With this method, you may use food to motivate your dog's cooperation throughout the day. Over a two-week period, you can gradually phase out treating for every correct response. Because your dog will be unsure when the food reward is going to be offered, his attention will remain sharp. Don't forget to praise him each time, though.

Tailoring Your Rewards to Your Dog's Personality

Regardless of your dog's priority, the Reward System works by increasing your dog's focus on the learning task and the speed at which she can identify your intention, and linking it to a specific word or signal. If the goal is to have your dog "Sit" or "Potty" when directed, then you must offer a reward when your dog acts appropriately.

You should also reward your dog based on his personality type.

Assertive

Some dogs are assertive because of their breed (see Chapter 6), while in others it's an individual personality trait (Chapter 5). In each litter of puppies, one or two puppies are generally bossy and controlling by nature. These puppies bring the same level of intensity into their human family. How can you tell whether you have a dominant puppy? If your puppy ignores or defies you often, stands in your way, or goes to great lengths to control situations (from greeting visitors to disrupting your quiet time), she's exhibiting a dominant personality.

Please note that these behaviors aren't signs of a "bad" dog, just one who has a strong sense of herself and prefers to give direction rather than take it. Fortunately, you can condition good behavior without breaking this dog's spirit. Use Chapters 3 and 12 to set reasonable boundaries and then begin with these exercises:

- ✔ Use a fanny pack filled with treats to center your dog's focus and encourage her to accept direction as a positive interaction, instead of issuing corrections, which are perceived as confrontational.

- ✔ Teach your dog "Excuse me" by moving her out of your way when she's in it. There's no faster way to remedy her delusions of grandeur than to remind her constantly that she needs to be more mindful of where you are, versus the other way around.

- ✔ Design a lesson plan (see Chapter 12) to highlight the directions most essential to your day. Reward each cooperative response. If you're using food rewards, consider employing a clicker as well.

- ✔ Once your dog is responding eagerly to your directions, involve other family members. Chaperone children, using a leash to enforce a respectful reaction to each direction.

Getting your dog to "Come"

Though your dog's response to the direction "Come" is not the be-all or end-all of the training process, it's especially important if your goal is off-lead control. Though Chapter 12 outlines the lesson "Come," you can use your dog's meals to create a positive association to the word.

Avoid repeating or overusing "Come": come inside, come while walking, and come before isolation or unpleasant handling experiences. Overuse dilutes its intended meaning and often turns your dog off just as a nagging spouse would. Your dog should think of "Come" as the human phrase equivalent of "Huddle." Here are two options:

✔ Place your dog's meal in your pocket or fanny pack. Either let your dog free in an enclosed yard or place her on a drag lead. Each time your dog returns to you, say "Come," and then praise and reward her with a handful of her meal.

Once your dog learns where her food stash is, she may Velcro to your side. Consider ways to encourage separation, such as throwing a toy or introducing another person or dog, or simply ignoring her until she loses interest.

✔ Fill a treat cup with kibble and run away from your dog as you call out her name. Reward your togetherness, linking "Come" to receiving a reward and playing a fun game as well.

As your dog quickly associates "Come" with being together, begin to say "Come" as your dog is in the process of running over to you. If you're having trouble prompting your dog's return, don't call her repetitively or run at her in a huff. Instead, act like another dog, either kneeling to poke inquisitively at the ground, or by taking out a treat cup or favorite toy and pretending to reward yourself.

Fearful

Timid dogs often look abused, although that's not always the case. By nature, some dogs have a low self-esteem, which may be an unintended result of how the dog is treated in their home environment. For example, dogs rarely approach each other from head on unless they're playing or attacking. Some dogs (especially the smaller ones) are cautious when approached and often back up defensively. If the person persists in trying to reach or touch him by following or chasing, the dog often becomes afraid and assumes a submissive posture to ward off the "attack."

Shouting is another example of miscommunication. Though a natural expression of human anger, this loud reaction (perceived as barking) can spell terror to a puppy/dog with low self-esteem.

Consider these thoughts and options:

- ✔ Reflect on the situations that initiate fear reactions for your dog and use her meals or treats to create a positive association to each.

- ✔ If your dog backs up when you reach down to hold/pet her, turn sideways and kneel down at her level *avoiding all eye contact*. Feed her handfuls of food as you caress the side of her head with your free hand. Also engage other family and friends to approach and pet her as you portion out her food.

- ✔ Dogs often back away when approached with a leash or to be medicated. Teach your dog the directions "Sit" and "Wait" (see Chapters 3 and 12) and link food to these directions. Practice simply approaching her, waiting to actually medicate or handle her until you've regained her trust.

Rescue dogs

Regardless of their age or situation, a dog that is rescued, having been abandoned or in a shelter, can have emotional problems due to the experience. Some dogs act manic, but that behavior is simply a mask for their being emotionally out of control. Even the best shelter situations are jarring, often prompting defensiveness and confusion (see Chapter 15).

Fortunately, dogs are an incredibly forgiving species and are eager to bond with new families and people who provide for and love them. Though these dogs need special consideration, many need merely to be reintroduced to the routine of everyday life. Here are a few tips to initiate your bond together:

- ✔ Give your dog's meal at the time of normal feeding to solidify your constant presence in her world and condition cooperative behavior. This approach goes a long way in shaping both her understanding of, and response to, your direction.

- ✔ If you have children, let them play a role in the reconditioning process. Place the treats/meal in a cup, and with the children, approach the dog when she is eating, resting on a mat, or chewing an appropriate toy. If she growls, stop immediately and call for help.

- ✔ Play training is essential with rescue dogs as the intensity of their former situation often overshadows their ability to have fun. Use treat cups to call your dog back and forth from one person to the next as you use her name. Hide from your dog and/or run away from her as you shake the cup — all the while rewarding and praising her.

Many rescue dogs equate the directional tone used in training with past corrections or disapproval. As you teach your dog new directions like "Sit" and "Down," lure her with her meal as described in Chapter 15; be generous with your praise, too.

Shaping Behaviors

You can break down many learned behaviors, from "Come" and "Down" to agility sequences and tricks, into several separate actions, allowing you to teach each separately before linking them altogether. The direction "Down," for example, can be broken into three sequences: looking down, moving the legs forward, and finally lowering the body into position. The direction "Come" also links three actions together: When a dog is called from a distance, she must respond to her name, leave the area and run toward the person, and, finally, slow down as she gets close and fully reconnects.

Any sequential behavior can be taught step by step before linking the steps together. This technique is ideal for young puppies or for dogs who are unable or unwilling to concentrate on the overall request. Building on your dog's success rate instantly lightens what can otherwise be a stressful situation.

In addition, simply saying a direction as your dog repeats a behavior enables you to practice shaping techniques throughout the day.

Luring with food

You may use food to practice luring. To lure your dog, simply think of the lure as attached to your dog's nose by a short thread. Then consider her movements to discover how to maneuver the food to lure her into a specific position (see Table 10-4).

When luring, move the reward very slowly. Jerky motions encourage jumping or moving and can confuse your dog. Though she may not catch on right away, she'll focus on the goal when you repeat the luring motion.

Table 10-4	Luring Your Dog
Command	*Method*
Sit	Take the lure from your dog's nose and lift it up and back just above her ears. Say "Sit" as your dog's bottom reaches the floor.

Command	Method
Down	From a sitting position, take the lure from your dog's nose straight down to the floor between her paws. Say "Down" as her elbow contacts the floor.
Stand	From a sitting or down position, take the lure and hold it between the bottom of your dog's nose and his lip. Draw the lure up and out at a slight angle until your dog stands; say "Stand" at this time.
Follow	Hold the lure in your right hand and cross it in front of you to your left side. Hold the lure at your dog's head level, saying "Follow" as he moves along cooperatively.
Come	When using a lure to encourage "Come," work indoors initially when your dog is eager to interact with you. Take the lure in front of your dog's nose and back up as you call out "Come." Kneel down and reward your dog as you pet her lovingly. "Come" should always encourage her desire to be with you.

Using pressure points to direct

Your dog has many pressure points on her body that, when touched gently, will induce her into a specific position (see Table 10-5).

Avoid manhandling or jerking your dog around as it is both unnecessary and hurtful.

Table 10-5	Using Pressure Points
Command	**Pressure Point**
Sit	Squeeze your dog's waist muscle just behind her last rib. If she resists at first, lure her with a treat. Say "Sit" as she moves into position.
Down	Place the flat of your thumb between your dog's shoulder blades, applying constant pressure. If she braces against you, lift one of her paws up gently to create a tripod effect. Say "Down" as she moves into position.
Forward	When moving your dog forward, hold her steadily with your right hand as you tuck her tail between her hind legs. Say "Forward" as she moves ahead of you. ("Forward" is helpful when leading a dog into a crate.)

(continued)

Table 10-5 *(continued)*

Command	*Pressure Point*
Side to side	If you're moving your dog side to side, hold her head steady with your right hand as you use your left to put gentle sideways pressure along the side of her waist (between her ribs and her rump).
Stand	To stand your dog, tickle the underside of her belly along her last rib and pull her buckle forward under her chin with your right hand. Say "Stand" as she stands steadily in a relaxed fashion.

Modeling as an example

Modeling can refer to both behavior and training. An obvious example of negative modeling is the chaos that often ensues when visitors arrive. If you rise to your dog's level of excitement, then you're modeling her reaction. For an example of positive modeling, consider the same situation as you remain calm, only including your dog after she models you by calming down. Though it may take many repetitions to note an improvement, it will come.

Modeling for training can be as goofy as lying down to encourage the same or as inclusive as using a well-trained dog to mirror the proper response to a new student.

Stay calm in any situation that confuses, excites, or startles your dog. Though your interaction may be heartfelt, reassuring postures and tone often convey confusion. Stand tall as though nothing were out of the ordinary: Your dog will feel secure in your confidence and learn to mirror your reaction in all situations.

Chapter 11

Helping Your Dog Learn from Everyday Living

*D*ogs and people really do want the same thing: They want to get along and spend time together. Unfortunately, no one can enjoy an ill-mannered dog, which leads to a vicious cycle: left at home or corralled into a kitchen, this dog learns nothing about the world and how to behave. When finally invited into the family circle, the dog is simply bursting with excitement but has never been adequately educated to know what to do. So his hyperactivity becomes annoying to his human family, resulting in further isolation but no further learning.

To survive as a good human companion, a dog must learn what to do in his life. He must not only learn how to respond to formal commands, such as "Sit," but he must learn to interpret and appropriately respond to human signals and frequently occurring situations. Given the opportunity, a dog will spend his entire life learning, and we must recognize that we're consciously or unconsciously teaching him all of the time. Understanding how your dog learns allows you to shape his behavior to make him a better and happier companion.

Consistency Counts

If you want a well-trained and civilized dog, you, and everyone who lives with you, should be consistent in your behaviors involving your dog. The first thing that you should do is to always use a word or phrase to signal what you want your dog to do. If you're going upstairs with him, say, "Upstairs." If you're going to put a leash on him, say, "Leash on." If your words always signal actions, the dog soon learns to pay attention to the sounds coming from your mouth because they signal what he's supposed to do next.

Always use the words before you act so that the dog can learn the meaning of your language. Everyone in your family must use the same words. If the aim is to get the dog off the sofa, make sure that everyone knows that you're all going to use the word "Off." If one person yells "Get away" and another "No!", this inconsistency only confuses matters. Whether you're starting your journey with a young pup or an older dog doesn't matter as much as maintaining a consistent approach.

Dogs respond very well to routines and repetition. Consider your morning ritual: rising out of bed, taking a shower, eating breakfast, letting the dog out, drinking coffee. When was your routine set? Probably in childhood. Whatever the sequence, you repeat the routine, quite unconsciously, day after day.

Shaping your dog's behavior is no different. Dogs actually love routines even more than you do: The more regular their schedule and the greater your predictability, the greater their feelings of safety and security and the more likely they are to behave in a cooperative fashion.

Begin by establishing routines around your dog's basic needs: eating, drinking, resting, playing, and eliminating. Assign a word and a specific routine for each need, creating a chart to help your household follow through (see Table 11-1). Though your dog's schedule will vary slightly throughout maturity, the constancy of these words and routines will tie him to the certainties of his everyday life and give you a mutual language base.

Table 11-1	Human Phrase Equivalents	
Direction	*Human Phrase Equivalent*	*Use When*
"Follow" or "Let's go"	I'm the leader! Follow me!	Walking together
"Stay"	Hold still.	Calming your dog
"Down"	Relax.	Enforcing mindfulness
"Come"	Huddle.	Reconnecting

Remember, your dog doesn't speak English (see Chapter 3). Though she listens to you, most of what you say sounds like gibberish. When a word pops in that she recognizes, it's as exciting to her as our hearing recognizable words when in a foreign land.

Though you need to take time out of your day to teach your dog the proper responses to your directions (for example, Sit-Stay), once she's learned those responses, you can use the directions throughout the day. Practicing these exercises with your dog is like your being taught in school the skills you need for everyday life: Counting fruit or balancing your checkbook can be thought of as learning to stay or behaving appropriately when greeting someone or on an outing.

Also, make sure that everyone understands that your dog loves attention. He'll repeat anything that guarantees interaction and, like a human child, he can't distinguish negative from positive. If a response guarantees anyone's reaction, it will be repeated: If you put his food dish down when he sits calmly, then he'll sit calmly. If you ignore hyperactivity and only interact with your dog when he's rational and responsive, then your dog will learn to behave rationally. Of course, the reverse is also true: If a dog's demanding posture is responded to, he'll learn those undesirable behaviors just as quickly.

Monitoring Human Behavior

Inconsistency will create confusion in your dog's mind and often intensifies her reactivity. All the people in your dog's life should know the rules and words to use around your dog.

Imagine trying to understand what to do based on the reactions that you get to your behavior. Imagine trying to work out the rules if one person insists on consistency while another welcomes chaos. Under such circumstances you or your dog won't be able to determine how best to behave when meeting someone new. In dogs, such inconsistency for different people in their lives invariably snowballs into maniac anxiety, and the resulting confusion guarantees only one thing: that your dog will not be welcomed into polite society or be the star attraction at family gatherings as he'd loved to be.

Of course, as anyone who has shared their life with a dog will tell you, that friends and family members can be the hardest "dogs" to train. Everyone has their own ideas as to how to control dog behavior, and many people are, by nature, very strong willed. Shouting, "Don't let him jump!" (or similar epithets) at someone to rally their support will fall on deaf ears: No one likes to hear the words "don't" or "no."

Of course, you can't train everyone

In a perfect world, you'd be able to control everyone, consistency would reign, and your dog would never be confused. Alas, it's no perfect world out there and, try as you might, some people just won't heed your advice. If it's an occasional stranger on the street, don't worry about it, but if it's a live-in companion that interacts frequently with your pup, then you must come up with a plan.

If your companion encourages jumping, exercise your dog prior to his or her interaction with your pet to tone things down a bit. If he urges your dog to jump on the furniture, agree upon one piece of furniture and teach your dog that the others are off-limits. If feeding from the table is the main issue, be sure to feed your dog first and reward her for staying on her bed during meals.

Be creative and think outside of the box: You'll find there's always another way around your problems with both four-footed and two-footed dogs.

It's hard for some people to see the downside to ecstatic joy. When asked, they'll tell you that the wild greeting they get from their dog at the door is one of the highlights of their day. Unfortunately, permitting and, in effect, rewarding hyperactivity takes its toll: A dog who manically greets his own people will greet everyone that way. Furthermore, if the dog suffers from separation anxiety, even the sound of someone nearing the door is likely to trigger hyperactive anticipation, which, when unfulfilled, may result in destructive behavior.

If you're trying to change the behaviors of people when interacting with your dog, it's sometimes easier if you control the dog's behavior. Do the problems arise when your kids get off the bus, or your partner walks in from a long day at the office, or your friend who just adores your dog comes for a visit? If you can predict their arrivals, considering *leading* your dog to the door to greet them as described in Chapters 3 and 12 or, alternatively, diverting your dog's attention with a new toy. If you can prevent your dog's manic behavior, then it has no chance to be rewarded, and your dog's calm demeanor may help change the expectations of the humans in your life. Some things to try include

   ✔ Substitute a response by refocusing your dog's attention on another object, such as a treat cup or clicker. In the case of doorway excitement, teach your dog to sit when you shake a cup filled with treats and then practice at the door, shaking the cup as you open, shut, and knock on the door yourself. When your dog is fully conditioned to the sound, ask visitors to shake the cup, rewarding your dog for sitting quietly.

✔ Try pitching your goal with a positive zinger, such as, "We're training our dog to say hello politely, which involves four paws on the floor." If you explain your goal this way, then teaching your dog becomes a group effort rather than an order, and most people like the opportunity to give the dog a treat for behaving. (See Chapter 13 for more information.)

✔ Teach your dog a greeting trick, such as paw, belly up, or roll over. Everyone can teach these cheerful interactions, and they're a wonderful way to break the ice and initiate positive interaction from the get-go.

Living with Kids and Dogs

Got kids? Your family dog will be one of their childhood memories, which puts the pressure on you to ensure that your dog is a civilized companion. Because the lion's share of the responsibility is resting squarely on your shoulders, here are a few techniques to encourage their participation and self-control:

✔ **Become a treat hero.** If your dog or puppy enjoys treats or (even better) food, place a handful in a cup and let your child dole them out when the dog responds to simple commands like "Sit" or "Come." Work through the directions in Chapter 12, transferring the directional skills to your entire family. Phase off using the treat cup after a week of cooperative responses. At this time, shake the cup only half the time as you position and praise your dog's cooperation. Although you'll gradually reduce the number of treats, remember that praise and petting should be continued as a reward.

✔ **Encourage more than you discourage.** Kids (like dogs) are very sensitive to language and tone. When you discourage their behavior, you are, in essence, throwing a wet blanket on their relationship with your dog. Be creative, teaching them appropriate games to play and using treats to shape more positive interactions. Focus on what your children are doing right with their dog. If you have to step in to control the interaction, immediately help them find a more positive activity so that you can end on a high note.

✔ **Create activity charts.** Kids are so easy to please: Sometimes just an activity chart with stickers for getting the dog to respond to simple commands or perform simple tricks can be enough to prompt their eager participation. If you're unsure how best to motivate your children to cooperate, ask their teachers for suggestions.

✔ **Catch the team spirit.** Kids (like dogs) love to be a part of a project! Try dispersing the responsibilities of caring for your dog so that not all the tasks rest on one person's shoulders. You will have to help out one way or another, but when encouraged to help, children feel needed and empowered. Table 11-2 outlines some age-appropriate activities.

Don't involve your children if your dog has shown any signs of aggression. Dogs naturally dominate young children: Asking them to care for an aggressive dog is putting them in grave danger. Get professional help.

✔ **Creatively contain your dog.** Create play stations for your dog (see Chapter 3) in each room, securing him when he's unable to contain himself. When you can supervise the interaction, ask your children to race about, thereby teaching your dog how to displace her urge to chase by offering her a favorite toy/bone for remaining calm. Provide a crate or secure a quiet area and take your dog there when the children are overwhelming or when her behavior is clearly evidencing that she's out of control. Think of this area not as a punishment zone, but as a quiet room where she can go to unwind. When dogs get stirred up, it's often due to being overstimulated or overtired.

If you're raising a puppy or teaching your old dog some new tricks, your children may seem to undermine the very principles you're working hard to instill. Don't get mad: after all they're kids. Think back: Did you always follow your parents' direction? On the whole, children, like puppies, are playful and interactive, and both are very attuned to negative attention. It may be simply that your dog views your kids more like playmates than respected leaders. Please consider the following:

✔ **If you get frustrated with your child, you'll look as though you're frustrated with your dog, too.** Sure, *we* know you're yelling at your child, but your dog can't decipher the focus of your feelings. Your reaction may lead her to feel more anxious or aggressive when your children are present, and may ultimately create a feeling of sibling rivalry between them.

✔ **Try not to tense up when your dog and child/children are together.** This reaction is understandable to us; however, your dog isn't human. If the tension is notable only when the child and dog are together, then (in the dog's mind) the child brings tension.

✔ **Don't lock up your dog when your children's friends come to play.** Your dog won't understand why and will get hyper or assertive whenever their friends come to call. Think of other creative options, such as leashing your dog, using treat cups to encourage contained greeting, or enclosing her in an open playpen or crate until she is accustomed to the new visitor.

Table 11-2	Age-Appropriate Activities
Age	**Activity**
2–4	(Adult supervision is required at all times. All activities must be closely supervised.) Scoop the dry meal into a bowl: As they get older, they can instruct the dog to sit as they put the meal down. This age can also play simple games, such as fetching thrown toys, with the help of an adult.
4–10	(Condition your dog to all games and training activities ahead of your child's involvement. Adult supervision is still required.) Games like soccer or Frisbee tossing can be a sure fit for children of this age, and their natural enthusiasm for play can go a long way toward tiring out your dog. Joint walks can give you time to be together, and even the act of scooping the poop can be shared! Of course, you can allocate feeding responsibilities, although do keep a check-off chart handy to ensure that your dog's needs aren't overlooked.
10 and Up	(Use your judgment. If you can't hold onto your dog, don't ask your children to walk him.) Children this age should be encouraged to care for the dog as though it was their baby. Passing on this or other training books can help them understand how their dog/puppy develops, thinks, and learns. If possible, sign up for a training class together and watch your child handle your dog: Your heart will swell at their success.

Early stress syndrome

Irresponsible breeders often push for the early adoption of puppies. While the cute factor of a 6-week-old puppy can't be disputed, it should be criminal to take such a young pup away from her mom. Undeveloped and emotionally weak, such a puppy will likely be brought into a home where people (unless educated) will coddle them ad nauseum. Too often, the result of this heartfelt adoration is the development of a *Super Alpha:* a puppy who never learns respect for anyone. These puppies are often excessively nippy and may show aggression prematurely. If these behaviors aren't arrested, the puppy may become a danger to live with and show behaviors that look as if he has a split personality: lovely when seeking a resource like food or attention, demonic when interrupted. If this description sounds familiar, please seek professional help.

Avoidance 101

No one likes to feel discomfort. Most people will go to great measures to avoid pain or disappointment and, as parents we strive to protect our children from physical and emotional harm. Your dog's instinct to protect himself from harm is no different. Still, it's here that we must examine the differences in our species, since sometimes what we consider as emotional support is often misconstrued by your pup, and your efforts to "discipline" her may, in fact, not be communicating any useful information..

Soothing your dog's fear

When your dog shows fear or discomfort, your immediate impulse may be to soothe her. It's heartfelt, but detrimental, too. Remember, your dog doesn't understand the reasoning behind human behavior and emotions: He merely reads your posture, eye contact, and tone of voice.

When we comfort an animal, we lower both our body and our head, speak in a moderated tone, and look concerned; to a dog, these body cues bespeak utter panic. To a dog, we look cornered, trapped, and cowering — enforcing their fear rather than assuaging it.

A better approach to soothing a dog's anxiety is to mimic canine confidence and let your dog hang in the shadow of your protection until he feels safe enough to stand on his own. To do so:

- ✔ **Teach your dog "Back,"** directing him there whenever you anticipate a reaction or when his posture bespeaks caution. Leaders, lead.

- ✔ **Use the direction "Under"** (see Chapter 3) if you're sitting, directing your dog under your legs instead of propping him on your lap or allowing him to dance about in front of you.

- ✔ **Instruct your dog to "Follow"** (see Chapter 12) whenever walking in unknown terrain or near a roadway. This message conveys guardianship and lets your dog depend on your protection.

- ✔ **Use "Stay" to teach your dog to be still.** This direction helps to contain his *flight* impulse and concentrates his attention on your pose.

- ✔ **Stand confidently in the face of any distraction.** If the object of your dog's fear is stationary, let his leash go loose, approach it, and feign sniffing. As dogs see by sniffing, your reaction shows him how to overcome his fears while instilling confidence in your authority.

When discipline instills fear

No one wants to frighten their dog, but many people do just that, often under the guise of disciplining them.

The truth of the matter is that puppy-rearing philosophies lag behind the newest theories on child-rearing, and we all would do well to take note. For example, physical abuse in response to parental frustration is illegal. Even the suspicion of emotional abuse will have school officials taking note.

Unfortunately, the same doesn't hold true with the raising of puppies. People still yell at their dog or puppy, though these methods have been proven ineffective. Others are locked into a vicious cycle of physical corrections, though they have no educational value and often instill aggression or make matters worse. If the goal of discipline is to teach a dog better manners, then the effort to communicate as much must be closely examined. Here's what doesn't work and why:

- **Hitting:** When a hand is raised in frustration, a dog immediately seizes on the rapid motion and not on any other previous behavior. The predatory response part of her brain that activates upon seeing motion is an entity unto itself: Any prior impulses are abandoned. When the hand makes contact (and stings the skin), that feeling must also be interpreted. Because hitting has no real world template (after all, dog's don't hit each other), fear is often shown as an appeasement gesture. The true emotional damage comes into the relationship, however, when it is the very person who is attacking her that a dog needs to turn to when life doesn't make sense . Sound like abuse? You're right — it is — and completely ineffective.

- **Yelling:** Yelling is barking to a dog. Loud and interruptive, it will likely stop a dog in her tracks and may even cause an appeasement gesture, although neither is a sure sign of comprehension. Please reference Chapter 3 for more insight.

- **Chasing:** Chasing a dog is insane and has no retentive value, save to guarantee a repeat performance. Put the shoe on your foot for a moment and imagine being chased by an enraged 400 pound gorilla who was also the very one you depended on for life's sustenance. A dog has no other option but to process this reaction as a game or offer an appeasement gesture so extreme as to assure your pity. Nothing can be learned, and while this *predatory attack* is damaging emotionally, it commonly results in manic displacement activities.

The ingredients of a good correction

The goal of any correction is to discourage behavior: Whether your dog is nipping, jumping, counter-cruising, or barking, the strategy you develop to react to the behavior either supports or extinguishes the behavior.

Before attempting to resolve a behavior that distresses you, make a short list of what your dog really likes, from attention to play to treats. Next, list your frustrations, why your dog is repeating those behaviors, and what *exactly* you'd like your dog to do instead (see Table 11-3).

Table 11-3		Creative Solutions
Frustration	*Why*	*Other Options*
Jumping	Joy in greeting	Fetch a toy
Nipping	Playful interaction	Kiss
Chewing	Teething	Choose an appropriate chew toy

Encouraging self-training

Dogs, like children and people, learn through cause and effect. If you want to get rid of a specific behavior, consider why your dog is doing it in the first place. Is he jumping up to get your attention or to get a resource or make himself comfortable? If these reactions are effective, he'll do them again.

If, however, when he jumps up, your hands consistently raise to cover your face and you ignore him, she won't keep jumping up for attention. If, at the same time, you encourage her to sit or fetch a toy and give her attention for that, she'll soon abandon jumping for sitting or play. If she jumps on the counter to steal food and nothing is there or she finds a distasteful snack (bread laced with wasabi sauce, for example), she'll avoid this activity all together.

With regards to jumping on the furnishings, your dog's just as much of an opportunist as you are: Offer her a comfortable alternative, such as a floor pillow or dog bed, and when you can't be there to control his choice, place something on the furnishings that make comfort impossible.

Next, outline the three ingredients of a good correction and how you can implement them:

- ✔ **A good correction should be seen as coming from the environment, not from you.** At no point should your dog see the correction as coming from the person upon whom she relies most.

- ✔ **A good correction should cause a withdrawal in group interaction.** The best corrections should cause an immediate departure or an emotional withdrawal of attention. (See Chapter 13.)

  Your attention is what most strongly motivates your dog's behavior.

- ✔ **Any good correction must end in prompting an appropriate displacement activity.** Never just tell your dog what he has done wrong; show him what he should have done instead. "Get your ball," "Give kisses," "Outside." Though the directions you give are individual to the infraction, each should allow you to reconnect with your dog and teach him what he should be doing instead.

Chapter 12

Happy Training, Happy Tails

. . . .

In This Chapter

▶ Adding levity to your training approach

▶ Discovering the best approach to suit your dog's age and personality

▶ Incorporating the directions into everyday life

▶ Trusting your dog off-lead

. . . .

*I*n this chapter, you not only discover how to teach your dog basic directions, but you find out what each exercise conveys from your dog's perspective. Though other books cover obedience exercises for competition at dog shows or focus on age appropriate puppy training, this book looks at daily interactions and the basic skills necessary to live peaceably with your dog. Dogs, like kids, need a sense of structure and predictability to feel safe and connected, but unlike children, they aren't born prewired to understand our language: We must teach them. Think of educating your dog like teaching a foreigner English as a second language; be patient and encouraging.

I'm the Leader! Follow Me!

When walking your dog, one of you leads, while the other follows. Though you may not consider this scenario to be of consequence, your dog does. From her perspective, the two of you constitute a pack, a team, if you will. When you leave your home to explore life beyond the den, there are untold possibilities. One of you simply must be the decision-maker.

If you walk your dog on a leash, the restriction is immediately noted. Your dog will choose to either trot at your side, trusting in your authority, or she will strain forth, eager to give direction and determined to break free of the asphyxiating restraint — a posture that ensures an alertness to all distractions.

If your dog has any protective instincts, your inattention will convey a dependence on his leadership. In this role, he'll react to whatever sight he deems unsafe, whether real or imagined. Though reactions run the spectrum from aggression to fear, all convey a perceived sense of duty.

If your dog is allowed to run free and is known to roam, he'll mark strategic points as he wanders, claiming a territory that may be quite large. On leash or off, he'll alert to and/or address anyone who enters this area. If he's confined, he'll still react to what he considers incursions on his turf and noises and sights from his enclosure. Common reactions to the stress of watching activities from his confinement may include barking, destructive chewing, digging, or marking.

Near-sighted and visually limited (see Chapter 4), the world looks filtered and distant to your dog. He depends on his sense of smell to recognize places. Though his olfactory recognition is a powerful tool, it's not comparable to our vision as a long-range interpreter. Unfamiliar objects "appear" foreign and can't be identified until they're thoroughly sniffed. When possible, let your dog smell an unfamiliar item. Otherwise, teach him to follow you so that you're perceived as the social director. The only thing your dog really needs to focus on is you!

The good news is that you can avoid many common frustrations by teaching your dog to follow your lead, passively conveying your role as your dog's guardian and protector. As you work with him, remember that he's programmed to look to you for direction: Use hand signals with your directions as often as possible (see Figure 12-1).

Whoever is in front is in charge

The first ingredient necessary to train your dog involves improving your attitude. Be the one to watch! If you act confidently, like a respected coach with good ideas, your dog will admire you and respond to your direction.

Whoever is in front is in charge. The first step in conditioning good behavior is to ensure that, inside your home den and out, your dog follows and looks for your direction.

Figure 12-1: Use hand signals with your directions.

The "Follow" command says, "I'm the leader follow me." Initially practice this form of direction in a low-distraction room or a quiet outdoor area:

1. **Place your dog on a leash and fitted collar.**

   See Chapter 10 to help you determine which leash and collar are best for your dog.

2. **Call out your dog's name and the direction "Follow" as you move about in a clockwise circle pattern.**

   If your dog tugs forward on the leash, either guide him back using your leash or simply reverse your direction and stride away, leaving the dog behind you at the end of his leash and forcing him to recognize that he's no longer in front but now must run to catch up with you.

3. **Slap your leg periodically as a body signal and praise and/or treat your dog to reward his cooperation.**

When walking your dog, throw your shoulders back, stick your chest out, and smile. If you poke along or putter, your dog will be concerned and hesitate. Keep your pace lively and consistent, and he'll eagerly anticipate following your direction.

4. **Repeat the dog's name "follow" periodically and praise her cooperation.**

5. **As your dog alerts to this word cue, use it in increasingly more distracting environments.**

6. **Continue to use treats or click-treat combinations to encourage your dog's cheerful cooperation.**

For more on rewarding your dog and using a clicker, see Chapter 10.

7. **Once your dog is familiar with the "Follow" direction, reinforce this skill on walks outside of your home and yard.**

What "training" and "civility" have in common

Does the concept of training your dog seem like a downer — something you do to him, rather than for or with him? Many people cringe at the thought of ordering their dog about.

Though we fully understand your hesitation, we must speak up for your dog. Just feeding, loving, and giving him shelter aren't enough: He longs for the direction. Like a child, he depends on you to civilize him and to teach him the best ways to act in every situation. When you do so, you become his hero.

As a young dog, he'll be unable to contain his impulses, but allowing unruly displays isn't kind. If you don't train him to behave, he'll become a brat. Your dog needs you to teach him how to manage each feeling, emotion, or impulse as it arises. Replace the word "training" with "civilizing" and then embrace your real responsibility to your dog: teacher, friend, coach, and hero, your direction is his ticket to a wonderful life.

Ask yourself, which dog has the greater freedom — the one that has never been trained and therefore must be left at home because his misbehaving is a problem, or the one that has been well trained and can accompany you anywhere? A well-trained dog is not only civilized, but he's earned his freedom.

Encourage your dog to walk to one side and be consistent. Dogs are as habitual as humans. Once they learn a walking position in relationship to you, they'll rarely vary. If you're right-handed, walk your dog on the left. Though it may seem awkward at first, it's better that your dog not get in the way when you're manipulating objects.

Permission training

When walking your dog, you may come to crosswalks, roadways, or streams. Teach your dog to stop and look to you frequently for permission before moving into new terrain. This exercise ensures adequate containment skills and enforces a feeling of trust and protection. When your dog stops and waits for your permission, you're communicating your responsibility and that you'll ensure his safety before proceeding into new environments.

When you get to a thoroughfare, curb, or other passageway, get your dog to stop moving by either telling him to "Sit" or "Wait." (If your dog is unfamiliar with these commands, see Chapter 4.)

Here are a few pointers to keep in mind about permission training:

- ✔ If your dog doesn't sit or stand still, brace him as described in Chapter 4.
- ✔ Be still until your dog is sitting or standing calmly.
- ✔ Say "okay" and proceed with confidence.

Meeting and greeting

As you progress to walking your dog in more distracting environments, you're likely to encounter other pets, as well as human admirers. Don't let your dog drag you across the yard or road to greet anyone. Not only is this unsafe behavior, it's extremely rude and could easily result in disaster.

A far better approach is to teach your dog to "Sit" or "Wait" for your permission. Once forewarned, if the other party is willing, you may release your dog with the direction "Okay." This training is all part of the dog learning to act only on your permission. To do it effectively, you may need to teach your dog to harness his impulses (see the next section).

Teaching Impulse Control

Keeping impulses in check is hard for anyone, and more so for your dog who responds much like a young child. Expecting him to ignore that squirrel in the front yard or that roast on your counter-top is like asking a young child to ignore cookies just sitting out on a tray in plain view. Expecting your dog to ignore a distraction, for no other reason than your saying so, takes a high level of control and an even higher level of respect for you. The three ingredients that go into mastering impulse control are

- **Maturity:** Maturity is the result of both experience and biological setting. A distraction becomes increasingly less enticing the more often your dog experiences it. As your dog ages, psychological and physiological changes will have a relaxing effect on his personality as well.

- **Your interaction:** If you correct your dog when he's reacting to a distraction, he'll think you're supporting him or competing for a prized item. Instead, focus on your surroundings, intervene, or just distract him before your dog has taken matters into his own hands.

- **T & C:** In professional circles, T & C stand for *time* and *consistency,* the two necessary ingredients to learn any skill. The more you expose your dog to distractions, routinely providing the same direction and structure, the faster he'll become conditioned to events and react automatically.

Verbal discouragements

"No" must be taught as a direction, not a correction. Using "No" as a punishment will only confuse your dog, who really doesn't have the mental or emotional capacity to understand the concept of being bad. Even though he's a relatively simple and spontaneous creature, your dog can learn to harness specific impulses out of trust in your direction and respect for your authority. Just like a child can adapt to a set structure, so can your dog. To teach him "No," place him on a leash and rig a situation to prompt his interest, such as placing a tissue on the floor or a tray of snacks on the coffee table. As you approach the distraction, watch your dog's ears, nose, and/or eyes to determine his focus. The moment he alerts to a distraction, lightly tug the leash and either slap your leg or rap loudly on the wall (with your hand). Don't interact with your dog until he's pulled away from the distraction and then redirect him to a positive activity and praise him warmly.

If you correct your dog in the midst of an action, he's likely to interpret your attention as interactive, not instructional. Instead, set up situations that allow you to correct your dog the moment he even considers a misdeed. If you're too late, you're far better off saying nothing and simply containing your dog until such time as your communication will make a lasting impression.

This may sound silly, but it works. If the thing that commonly distracts or attracts your dog is an inanimate object, such as a tissue or a sandwich, slap and angrily admonish it by saying "Bad Sandwich!" Don't look at your dog. Following several repetitions, dogs often come to avoid or look away from the punished object.

Here are a few other directions to offer:

✔ **No!** This direction must carry a tone of finality that your dog will learn to respect. Use it very selectively for impulsive actions that will endanger your dog or others.

✔ **Don't even think about it!** If you catch your dog warily eyeing or sniffing an item or activity, he's considering it. Nip it in the bud with a well-toned, growl-sounding utterance, "Don't even think about it!" If he's unimpressed, back yourself up with a firm leash tug and set up situations to allow practice of this direction.

For example, once your dog has learned to avoid the countertops, leave a sandwich close to the edge. Place a can full of pennies just in front of the plate to facilitate your interference should he ignore you. As you leave the room, look seriously at your dog and instruct "Don't even think about it." If you hear the can rustle, come back into the room swiftly.

If your dog hasn't nabbed the sandwich, slap the table and say "Bad Table," and then direct your dog back to a bone or bed. Repeat this process in two days and again until this direction begins to make an impression.

If your dog is too quick and is enjoying his prize, let him have it as you flip back a few paragraphs and review how to teach the direction "No."

An untrained dog often needs a leash tug to maintain control. Think of a leash as an extension of your hand, which is always in contact with your dog — which is the way your dog thinks of it! The tug, however, should be gentle. It's a reminder that you're in contact with him, and is a way of getting his attention; it's not a punishment.

In addition to general praise, teach your dog a specific word or phrase, such as "Yes" or "Good dog," to tell him that you're pleased and to reinforce his cooperation. In the early stages, follow each "Yes" or "Good dog" with a treat or other reward. After a while, just the sounds of the words will get a happy response from your dog, and you can use the word as a reward, even if the dog is off leash and some distance away.

Teaching the down

The direction "down" asks your dog to move into a vulnerable, submissive pose. Initially, he may not be a big fan of this direction, especially if he doesn't think of you as the leader of his pack. Your first job is to convey a sense of neutrality, so that your dog neither fears the direction nor reacts defensively. As you practice, he'll be more cooperative in familiar, peaceful environments and around distractions.

When teaching down, give the direction once. It is important to get your dog used to responding to one-word commands. Also successively repeating any direction changes the command: "Down, down, down" sounds different than the direction "Down."

Start with the dog sitting beside you. If your dog is unfamiliar with this direction, use lures to guide him into position. For example, show him a treat and then move it from a position above his head in a downward arc that ends a foot or so in front of the dog's paws at the level of the floor. As he lowers himself to the floor, say "Down" as you release the prize. Don't be concerned if he pops up immediately: You can teach the "Stay" command another time.

When your dog is routinely cooperating, hold the reward in your other hand as you say "Down" and give him a hand signal that looks like the motion you used to lure him down. If he doesn't cooperate, you might physically correct him by using the pressure point (between his shoulder blades), pause as you bring the treat to his mouth, and then praise and reward him. Incrementally increase the duration of the pause: When your dog is showing signs of self-control, say "Stay" during the pause.

When you're luring your dog into this position, slowly move the prize downward from your dog's nose directly between his front paws. Point training, as described in Chapter 10, is ideal for signaling all your directions: Point as you lure and then continue to use this signal as you faze off luring him.

✔ **Straight back down:** Once your dog is cooperating with the preceding command, kneel next to him or sit at his side in a low chair. Keep your back straight: Your goal is to direct him from an upright posture. If you don't eliminate your bending, it will become a body cue necessary for his cooperation.

In this posture, don't lower your hand to the floor, but signal him by moving your hand in a short downward movement in front of his face. If your dog stops moving when your hand stops, use your free hand to press him into position gently.

✔ **Standing down:** Once you've completed the preceding command, gradually begin to direct your dog when you're in a standing pose. If necessary, bend at your knee or curtsy in order to lower your body without bending your back. Use "Stay" once your dog has lowered himself, sliding a leash under your foot to anchor him if he fidgets, and repositioning him until you release him with "Okay."

✔ **Distraction down:** As you bring this direction into normal everyday situations, you may notice that your dog is notably less responsive. Although she may react immediately in the quiet of your home, when distracted, this direction can take on a whole new meaning. Loss of face, end of interaction, submission . . . your dog may look at you like you've never met. Don't be discouraged, and above all else, don't repeat yourself! By keeping a few treats in your pocket at all times, you can turn any situation where the dog isn't responding into a training opportunity. Eventually, the dog learns that the same commands have the same meanings and potential for rewards in every situation.

Stay

This direction instructs your dog to stay put and contain his impulses. In addition to enhancing his focusing skills, long-distance stays can help to ease separation anxiety (see Chapter 14).

It's best to begin in a low-distraction environment where your dog can concentrate on learning this skill:

1. **Begin with your dog in a "Sit" position.**

2. **Turn around so that you're in front of your dog with his nose close to your knees.**

3. **Quickly flash an open palm signal in front of his face, confidently tell him to "Stay."**

4. **If he moves, tell him to "Sit" again, repeating the "Stay" command and the hand signal.**

In the beginning, you can expect him to hold his position only for a few seconds. Later, you can stretch out the time and increase your distance from him.

Keep your lessons short, upbeat, and fun to ensure your dog's interest and enthusiasm. Simplify each exercise, building your dog's confidence before proceeding to more difficult distractions or long durations. If your dog routinely breaks the command, consider whether you're asking too much of him. Make the exercise easier by making the stay times shorter, thus enabling his success rather than setting him up for failure.

In addition to short, concentrated lessons, practice the "Stay" exercise with the dog at various distances from you throughout the day.

Settle down

Use the "Stay" command for short periods where you want your dog to hold a position and not move. If you want to have your dog simply remain in a particular place, but don't care much whether he sits or lies down, and you intend to leave him for a relatively long time, use the "Settle down" command. To teach this command:

1. **Secure a short 3-foot leash in a familiar area, such as a play station (see Chapter 3).**

   Place bedding and toys within reach.

2. **Bring your dog to this area, directing him with a phrase, such as "Go lie down."**

3. **Secure the pre-attached leash to his regular collar or harness, helping him to sit or lie down.**

4. **Instruct him to "Settle down" (see Chapter 4).**

   If your dog is nervous, stay close by him until he seems more settled. Walk about the room or relax nearby. Don't pay attention to him if he whines or barks in protest, though you may praise him when he's chewing a toy or resting calmly.

5. **Once your dog is comfortable with this routine, instruct him to "Settle down" and leave the room for gradually increasing periods of time (not to exceed 30 minutes).**

   If he protests wildly, watch him in order to prevent injury or household destruction. Then continue practicing until he's more comfortable settling down with you in the room.

   If your dog seems agitated upon your return, don't look at or address him until he's calmed down. Remember, you reinforce whatever you pay attention to. Concentrate your attention on your dog only when he is calm. He'll quickly learn to accept your departures or chew his bone, which is an appropriate activity to relieve anxiety.

Reconnection

Your dog's response to the command "Come," or to any command when he is off leash, depends upon his desire to be near you. This pack mentality stems from a dog's social instinct to reconnect with and look to others before acting. Provided your dog respects your direction, and has confidence in your control, he will respond. Taught in an upbeat, fun manner, the following instructions will ensure that the direction "Come" will be one your dog's favorites.

The indispensable "Come"

Being able to bring your dog to you when he's at a distance is one of the most vital things that you must teach him. It can save his life if he's moving toward a dangerous place or situation. If he doesn't respond to your call, your dog really can't be considered to be under control.

Psychologically, however, responding to your "Come" command isn't easy. Consider what you're asking your dog to do when you ask him to come. You demand that he curtail his activities instantly. Then he's suppose to drop everything and race over to you full throttle — a wholly unnatural behavior whether you're dog or human. If that weren't enough, your dog is then supposed to gauge his speed and do a perfect four-point stop at your feet. And then, well maybe you'll offer him praise or a little treat. It takes a lot of effort and self-control for a dog to respond, especially if your dog is young or untrained.

Try this little "Come" exercise on your significant other. Wait until he's fully engrossed in a pleasurable activity, such as golfing, reading, or watching the television. Call out his name. Does he look up? Regardless, ask him to come with you. Any luck? Unlikely!

If you habitually use this term to call the dog to you when you want to punish or scold him, then don't be surprised if he doesn't respond or even turns and runs.

To teach or reteach this direction, divide "Come" into three parts, working on each part separately before uniting the entire exercise:

1. **Encourage your dog to cheerfully alert to his name.**

   Call his name as you shake a treat cup, wave a toy, or use your clicker (Chapter 10). Call his name in an inviting manner to encourage his enthusiasm. Avoid using your dog's name if you're preparing to isolate or groom him. "Come" should always invite generous tail wagging.

2. **To teach your dog that "Come" means togetherness, not separation, use this direction whenever you're physically interacting or rewarding him.**

   Suddenly, "Come" becomes a welcome command, rather than an uncertain one.

3. **Now use the word "Come" to bring the dog with you from a distance.**

   Begin calling him on leash from short distances. Call your dog's name, cheering him on when he responds to you, or pat your legs or back away to encourage him to move and then praise him or give him a treat when he responds.

"Come" should be your dog's favorite direction. Don't call your dog every other second. If you default to "Come" as a means of controlling or curtailing your dog's every move, he won't like it. Come must be a welcome invitation to reconnect.

When your dog is running at you from a distance, use the human exclamation point (arms enthusiastically thrown up in the air), the praise words "Yes" or "Good dog" or a quick clap of your hands to signal your delight.

How to make this lesson fun

Steer clear of making "Come" a serious direction. The more your dog views this direction as fun, the more you'll guarantee his quick response when it matters most. Use it throughout the day when you're playing with or treating your dog.

Run away come game: Place your dog on a drag leash (Chapter 10) inside or out. When you have his attention, run away from him as you say "Come." Vary the distance of the chase, kneel down, and give him a treat and a pat.

Hide and seek: You can play this one-on-one or with a partner. With treat cup in hand, wait for your dog to be distracted and then hide behind a tree or sofa. Call your dog's name and shake the cup, ducking out if you sense your dog is confused. When he finds you, say "Come" and reward him.

Off-leash control

The goal of off lead training is that your dog responds to you with a higher priority than he gives to anything else. Dog owners often desire off-leash long before a dog is mature or fully capable of containing his impulses. This level of control requires a comfortable response to all directions, including "No," which, when used appropriately, can arrest an instinct to chase or explore. As you practice your distance skill, use an extendible leash or long line to restrict your dog's freedom to roam while you work on your greater distance control.

Please don't allow your dog off leash near civilization. Even a well-trained dog can lose focus and dart off impulsively, racing into a street and putting himself in danger or frightening children or others who don't know him.

As your dog learns to take direction, he'll become more focused and fully entwined with your daily interactions. He'll grow increasingly aware of your moods and what distracts you. Your dog may note that you don't follow through with your directions when company visits, or that off leash you don't have the same level of control.

If your goal is to have a responsive, off-leash dog, pay close attention to your behavior. When practicing your long-range skills, be mindfully aware to only ask your dog to do something when you can follow through, when you're sure that he'll respond correctly, or when you're able to enforce your command.

The first three things to work on are your dog's name, "Wait" and "okay," and "Let's go":

- **Name:** A dog's name should really mean "Look at me. The next sound that comes out of my mouth is an instruction for you." It should precede any command. Thus "Lassie, sit" or "Lassie, down" is proper grammar when talking to your dog, while "Sit, Lassie" isn't because the dog will be looking at you and waiting for a command that has already disappeared into the ether.

  A quick check-in is all you're looking for here — the human equivalent of looking up from an activity when your name is called. When your dog looks to you, give him a cheer. If he continues by coming to you, you may offer a treat, although you don't require this response. If your dog ignores you, leash him and issue a light tug, or step close to him and touch him to attract his attention or even hold the leash and step off in the opposite direction. Ignoring your calling his name isn't an option.

- **Wait and okay:** This duo of commands instructs your dog to stop in his tracks. A sudden freeze in motion is your goal. Vary the time he must remain still before releasing him with "Okay!"

- **Let's go!:** This direction is slightly looser than "Follow," which instructs your dog to walk by your left side. "Let's go!" doesn't direct your dog to your side per se, but does encourage him to follow you. Use it whenever you're changing directions. If your dog is unresponsive, simply leave him on lead and give him a light reminder tug; like other directions, not following you is not an option.

Remember the direction "Come" is a three-part exercise. If you call out your dog's name and he ignores you, he's unlikely to respond to "Come." Should he ignore your call, give a light tug on his leash and repeat his name. Once you have his attention, say "Yes" or "Good" and then call "Come" as you either kneel down or run backward to encourage his cooperation. If your dog races over but doesn't slow down to reconnect with you, whip a treat out of your pocket and show it to him to lure him in. After all, "Come" is supposed to mean "We're together, and when we are, good things happen to obedient puppies!"

Part IV

Dogs Don't Misbehave: Misperceptions and Solutions

"Arthur, will you please look at this? I don't like Sparky's body language."

In this part . . .

Though a dog's misbehavior can be frustrating at times, when you boil it down, it is often a sign of restlessness, discomfort, or a need for attention. Most often it is a reaction to a breakdown in communication between the dog and his owner or the lack of leadership or an organized family.

In this part, you get insight into your dog's perspective: not only why he does what he does, but what he's trying to communicate when he does it. Through this understanding, you discover appropriate ways to extinguishing the "bad" behavior, while simultaneously encouraging more appropriate ways for your dog to communicate his frustrations. In addition, you get the tools to cope with the set of anxiety-related and aggressive behaviors that are most likely to damage the relationship between you and your dog.

Chapter 13

Addressing and Solving Problem Behavior

*P*roblem behavior is a very subjective thing. Of course, chewing on the carpet is a universal issue, as is housesoiling, but many people enjoy a lively, spirited dog jumping on them when they come home and don't mind a few unearthed holes in the front yard. In this chapter, we put a few common frustrations under the microscope, looking at each from your dog's perspective and offering simple straightforward remedies if, in fact, you're seeking one.

Personal Philosophy and the Problem Dog

Consider two 4-month-old Cairn terriers who have started to do what growing terriers normally do — namely bark at every sound near your door, your window, your front walk, your street, your city. Remember, terriers are born to bark (see Chapter 6). Whether any given behavior that a dog displays is a problem is a matter of psychology — not psychology of the dog, but rather the psychological reactions of the people who live with and interact with that dog.

Sonya Brown is a young woman working her way up in an advertising firm. She has been living with one of these terriers, Toto, for nearly eight weeks, and she's beginning to think that purchasing this lively puppy was a major mistake. She wanted a playful and affectionate dog, and Toto is certainly that. However, the dog's continuous barking is becoming very annoying. Toto barks at everyone and everything, and it seems to her that she can no longer have a phone conversation with friends or business associates without being interrupted by her noisy dog.

Compare this to Sibyl White, a school teacher, who bought Toto's littermate. This pup, Ozzie, was supposed to keep her semi-invalid mother company, especially while Sibyl was at work. Sibyl's mother, Edith, was always a timid woman, and she became anxious about moving to the city to be with her daughter after her husband died and her health became worse. Edith had heard stories about how urban gang members and hardened thieves would break into homes that they thought were unoccupied or easy marks and often injure any occupants that they found. For this elderly woman, Ozzie's alertness and noise were a great comfort, and, when not on alert, he would provide her with another form of comfort by resting close to her and allowing himself to be petted. Edith showed Sibyl an article that said that the likelihood that a home would suffer a break-in was massively reduced by simply having a dog that barked inside — regardless of the size of the dog. Sibyl could not remember her mother feeling this secure since she had moved to the city. With each outburst of barking, Edith would say, "Ozzie's just doing his job. He's letting them know that this house is protected."

When mechanics conquers psychology

Many times a mechanical solution is better than a behavioral solution, so it always helps to look at the possibility of changing the environment rather than the dog. Consider the following quick mechanical solutions to common dog behavior problems:

✔ **The dog gets into kitchen cabinets:** Solved by childproof locks on cabinet doors.

✔ **The dog races out the door when it's opened:** Solved by slipping the leash on the dog before opening the door.

✔ **The dog chews shoes:** Solved by keeping shoes you're not wearing in the closet.

✔ **The dog cruises the counter for food:** Solved by keeping the dog out of the kitchen when you're not present or putting food away rather than leaving it on the counter. (If the dog tries to get food from the counter when you're present, a sharp "No!" reinforced with a loud sound, like a pot hitting the floor, usually works.)

✔ **The dog jumps on the bed and tries to sleep with people:** Solved by closing the bedroom door or putting the dog in a kennel beside the bed.

None of these solutions require a Harvard degree. Look around and see whether you can change the environment to quickly eliminate the unwanted behavior, and you may be able to save lots of training time or the cost of hiring an animal behaviorist.

Both dogs are exhibiting the same behaviors. However, Sonya considers the behavior a problem while Sibyl feels that she has the perfect dog for her situation. The issue isn't just what the dogs are doing, but more importantly, it's how the dogs' owners interpret and respond to the behavior.

No matter what kind of behavior problem your dog has, the options open to you are the same ones available to everyone:

- ✔ **Live with the behavior.** Obviously, if the behavior isn't bothering you, as in the case of Sibyl and her mother, you don't have a problem, and life can go on undisturbed. If the problem bothers you a little, then you can reorganize yourself and your environment to eliminate the immediate annoying effect of the behavior and be satisfied with that. Thus, if Sonya normally talks on the phone in the kitchen where Toto barks at the kitchen window, she can simply walk into the living room.

- ✔ **Let the dog continue the behavior, but change how you feel about it.** Changing a person's attitudes and emotional responses to a dog's behaviors is sometimes easier than you may imagine. For example, Sonya is a woman living alone. Perhaps if she were shown that article about how a barking dog reduces the rate of burglary and home invasions, then she might come to be comforted at the sound of Toto's protective barking.

  In our casebook, we have an example of changing attitudes toward a dog's behavior involving a woman named Sharon and her manic retriever. Sharon's pet was a Labrador Retriever named Magnet who, like all Labs, was extremely sociable and loved to retrieve. Magnet would drive Sharon crazy by picking up anything that he found on the floor and carrying it to her. Plush toys, stray slippers, socks, and magazines all ended up being offered to her. Then one day Magnet showed up with a pair of glasses that Sharon's daughter had dropped, and another day he appeared with the car keys that she had been frantically looking for. It was then that Sharon realized that perhaps this behavior was not all bad. She has now even turned Magnet's retrieving behavior into a game. She'll walk into a room and happily call, "Magnet, find stuff!" and the dog scours the floor for anything laying around. It helps her keep the house neat, recover lost items, and redefine her dog's behavior so that it's no longer a problem but rather simply something that her dog does.

- ✔ **Don't change the dog's behavior, but change the environment so that the behavior is limited, blocked, or is no longer seen as a problem.** Many people, when confronted with a behavior problem, tend to focus too much on the behavior. Consider the story of Kevin and Noodles.

Kevin shared his life with a lovely, though garbage-obsessed, collie, aptly named Noodles. In every regard, Kevin loved his dog, though he was plagued by the frustration of her garbage escapades each morning when he left to run errands. No matter how long he'd be out, he'd come home to find the kitchen floor strewn with refuse. Though he had attempted every remedy from yelling at her to dragging her over to the scene and hitting her, nothing worked.

However, the real solution was easy and obvious, once Kevin was convinced to look at his own involvement in this cycle. Because Kevin's reaction frightened Noodles, she grew more nervous as he got ready to leave. Equipped with more appropriate toys like chews and treat cubes, Kevin was also encouraged to take one simple step that cured the issue in one instant. He purchased a garbage can with a latched lid.

✔ **Change the dog's behaviors so that they match what you believe to be appropriate.** Actually, this approach is the psychological or training option that most people immediately think about. The rest of this chapter focuses on solutions of this sort; however, note that you have to make certain choices when you decide to change the dog's behaviors:

- How much time do you want to spend? Often, completely changing a dog's behavior can be time consuming or involve an expensive dog trainer.

- How drastically do you want the behavior changed? Often, a small amount of training can greatly reduce, but not completely eliminate, a dog's problem behavior.

Suppose that your dog is messing in the house every day — obviously a problem. Do you require that your dog never, ever eliminate in the house again, or can you put up with one accident every month or so? The first solution may be very laborious and time consuming, while the second may be accomplished quite quickly. Of course, adopting the second alternative may require that you also have to change your attitudes a bit to accept an occasional transgression by your pet.

✔ **Get rid of the dog.** Your original reason to get your dog was to improve your life and give your dog a good home. If neither is the case — your life quality is not great and your home is less than ideal for a dog's lifestyle — then it's time to rethink matters. If you're unwilling to cope with problem behaviors, to take the time to modify them, or to change your attitude to accommodate such a situation, then everyone may be better off if you found your dog a different household that will appreciate all her special qualities. It's a difficult choice to make, but please keep your family's and your dog's interests and happiness at heart.

It may well be that you got the wrong breed of dog for your needs and living conditions (such as Sonya who may be better off with a breed of dog that seldom barks), or, sadly, you may be at a time and place in your life where you're better off without a dog.

Denning Your Dog

Having an enclosed area, such as a crate, sectioned off playpen or room, or stationed corner (see Chapter 4), is useful as it provides your dog with a sense of security and comfort in your home. Your dog's wild cousins lived in a den, either a hollow area (enclosed on all sides except one), cave, or a deliberately dug-out hole. This den provided comfort and security, and was a safe place to go when its occupants chose to be undisturbed. Inside your home, the crate or small-secluded area is simply a substitute for the den.

Crates come in several materials and sizes, as do playpens. Whether you purchase or manufacture a den, or choose to enclose your dog in a small gated room, the area should be large enough in which to stand, turn around, and lie with outstretched paws. Place a soft bedding material in this area, provided your dog doesn't chew or soil it.

Although the crate (such as those shown in Figure 13-1) may look like a cage to a human, most dogs actually like them. Locate your crate in a familiar room, ideally placing it at your bedside at night and in a populated room during the day.

Figure 13-1: Typical kennel crates. Drape a sheet over three sides of wire crates to give it a denlike feeling.

The fastest way to encourage your puppy into his kennel is with food lures and a reward system. Once all hesitation is gone, direct your dog with a verbal cue, such as "In your house." If you're teaching an older dog, gradually increase the amount of time she's expected to stay. Initially shut the crate door for just a minute or two and reward her for her accomplishment. Next, close the door and try leaving the room for a few moments. Return, give her a treat, and let her out. Then gradually increase the time away from your pet.

If your new puppy or dog is whining in the crate at night, determine whether anything is wrong or if she's in physical discomfort. (Puppies under 12 weeks should be taken out in the middle of the night if they whine.) If nothing is wrong, ignore your dog because your attempts at comforting provide attention, which is rewarding to the dog, and thus the whining will become a habit.

Silencing Excessive Barking

Rewind to ancestral times, and you'll quickly note that a dog's barking was one of the chief assets of the canine/human union. More vocal alert than a wolf who howls at night, a dog's bark provided warning to our primitive ancestors.

Though dogs still bark out their alarm or warning, few people appreciate the depth of their skill and devotion to this task. Furthermore, dogs that bark continuously at night, in their yard, in an empty home or apartment, at every dog or person that they see, and so on are considered a nuisance and often bring unwanted attention from the community and even fines for breaking anti-noise bylaws. This situation may pose a problem for the ever-eager, constantly vigil, and slightly bored dog of our modern era.

Every dog behaviorist's casebook is filled with complaints that go something like this: "My dog barks at every little thing, even when I'm at home. She stands at the door or window and barks. I tell her to stop, I shout at her to be quiet, but nothing stops her. I think my trying to correct her may even be making her barking worse!"

Dogs bark as part of defending their territory, so it's quite natural for a dog to bark more when he's at home than when he's away from home. It is important to understand what is triggering the barking response and what the dog is trying to tell you.

Barking is an alarm sound (see Chapter 3). There is no threat of aggression signaled by the dog unless it's mixed with growls.

The most common bark heard around the house involves rapid strings of two to four barks with pauses between each set, sounding something like "Woof-woof . . . Woof-woof-woof . . . Woof-woof." You can translate this classic alarm bark as, "Call the pack.

Something is going on that should be looked into." It indicates that the dog senses something nearing or outside the home and is trying to bring it to the attention of his pack and pack leader. The problem is that most people fail to recognize that the dog is trying to communicate to them and that what's required is an answer.

Because the dog is being noisy, they usually try to silence their pet by shouting, "Be quiet," "Stop that noise," "Shut up!" This response is exactly the wrong one because the dog interprets your yelling as "Woof-woof . . . Woof-woof-woof . . . Woof-woof." Instead of reassuring him, your involvement now confirms that you feel the same way that he does, so don't be surprised that your dog feels he's done the right thing and continues to bark — perhaps even louder. After all, you're encouraging it!

The appropriate way to stop his barking is to recognize that his noise is really a signal with a specific meaning. He wants you to investigate something. A more appropriate response is to look out the window or check the door where he's barking. Then calmly tell him, "Good guarding," give him a pat, and call him back over to you when you sit down again. He'll interpret this sequence as, "I asked the leader of the pack to check things out, and my leader sees no problem. Therefore, I don't need to continue barking." Eventually, "good guarding" will quiet him and bring him to your side.

Notice that this solution doesn't prevent barking. It's normal for your dog to bark at animals and people that come onto your property or approach your door. Many cities have gone so far as to define this type of barking as "reasonable" when they've drafted laws concerning nuisance barking. You don't want to completely eliminate the barking because it serves the useful purpose of alerting you to someone's presence. However, you do want to stop it quickly and keep it under control, and communication is the way to do so.

Dogs that bark at neighbors

When your dog barks at a neighbor, he's protecting his territory. Although his protection is warranted, the neighbors are there to stay, so it is better for everyone if you resolve this daily confrontation.

The trick is to arrange things so that the neighbors are no longer seen as trespassing marauders. Follow this simple three-step process:

1. **Introduce your dog to the neighbors on common or neutral ground, such as the area between the two properties.**

   Let the dog make the first move to sniff or greet your neighbor, who should stand still and not stare or reach until the dog has settled down. If your dog is fearful or overly aggressive, handle him on a leash and bribe his acceptance of them with a treat or toy. If he doesn't relax, seek professional help. Don't force him onto anyone, or he may react in self-defense.

2. **Have the neighbors come into your yard and stay for a bit.**

   Be sure that they interact with your dog. Have them use his name, call him a few times, offer him treats, play a bit of fetch, and so on.

3. **Have the neighbors return to their own yard with some of the treats that you have provided and then have them approach the fence.**

   They should talk happily to the dog, use its name, and offer him a treat through the fence. If it is a solid fence, any crack or knothole will do.

Remind the neighbors that if your dog does bark at them again, they should just use her name and approach the fence to say "Hello." Remember, the dog usually only barks to warn of strangers, and now the neighbors should no longer fit into this category.

Excessive barking in the yard

Many dogs bark when left alone outside. Though barking can drive everyone to distraction, the typical approach of screaming rarely has the desired effect. The solution lies in examining why this barking occurs in the first place.

First recognize that dogs are social animals and are most comfortable and happy when they're in the presence of others, whether people or other dogs. Second, consider your home as your dog's den. Isolated from entry, your dog is frustrated, lonely, and bored, which can easily escalate to fear and insecurity if the surrounding environment is noisy or unpredictable.

The solution to this kind of barking is simple: Limit your dog's outdoor isolation and bring the dog inside the house. Even if your schedule leaves him alone, you can enclose him in a crate or room and be assured that he'll be much happier surrounded by sights and smells that are associated with his family.

If your dog does bark when you're away, remember that a barking dog in a home reduces the rate of burglary to one-seventh of the normal rate. A barking dog can be quite useful because he's now protecting your home!

Other nuisance barking

Dogs that love to bark — at moving objects, noises, and sights — and those who seem to bark just for the fun of it are the hardest group to quiet. The first step in controlling the persistent noise is to help bring attention to the sounds they're making. Like chatty children, their motto may be, "I bark, therefore I am."

The most clever and quickest way to turn off unwanted barking is to teach the dog to bark on command! One simple way to do so is to follow this training routine:

1. **Place your dog on leash and attach the leash to a fence or other stationary object.**

2. **Stand a few feet away and tease him with a toy; when the dog gets excited and/or frustrated and starts to bark, immediately give the direction "Speak" and then give the toy as a reward.**

3. **When the dog is consistently barking to the word "Speak" with the toy as a reward, switch the reward — first to a treat and later to a verbal praise.**

4. **At the end of a barking tirade, say "Quiet" and then reward him; after your dog recognizes "Quiet," move a short distance away.**

   Learning this step may take several repetitions. Be patient.

5. **When your dog responds appropriately to your commands, return to give the reward.**

   Eventually, you can move farther away and change to verbal rewards.

6. **Finally, with a pocket full of treats, take the dog out to situations where he normally barks; each time he begins to bark, vary the duration he's allowed to sound off before instructing "Quiet." Reward his cooperation immediately.**

You can use the "Quiet" command as an off switch to stop most barking when you're present. However, the length of time that the dog stays quiet will depend upon what you do next. Distracting the dog with play, attention, or a brief training session can help keep him focused on you rather than the bark-inducing situation. Eventually, his silence will evolve into longer periods of silence and greater self-control on the part of your pet.

Barking in the car

Dogs often turn into frantic barkers when left alone in the car due to two factors:

- ✔ A dog's natural instinct when something startles or frightens them is to run away, which can't happen while riding in a car. Barking is an attempt to call his pack mates back for help.

- ✔ The car becomes the limits of their territory, and its compact area must be vigorously defended. Because no help is arriving, the barking may change to a combination of warning and threats. When the object that worried him, such as a person walking by, moves away, it rewards your dog and makes it more likely that he'll bark again in a similar situation.

Manic behavior in the car can be annoying and frighten passing pedestrians. If the car is moving, the dog noisily ricocheting around the interior can distract the driver and even lead to accidents.

The simplest solution to this problem actually takes less time to present than it takes to describe the behavior problem itself. This is the perfect place to use the dog's kennel crate. If you have a hatchback car, van, or station wagon, just pop the kennel crate in the back. If you have a sedan and a small- to medium-sized dog, you can put the kennel crate on the back seat and secure it from moving during sudden stops by using a strap or the seatbelts. Now all that you need to do is to put the dog into the crate with a treat and a chew toy. The kennel walls will screen many of the exciting sights from view, which helps some dogs. However, the major benefit is that the dog understands that the crate is his den, and he's always safe, secure, and undisturbed in his den. With no threats or anxiety, he has no need to bark, and the problem is solved.

Chewing

Chewing is as natural to dogs as touching is to kids and people. To recognize your dog's motivation in chewing, consider his age, as well as outside disturbances that often trigger the chewing in adult dogs:

- ✔ **Curiosity:** Very young puppies (up to 12 weeks) mouth to experience new objects, much as young babies want to touch and hold anything within reach. The best approach is to puppy-proof your home, clearing shelves and anything else within your puppy's grasp. If he gets an object, calmly remove it and replace it with an appropriate item, such as a treat or chew toy. Don't issue even a verbal admonishment at this age. It will make no sense and create friction in your household; it's like yelling at a 6-month-old baby for pulling your hair.

✔ **Teething:** Young puppies do teethe, just like children. Their "milk teeth" (or first set of choppers) are displaced by the arrival of their permanent set, causing itching, pain, and sometimes bleeding. This is usually about the time your puppy may start chewing the furnishings or molding. Frankly, this reaction makes perfect sense: If he can't locate a toy immediately, at least he always knows the whereabouts of a table leg or wall. Regardless, you need to arrange areas for your dog in each room, equipping each spot with desirable chew toys (and tying them down so they're not carried off). In addition, spray your items at risk with a distasteful solution.

The teething stage is also the time when many dogs learn the artful game of grab-and-go, and who can blame them? It's fun and exciting to grab an object and entice you to chase after him for it. Because the behavior is primarily attention-getting, the best response is to simply walk away or leave your home for three minutes. At another time, prompt your dog's interest by placing the object nearby and walking him toward it on leash. The moment he shows interest in it, tug the leash back and say, "No." Then direct your dog to a more appropriate activity.

We often liken excessive chewing in adult dogs to an adolescent acting out: The behavior itself represents a deeper unrest, and the worst thing you can do is scold your dog after the fact. To address this issue, you must first determine whether the behavior is age-appropriate; if not, ask yourself what environmental disturbances or changes in your relationship may have prompted this restless behavior. If chewing has evolved recently, consider whether it's occurring due to boredom, frustration/anxiety, or attention seeking. (We cover alternatives to these situations in Chapters 14 and 15.)

Putting a Damper on Jumping

In movies and cartoons, it may be funny when the big dog heads directly to the woman in white clothes, jumps up to greet her, knocks her down, and leaves muddy footprints on her dress. In real life, however, this behavior is rarely welcomed. How you stop it depends on what's prompting your dog to jump up in the first place.

Competing behaviors

To stop a dog's annoying jumping, all that you need to do is to find a "competing behavior" that is incompatible with the act of jumping. In dogs, the easiest competing behavior for jumping and a variety of other active behaviors is to have the dog sit. One reason why it's easy is because most people have already taught their dog to sit when given a verbal command or a hand signal. Obviously, if the dog is sitting, he can't be jumping at the same time.

To get rid of jumping behaviors as a greeting, simply tell the dog to "Sit" when you walk in the door or greet the dog in the morning. Praising, petting, or offering a bit of a treat serves as a reward.

Another example of a competing behavior is when dogs jump onto the furniture. They're seeking a soft comfortable place to rest, so providing a dog bed or floor cushion in the same room is the solution. The dog must be shown this alternative and placed there if he jumps on the sofa. Obviously, the dog can't rest on the sofa and his bed simultaneously!

Your dog may have many reasons for jumping up. If jumping occurs during greeting rituals, his intention is to make contact with your face.

Because attention (negative or positive) reinforces behavior, many people unintentionally reward jumping. Any reaction that involves touching is considered interaction. Do you find yourself pushing or grabbing your dog's coat as he leaps about? You may be encouraging this behavior.

Some training books suggest harsh measures, such as kneeing the dog in the chest when he jumps on you. Such methods don't work very well, and even when they do, they only stop the dog from jumping on the person who punishes him for it.

Greeting jumping

It's important that you praise your dog for sitting instead of jumping. However, it's equally important that the dog be completely ignored when jumping. Don't say, "Bad dog" or "No" because that means that you're paying attention to him, and attention is rewarding. Don't push the dog away because touch is rewarding. Simply act as if the dog isn't there, except when you're telling the dog to sit. When the dog does sit, lots of attention and rewards are the result.

If ignoring your dog is ineffective, fold your arms over you face and continue to ignore him until he's stopped and calmed down. Redirect him to sit or to fetch a toy.

Company jumping

If your dog is jumping on other people and you're present, the solution is simple — just tell your dog to sit before he jumps, reward him, and then allow your visitor to pet him or give him a treat for sitting politely. If he's too rambunctious, keep him on a leash, either stepping on it to prevent interference, holding it, or tying him back away from the door until he's calmed down.

Of course, that approach doesn't work when you're not around and your visitors don't know that they must give the "Sit" command to prevent being jumped on. There is an easy solution, however.

Most people train their dog to sit when they say the word or give a hand signal. What you must do is train the dog to sit to an additional hand signal that can be used during the greeting rituals. In this case, the hand signal that you want to use is to have both hands flat, palms up, facing the dog, as shown in Figure 13-2.

Figure 13-2: Hand signal for "Sit" to reduce jumping behavior.

To train the dog to respond to this hand signal is easy. Stand in front of the dog, say "Sit" (which he already understands), and give the hand signal. Give him a treat when he responds. Once he gets used to seeing the hand signal along with the verbal command, try just the hand signal and see whether he's figured it out. If not, keep practicing using both the hand and voice commands. When the dog understands that when both hands go up, he's supposed to sit, you're then ready for the dog to meet strangers, even when you're not present.

The reason that this new hand signal prevents jumping is that it's the same as the defensive motion that most people make to protect themselves when they're afraid that something (like a large dog) is about to collide with them. So your visitor sees your dog approaching and makes automatic defensive hand movements (with no need of instructions from you). Your well-trained dog interprets this as a "Sit!" command, and the problem is solved. Remember, a sitting dog is not jumping up.

Housetraining

Though several scientific studies show housetraining to be the No. 1 frustration of dog owners, it doesn't take a pie chart or graph to convince you that a dog that is not housebroken isn't any fun. If you're still struggling in this area, help lies just ahead.

If your puppy is young and is used to sleeping in his kennel, your efforts will be straightforward, as he'll instinctively avoid messing in it. One of the first lessons the puppy learns from his house-proud mother is the need to be clean in the sleeping area, which she teaches by consuming all the waste that the pups produce.

Every facet of your dog's behavior draws on his evolution. Before domestication, birth dens were kept clean to remove the scent of droppings that could lead a predator to a young litter of defenseless pups.

If your puppy is eliminating in his kennel crate, it may simply be too large. A large crate allows the pup to eliminate at one end and rest in the other. The goal is, of course, for your puppy to build control and not go until he's released from this confinement. If you purchased an adult-sized crate, purchase or fashion a barrier to limit your puppy's free space. Inserting a cardboard box of the right size to leave room only for the pup to turn around and lie down is an easy solution.

Bathroom buddies

Experienced dog owners will tell you that it is a lot easier to housetrain a puppy if you already have a housetrained dog in the home who knows the routine. The trick is to let both the older dog and the pup out at the same time or take them on their walks together. The puppy watches the adult dog and, from simple observation, learns what is expected of him.

This advice leads to an obvious recommendation. If you have an older dog in the house and fear that he is nearing the end of his life, it may be helpful to bring a new pup into your home before the older one dies. This early arrival gives the puppy a chance to be mentored in house cleanliness and other basic skills by the already trained senior dog. A side benefit is that having a new pup in the family often improves the quality of life and the activity level of the older dog and may even extend his life.

To insure you choose a puppy who is compatible with your older dog, please refer to Chapter 5. A dominant puppy can emotionally undo a peace-loving senior.

The housetraining routine

Routine is a key feature of housetraining. Draw up a master schedule and insist that everyone take part in ensuring adherence. Schedule feeding times, toilet breaks, and organized play periods. Here's a quick list of tips:

✔ Young puppies and untrained dogs need to go outside after napping or after being crated for a while, because increases in activity after a period of quiet often trigger elimination. This means that the first thing in the morning, immediately after you take him out of the crate, he has to get a chance to eliminate. After a long night, puppies often can't even make it to the door before they have to go, so you may have to carry him to the door for a week or so.

✔ A young puppy hasn't developed strong bladder muscles and must be taken out frequently, particularly after eating, drinking, play, resting, and isolation. A young puppy (6 to 14 weeks of age) may benefit from being taken out eight or more times a day. This number will gradually reduce over the next six months.

✔ If your dog is eliminating very frequently, he may have an internal infection or parasites. Speak to your veterinarian immediately.

✔ Bring your dog to the same area to relieve himself. You may highlight this area with pine chips or designate a specific tree or outcropping. Have a fenced-in yard? Until your pup is housetrained, you'll still need to accompany him to encourage and reinforce his habits.

✔ Don't confuse your goals. When you take your dog out to potty, bring him to his area and ignore him until he does his business. Don't give him walk time or play time until afterward.

✔ Teach your dog word cues and routines to highlight your participation, such as ringing a bell or barking before you go out. Say, "Outside" or "Papers" as you escort your dog to his area. Then cue him with another phrase, such as "Be quick" or "Get busy," as he's in the process of eliminating.

By repeating a phrase each time your dog eliminates, you're indicating what you want the dog to do, and ultimately he can learn to eliminate on cue.

✔ Once your dog has eliminated, take time out to reward him with your attention, a fun game, or a walk. If you rush back inside immediately, your dog will learn to delay eliminating in order to spend more time outside with you.

✔ Most puppies can hold their bladder muscles for six to eight hours. Take your puppy out just before your bedtime, even when you must rouse him from a deep sleep.

When accidents happen

Face it — accidents happen. Although dogs catch on to the house-breaking routine quickly, no one is immune to an occasional lapse. Accidents happen for a variety of reasons:

✔ The dog was isolated too long or not given adequate time to relieve herself during the last outing.

✔ He's suffering an infection or illness.

✔ He awakened from a nap or had a large drink of water and no one noticed, so he wasn't let out.

✔ You got home later than usual, and the dog couldn't hold it.

If the dog messes, don't hit him, yell at him, or rub his nose in it. A dog rarely makes the connection between your punishment and his earlier behavior. Such heavy-handed behaviors only teach the dog to be afraid of you. If you catch the dog in the act and punish him, all that you may have taught him is to make his messes in hidden places out of your sight.

If you actually catch your dog in the process of eliminating inside the house, interrupt him and take him outside to the proper place (without harsh words or punishment). If he eliminates outside, praise him. Remember to be patient; some dogs take longer than others to housebreak.

Your best course of action when faced with an occasional mess is to simply clean it up. Then use a commercial odor eliminator (many are enzyme-containing products) or simply clean the area with white vinegar or rubbing alcohol. These cleaners kill any trace scents that may trigger elimination.

Laugh a little

Your interpretation and response to your dog's behavior really determines how disruptive his delinquency is to your life. Often, a sense of humor will save your relationship with your pet.

One day, Stan had done some shopping and then left the bag of groceries on the kitchen counter while he went off to a meeting. When he returned, the kitchen was a disaster area. His retriever Dancer had pulled the bag off the counter and eaten a bag of cookies and a loaf of bread from it. In the process, a plastic bottle of cola and another bottle of pink liquid stomach upset remedy had split open, covering the floor with a sticky brown and pink mess with lots of crumbs floating in it. Meanwhile, Dancer stood in the middle of this mess with his stomach distended and rumbling.

Obviously, disciplining Dancer for something he'd done a couple of hours ago was useless because he wouldn't understand the connection. Stan had the following alternatives:

✔ Yell at the dog anyway.

✔ Ignore the dog and angrily clean up the mess.

✔ Feel guilty about the fact that his dog was now in great discomfort because of his own negligence in leaving the bag so close to the edge of the counter.

✔ Laugh at the idea that his dog had not only gorged himself on forbidden sweets and washed it down with cola, but also had the foresight to drink a dose of stomachache remedy.

So he laughed. It doesn't mean that he doesn't care or likes cleaning up sticky messes, or that he'll ever leave things like that on the counter edge again. He laughed because it was too late to do anything but clean up and because he knew that this would be a funny story to tell to his friends.

Anger only confuses the dog and weakens your relationship with your pet. It doesn't solve any problem. Before punishing the dog for a transgression, ask yourself, "Will I laugh about this incident later or when I tell it to someone else?" If the answer is yes, why not laugh now and then get on with the business of making things right again?

Don't use products containing ammonia, because it smells enough like urine that it actually attracts the dog to eliminate in that place again. Also, don't let the pup watch you clean up because your activities may draw him back to that spot again.

For more information on housetraining, see *Housetraining For Dummies* (Wiley), by Susan McCullough.

Chapter 14

Countering Anxiety-Based Behavior

*F*ear, anxiety, and stress are the big three ingredients when it comes to psychological problems in humans, and they're equally important in the psychology of dogs. Sometimes it's quite clear that your dog is worried and afraid. In other instances, you only know your dog is afraid after he engages in certain unpleasant behaviors, which can run the gamut from destroying furniture and objects, loud barking and howling in your absence, or even behaviors that look much like unprovoked aggression, such as nipping or biting someone. The first step in helping your dog with his anxiety is being able to recognize it in the first place.

The Face of Fear

The more obvious signs that a dog is anxious or afraid include ears slicked back, tail down, whining, whimpering and other high pitched sounds, and cringing or rolling on the ground (see Figure 14-1). An anxious dog may respond in different ways, however, depending upon the type of fear it is dealing with.

Fear isn't a simple emotion, and often surfaces in unique ways and to varying degrees. The strongest and most obvious form comes when the dog feels that its very life and safety are threatened. In such situations, only two courses of action are open to the dog. It can escape the fearful situation, or it can fight the individual who is the source of the threat.

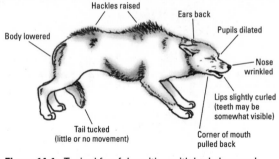

Figure 14-1: Typical fearful position with body lowered.

Among fearful dogs, you find a number of *fear biters*. These dogs are virtually swamped by their fear and may seem to be acting both inappropriately and unpredictably to otherwise everyday situations. If a trauma has left a dog legitimately so afraid of a person or situation that he is willing to attack to save himself from harm, he desperately needs to be reconditioned to accept the stimulus. Though this process may take time and patience, it's not impossible.

A fearful dog prefers to head for the hills and run away from situations or people that frighten him, whether threat is real or imagined. Consider the dog who is afraid of newcomers and who will immediately hide the moment the doorbell rings. In the wild, this reaction is a survival skill; in the home, it creates confusion, as most people love to introduce and share their pet's love as though it were another family member. Of course, if anyone in your family hid when a visitor knocked, you'd immediately seek help. So, too, should you be alerted if your dog is showing this level of anxiety.

Normal social fear and communication

It is fascinating that more dogs don't use aggression when fearful or threatened, though as with many behaviors, an evolutionary explanation exists. It seems that evolution took a dislike to aggression among members of the same group, unless there is no other recourse. In a pack of wolves, for example, it's important to their survival that they stay together, which requires strong social bonds. Within a pack of wolves, a hierarchy evolved to organize group interaction, with the brightest and most sensible wolves guiding the rest of the pack.

A nervous or fearful wolf might feel intense conflict when addressed by a more dominant pack member, but running away or showing aggression would not be an appropriate social response. Instead, wolves, and in turn dogs, learned more appropriate gestures to communicate respect, submission, and fear. In effect, this social skill allows them to stay in the group, share in companionship, and yet avoid conflict.

The eyes have it

If your dog is panting or showing any other signs of stress, look carefully at his eyes. In human beings, stress, anxiety, and excitement cause the pupils of our eyes to dilate. The same is true in dogs. If you have a breed where you can see the size of his pupils, check whether they're larger than usual. If so, your dog is under pressure of some sort.

Of course, this assessment requires that you first know how large your dog's pupils are when he's not worried, so take this opportunity to look into his eyes now so that you have something to compare with later if you think your dog is going through an anxious period.

At times, a fear is manifested, and a dog can't retreat. This situation creates an impulse of fight or flight, and when left no other option, a dog will react aggressively in its natural impulse to simply survive. In the wild, this reaction may be seen if a dog were cornered by a larger predator, such as a bear or a mountain lion, but in everyday life, this reaction can evolve when a dog is tethered, caged, or cornered.

Using social skills to resolve conflict

Fortunately, dogs who bite humans out of fear are in the minority. Dogs accept humans as other dogs, and they often use the same social skills that help them adapt to social living throughout evolution.

Truly fearful dogs often have a history of social isolation or neglect in puppyhood. If a young dog is isolated from humans and/or other dogs during her early socialization period (see Chapter 8), she'll be unable to learn appropriate play and communication skills. When placed in "normal" social situations as an adult, the social "handicap" will be readily noted through fearful/aggressive displays.

When a dog is socialized normally, he develops natural communication skills to avoid conflict and stress with other group members. Obviously, in the case of conflict, escape and fighting are still options open to the dog. Of the two, fighting is a less likely outcome.

The major communication signal that submissive dogs use to avoid conflict is to lower their body frame as they cringe with both belly and head near the ground while looking up. Designed to shrink appearances, it's exactly the opposite of expressing dominance, which involves standing tall, tail up, ears up, fur standing erect to make an individual look larger. In this case of submission, the dog is basically saying, "Let's not argue" or "I accept your leadership and higher social status."

The presence of a ritualized signal, such as the lowered body, isn't a sign of physical fear, but rather a means of avoiding the frightening possibility of confrontation. This stance is no different than a peasant bowing before a king to show respect and acknowledge his rank.

Recognizing signs of stress

Fortunately, most of our dogs don't often have full-blown bouts of fear, but they can suffer from a variety of stressors and worries. The following signs and signals indicate stress:

✔ **Panting:** In addition to panting or perspiring when a dog is overheated, a dog may also pant or appear distressed when he's experiencing excitement or anxiety. Thus, when a dog that isn't moving and that isn't exposed to warm conditions starts to vigorously pant, this means that he is excited or anxious. Obviously, excitement can come about because of positive events, such as anticipating a walk, but if such a happy event isn't impending, it's likely that the dog is anxious, worried, or perhaps even in pain.

✔ **Submissive paw:** A subtle sign of distress is a lifted front paw. Though many people may interpret this as cute, it signals emotional conflict, combining social fear with a reasonable dose of insecurity. For example, the raised paw signal for stress evolved from the earliest submissive behavior that puppies display in their litter. This raised paw gesture is also quite common in puppies and means not only mild stress, but a request to be interpreted as, "I need you to do something for me."

The submissive paw is a common site in the early stages of obedience training classes where the dogs are quite unsure as to what's expected of them. If the dog has been placed in a sit position and told to stay, for example, the dogs with their paws raised are also the ones that are most likely to lie down or to break and run to the safety of their master's side before the time has been completed.

✔ **Obsessive licking:** An interesting variation of this licking behavior is a sure sign of stress or anxiety. Adult dogs can show their stress by something that looks like they're licking the air. They flick their tongues in and out as though licking something when they're too far away to actually touch the individual who is causing their worry, or when they're too frightened to actually come close and make physical contact. Air licking is almost always a good indicator of an anxious dog.

Litter tales

Many of the gestures that indicate anxiety, worry, or submissive behavior that results from fear actually evolve from things that happened in the litter. After puppies are fed, the mother nudges each pup over onto his back or side with her nose. She then holds him down and licks him from top to bottom. When she starts to lick his face and neck, the puppy's reaction is to raise his paw and lie there submissively until his mother is finished with her task. Later, when the puppy's eyes are functioning well, it takes only a hard dominant stare from his mother to cause him to roll over while lifting his paw.

Puppies often try to pacify their mother or other members of their litter by licking them when they're acting hostile or threatening. Later, when the dog is more mature, he may use licking behavior for the same reason. He may lick the hand of his master who has been angry at him, for example.

The Leaky Dog Syndrome

The scene isn't uncommon. You arrive home, a guest arrives at your house, or you meet someone in the street, and when an attempt is made to greet your dog, you see her crouching on the ground with yellow droplets or a pool of piddle around her. This anxiety-based behavior isn't a lapse in housetraining. It is a sign that something about the situation is stimulating some extreme feelings of worry, and technically behaviorists refer to this problem as *submissive urination*.

Like many dog behaviors, you can trace the origin of this one back to the litter. Young pups need to be stimulated by their mother's licking and nudging before they can urinate or defecate. If the pup doesn't respond quickly enough, the mother may nudge the genital area quite hard to get things moving, and the resulting yelps from the pups indicate that this action can be unpleasant. Later, when the puppy is older and is effectively using his eyesight, the mother simply has to look as if she intends to roll the pup over to start the toilet ritual to trigger urination. This step saves the mother time (and the pups the discomfort of hard nudges) and prepares the pups to become "housetrained" when they're capable of following their mother outside to eliminate.

Psychologically, puppies learn early to respond to a dominant look or gesture with submissive urination. As the puppies become more mature, they do gain control over this behavior, and depending upon their life experience, it may never again appear in adulthood. However, in cases of severe stress (which varies, depending on a puppy's temperament or life experiences), submissive urination can occur and can become a messy and embarrassing problem to the dog's owners.

Submissive urination is an involuntary behavior that you can't correct by becoming angry or upset. Solving the problem requires you to control any display of emotion.

Before addressing the problem, analyze it. When does it occur?

- ✔ When you arrive home?
- ✔ When you or others are facing the dog?
- ✔ When you are angry, scolding, or raising your voice to the dog?
- ✔ When you lean over or try to pick him up?
- ✔ When the dog meets new people or enters strange places?

Once the situations that trigger the urination are identified, you can clear up the problem in a few weeks, depending upon your skill, consistency, and severity of the problem.

Stopping the leak

Because submissive urination predictably results when your dog is greeting a person whose stature or vocal tones convey authority, you can easily predict when this behavior will occur. When interacting with these authority-type figures, inform them of your efforts and ask them to ignore your dog, either completely or at least until you've equipped them with a treat cup or your dog approaches them.

The good news is that a puppy or a young dog usually outgrows the problem as he matures and can predict interactions. Building your dog's self-confidence is also critical in resolving this anxiety-based problem. Punishment, on the other hand, only intensifies his anxiety and makes matters worse.

The essence of the correction is to remove any signs of threat at those critical times that you've identified as the triggers for this behavior. For example:

- ✔ If your dog piddles when you approach, don't approach directly. Stand quietly and then turn sideways and crouch down.
- ✔ Don't say anything to the dog.
- ✔ Don't make eye contact.
- ✔ Don't hold out your hand.

✔ Let the dog approach you.

✔ When the dog reaches you, pet him lightly under the chin. Don't reach out palm down or over the dog's head. If petting causes further wetting, withhold it for a few days and then try again.

If your dog is treat motivated, use a treat cup, clicker, or hand-held goodies to externalize his focus as you encourage him to approach you (see Chapter 10).

In addition, make every effort to build your dog's confidence in your day-to-day interactions:

✔ Tone down your voice levels when interacting with your dog on a day-to-day basis.

✔ Use obedience training or other athletic courses (such as agility) using food and praise to encourage your dog's interest and cooperation. Using simple directions like "Sit" can calm him when meeting new people.

✔ When a new person approaches, ask her to hold out a treat and avert her eyes (preferably to the ground) as she calls your dog's name.

✔ If your dog is truly afraid of strangers, ask to hold your visitor's hand in yours as your dog sniffs your mutual scent.

The effect of this carefully planned social encounter can slowly recondition your dog's fear into eager anticipation of positive social encounters. Submissive peeing no more!

Curbing Separation Anxiety

Separation anxiety is a term used to cover a whole collection of extreme reactions that dogs have when their owners leave them alone in their home. Classic responses include

✔ Destructive chewing or clawing of door, clothing articles, furnishings, counter objects, and so on

✔ Self-mutilating behaviors, such as excessive licking, scratching, or clawing, referred to as *self-micturation*

✔ Digging garden beds, plants, carpets, or bedding

✔ Indoor micturation (marking, other eliminations)

✔ Vocal protest, including howling and barking

✔ Frantic/hyperactive displays upon your departure and arrivals

Our casebooks are filled with such instances: Jet, the border collie who quite literally stripped the kitchen wallpaper by the back door; Billy, the boxer who chewed and dug a hole through a wall between two rooms; and countless other dogs who daily destroy furnishings and clothing when they're left alone. Separation anxiety is all too common in today's world where dogs are left alone for prolonged hours and simply expected to entertain themselves. These poor social creatures don't perform these acts joyfully — each animal was in a heighten state of anxiety, to the point of sheer panic.

Accept it or not, but people are the chief cause of a dog's prolonged separation anxiety experience. Though most dogs experience separation anxiety during adolescence, handled properly, this developmental phase passes quickly. Handled inappropriately, however, this psychological issue can last a lifetime.

The experience of separation anxiety has evolutionary roots. In a pack, young puppies remain at the den with a chaperone, as the adult wolves/dogs would venture to a field to hunt or explore. As the puppies matured into adolescents, the release of adult hormones would herald a rite of passage, and the same puppies were included in all adult rituals. Fast forward to present day. Though young puppies readily accept your comings and goings, adolescent dogs must emotionally adjust to your separation as their impulses are quite literally telling them to join you.

Metaphorically speaking

Consider yourself a young child, say 8 years old. Suppose that your guardian leaves you alone in the house without telling you when she'll be back. As the minutes tick by, you'll likely grow bored, anxious, and/or concerned. You may find yourself involuntarily glancing at her photograph on the wall or finding a familiar object to reassure yourself. When your guardian does finally come home, you're happy and relieved and show this feeling with a strong display of emotion.

Dogs experience a similar anxiety, especially heightened when it's first experienced during adolescence. If you enjoy indulging your dog or you respond to every request for attention, your departure and consequent separation will be more pronounced. Because a quick phone conversation is out of the question, your dog may try to reach you by barking or howling. If your dog is a nonverbal type, he may visualize your presence and recall images of your activities around the house, such as your reading or television activities or clothing that is familiar and worn.

How can shoes or boots that are dragged from the closet be a sign of love and bonding? Though this dog isn't happy at the moment, his thoughts are most certainly with you when you leave him behind.

How it all begins . . .

Here's how a common reaction can take an understandably stressful situation for a dog and turn it into an anxiety-producing event: You get a new puppy that you leave at home while you go to work. Each time you return home, you joyfully greet the puppy with lots of touching, praise, and attention. Because, at least initially, you keep regular hours, the dog begins to anticipate these interactions.

But, of course, no matter how regular your routine is, there will be a day that you'll be late. Because dogs have a reasonable sense of time, your pup will begin to fret and worry. He may imagine hearing the expected sound of your footsteps or seeing you enter the door, but when it doesn't happen, he becomes anxious and wants to experience your presence. It's then that he comes upon the book you were reading, slippers you were wearing, or the TV remote control that you handled. If he can't have you, then at least he can have your scent and the taste associated with your body oils and sweat. So he sniffs, tastes, and ultimately chews the article to gain something akin to your presence.

Finally, you come home — only this time it's not going to be a happily-ever-after finish. The puppy sees you and, in full innocence, begins the usual greeting routine, perhaps with an added nearly hysterical component of relief at your return. You join in because this display of love is comforting — that is, until your eye falls on the shredded paper that was the book you were reading, the chewed remainder of your slippers, or the bits of plastic that once housed the remote control. Understandably, a frustrated reaction, such as a verbal outlash or a grab-n-drag to what remains of a chewed possession, follows.

The puppy, however, is unlikely to register the object as his simple one-track mind is currently focused on your homecoming. When this confused pup yelps and tries to escape, he's also filled with terror because the very person he instinctively turns to when distressed is, in fact, the one who is turning on him. Furthermore, because the punishment wasn't associated with the impulse to chew, he can't make any psychological connection to the behavior and instead links your reaction to your return and your separation to the events that are sure to follow, which in anyone's dictionary spells S-E-P-A-R-A-T-I-O-N A-N-X-I-E-T-Y!!!

So when you're away, your dog impulsively seeks objects that comfort him and grows exceedingly more anxious of your departures. Not only does this whole interaction not correct the puppy's anxiety-based behavior, but he now is likely to develop a conflicted view of you. In his mind, you become an angel and a devil, or Dr. Jekyll and

Mr. Hyde, in the same body. If this pattern is repeated a few times, it can lead to anxiety about your homecomings, which add to the anxieties concerning your absence. One consequence of this may be submissive urination. (See "The Leaky Dog Syndrome," earlier in this chapter.) The puppy now more actively solicits your attention when you're home because he needs the comfort and security that your interaction gives him. When you respond, this causes him to miss you even more when you're away, and this cycle of comfort-seeking destruction, followed by more, perhaps harsher, punishment continues. This pattern eventually leads to other problems and ultimately can destroy your relationship with your dog. Egad!

Solving isolation and anxiety problems

To resolve the issue of separation anxiety, all efforts must be two-fold:

✔ Your dog's emotional experience must be both understood and addressed.

✔ Your dog's inappropriate displacement behavior must be rechannelled to more appropriate activity.

Resolving a dog's anxiety requires more human behavior modification than anything else.

Secondhand dog separation anxiety syndrome

An adopted dog often shows signs of separation anxiety, many times resulting from the ultimate separation: sheer abandonment. Most shelter dogs, in fact, exhibit some form of separation anxiety in new homes. Suddenly transported from a familiar, predictable home environment to the unavoidable chaos of a shelter existence, they're then placed into a new home, where they're unsure of their new family members and the rules and rituals. These dogs are often left wholly undirected, especially when left alone.

In these situations, it's best to isolate or crate a dog until he's comfortable with his surroundings and routines. Follow the same conditioning exercises in this chapter to relieve separation anxiety.

Coming and goings

Although each of us loves our dogs and revels in their happy greetings, comings and goings need to become a far less dramatic event. If each time you (or anyone else) arrive or depart, a maniac scene ensues, your dog will never calm down when left alone. Each noise becomes cause for alert, each knock on the door a reason to kick into high gear. Though your reassurance upon departure may soothe your disappointment, it only highlights your inevitable separation, leaving your dog in an agitated state.

These simple efforts go far in de-emphasizing your absence and to condition your dog to being left alone:

✔ **When you leave,** draw the curtains or shades, if necessary, to screen out sights. Turn on a radio or television to provide human sounds and also to mask noises from outside. Simply put on your outside clothing and, *without saying anything to the dog,* leave.

Consider your door as the mouth of the den. Whether you're greeting your dog or a visitor has arrived, always address your dog after he's calmed down and is away from the doorway.

✔ **When you return,** be equally as quiet. Though your dog may be overexcited to see you, ignore your dog for a minute or two before acknowledging her presence. Take off your coat and hat and hang them up. Put away the bags or briefcase that you're carrying, if any, and enter the main area of the household. When your dog has calmed down, greet him quietly, and then continue on the course of your day. If you're eager for a more ecstatic interchange, promote play in an appropriate environment, whether inside or out.

When boredom masks as anxiety

Some destructive dogs aren't anxious at all! They're simply not getting enough exercise and are bored. Upon close observation, these dogs are simply revved up and in need of a good romp in the park. To break their pattern of destruction, increase their exercise. When you leave, provide favorite bones or toys specifically designed to alleviate restless energy, such as food-filled hollow toys or boxes that dispense treats as they're moved.

Toys that contain food items should be washed between every use and removed when you're home.

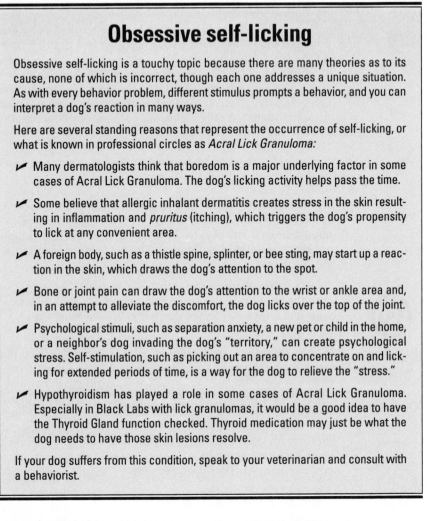

Obsessive self-licking

Obsessive self-licking is a touchy topic because there are many theories as to its cause, none of which is incorrect, though each one addresses a unique situation. As with every behavior problem, different stimulus prompts a behavior, and you can interpret a dog's reaction in many ways.

Here are several standing reasons that represent the occurrence of self-licking, or what is known in professional circles as *Acral Lick Granuloma:*

✔ Many dermatologists think that boredom is a major underlying factor in some cases of Acral Lick Granuloma. The dog's licking activity helps pass the time.

✔ Some believe that allergic inhalant dermatitis creates stress in the skin resulting in inflammation and *pruritus* (itching), which triggers the dog's propensity to lick at any convenient area.

✔ A foreign body, such as a thistle spine, splinter, or bee sting, may start up a reaction in the skin, which draws the dog's attention to the spot.

✔ Bone or joint pain can draw the dog's attention to the wrist or ankle area and, in an attempt to alleviate the discomfort, the dog licks over the top of the joint.

✔ Psychological stimuli, such as separation anxiety, a new pet or child in the home, or a neighbor's dog invading the dog's "territory," can create psychological stress. Self-stimulation, such as picking out an area to concentrate on and licking for extended periods of time, is a way for the dog to relieve the "stress."

✔ Hypothyroidism has played a role in some cases of Acral Lick Granuloma. Especially in Black Labs with lick granulomas, it would be a good idea to have the Thyroid Gland function checked. Thyroid medication may just be what the dog needs to have those skin lesions resolve.

If your dog suffers from this condition, speak to your veterinarian and consult with a behaviorist.

Soothing Fears and Phobias

Many dogs exhibit a fear response to specific situations, places, or people at some point in their life. It's a natural reaction to inexperience: Presented with an unfamiliar string of sensory stimulations, a puppy acts startled and looks to authority figures for direction. Handled properly, a puppy will condition to the event and integrate it into memory. For example, the first time the phone rings, a puppy may be startled, but after experiencing the routine aftermath of a telephone call, the noise no longer even wakes him from a deep sleep.

Handled improperly, however, a dog may harbor residual fear or, worse, develop a phobic reaction, trying to hide whenever the stimulus is presented. Do you know any dogs who try to hide whenever an electrical storm occurs? Are you living with one? Dogs can develop a fear or a *phobia* (which is an irrational but strong fearful response) to just about anything. Here are just a handful of situations from our casebook:

- ✔ Police sirens
- ✔ Vacuum cleaners
- ✔ Rain pelting a roof
- ✔ Linoleum floors
- ✔ Reflection of a metal pan on the kitchen ceiling
- ✔ Large men
- ✔ Lawn mowers
- ✔ Loud trucks
- ✔ Sound of a violin
- ✔ Pop-up sound of a toaster
- ✔ Sight of a body of water, such as a lake

Humans can contribute to a dog's fearfulness in a number of ways. Some involve what a person does, and some involve what a person hasn't done — for example, a lack of socialization (see Chapter 8). The more experience a dog has with different situations, especially during the first six months of its life, the more familiar he is with everyday life.

The best way to prevent a dog from being immobilized by fear of something is to fully socialize your dog.

Some dogs learn fears by *mirroring* their people's reaction to certain events. One common situation is when a small dog is lifted at the sight of a larger dog. Though there may be a reality element to this protectiveness, it's far better for people to socialize small dogs with familiar dogs of every age and size to ensure their comfort in the world surrounding them.

Another case involves a woman who is worried or apprehensive when she encounters large male strangers on the street. Every time she's walking her dog and she meets a strange man, she becomes nervous. Because all dogs are sensitive to body language and are literally attuned to the scent of fear, this dog learns that every time his mistress meets a man, she becomes frightened. Not surprisingly, the dog learns to be anxious in such situations as well. In this way dogs can learn to be frightened of particular classes of people, defined by their sex, size, or race.

The second way dogs can learn fears and phobias is to be rewarded for being afraid. Though no one would consciously reward a dog's fear, the difference between our languages can sometimes spell miscommunication. If, for example, your dog acts startled when he hears a sudden clap of thunder, your natural response may be to speak empathetically and bend down to sooth your dog. Though it's a nurturing and effective response with human children, the lowered posture, soft tones, and soothing pats communicate a very different message to your dog. In essence, your shrinking posture conveys that you're as unsure as he is and, at a very basic psychological level, you're rewarding your dog for being fearful.

The key to solving many problem behaviors in dogs is to "reward the behaviors that you want and ignore the behaviors that you don't want." Applying this philosophy to fearful behaviors takes some ingenuity, as it's often hard to highlight good behavior when your dog is in a fearful state, but you can get around this dilemma by playing through fear and working through fear.

Playing through fear

To solve fearful behaviors, it's helpful to reproduce the conditions that cause the fear. Thus, if a dog is afraid of thunder, you need to produce the sound of thunder, while if the dog is afraid of men wearing hats, you need a man willing to wear a hat in front of your dog. It's also better if you can control the intensity or distance your dog is standing from the fear-producing stimulus. Fortunately, if your dog is afraid of certain sounds, sound effect recordings are available, or you can download sound clips from many Web sites, often for free.

Here's what you need to do:

1. **Prepare a favorite game, activity, or pastime as you stimulate his fear reactions.**

   Chasing activities, tug, or catch are great options. (If your dog doesn't know them, teach him!)

2. **Introduce the fear-producing stimulus (at a low level or at a specified distance) and instantaneously (before your dog has time to become fearful) start your play routine.**

Here's what should happen. At first, your dog may act confused or may even revert to his usual fearful behavior.

3. **If your dog is confused or afraid, continue the happy play (perhaps while making the stimulus a bit weaker) for a couple of minutes and then stop.**

4. **Go do something else for about five minutes, while paying no attention to the dog.**

5. **Repeat the whole process.**

You can repeat this process about four times, twice a day. You'll know that you're making progress when the dog starts to wag his tail and looks at you when the fear-producing stimulus starts. Then simply turn up the intensity of the stimulus a bit and continue.

Working through fear

If you've taught your dog basic obedience (see Chapter 12), use these directions to help your dog through these frightening moments. Your direction is communicating several things:

- ✔ You're not afraid

- ✔ This stimulation is an everyday experience and nothing to be worried about.

- ✔ When your dog is afraid, he should look to you for direction, not collapse in fear.

Begin with a low level of the fear-producing stimulus (see the preceding section). Instead of play, use a leash/training collar and food rewards to direct and encourage your dog's cooperation. The moment that the stimulation is noted, direct your dog to "follow" you and proceed to lead him about the home, yard, or sidewalk. Stop occasionally and tell him to sit, or perhaps lie down, and give him lots of treats for paying attention and responding.

Your dog may act disoriented, looking at you as if you've lost your mind. However, confidence is catching; by simply attending to him when he's calm and not fearful, he'll soon learn to incorporate the situation into his memory bank of everyday experiences. Gradually, increase the intensity of the fearful stimulus a bit and continue your work routine.

Using a leash and food rewards to direct your dog through fearful situations has a great advantage: It's equivalent to holding a child's hand who is afraid. Consider using this procedure to get your dog through a fearful, real-life episode. For example, if you're out with your dog and an actual thunderstorm begins, tell your dog to heel and start to practice. No one needs to know that you're giving psychotherapy to your dog for his thunder phobia, although they may wonder about the soggy person walking a soggy dog in the rain, and giving him lots of soggy treats.

Chapter 15

Understanding and Resolving Aggressive Behavior

*M*ost people misunderstand the fact that the primary purpose of canine aggression is usually not to hurt and maim, but rather to change the behavior of another creature. Canine aggression is a tricky topic. Like human anger, it's a healthy form of communication, but it can get out of control if it's not comprehended properly, curbed, or redirected. Fortunately, only a small percentage of dogs elevate their responses to frustration, fear, or social challenge to a dangerous level. Out-of-control aggression can generally be traced to genetic or physiological sources, insufficient nurturing, lack of socialization, and/or rough or unintentionally confrontational handling.

Recognizing the Signs

Dogs don't bite just because they can. They react for a set number of situations, and once you recognize each, you'll be better equipped to understand your dog's angry or tense reaction. Not every dog reacts to every stress, and many dogs are wholly unaggressive. If your dog is showing aggression, ask yourself the following questions about when your dog seems to be threatening:

✔ Does it happen when someone is staring at or threatening him, such as during discipline or greetings?

✔ Does it happen when he feels cornered?

✔ Does it happen when a food resource or object is at risk?

✔ Does it happen when competing for a limited resource (such as food, toys, or attention) with another dog or person?

✔ Does it happen when he's disturbed during sleep?

✔ Does it happen when a territory is approached?

✔ Does it happen when competing for an object or resting space?

Reading body language

Dogs signal their aggressive intentions through certain clear changes in their facial expressions, their body posture, movements, or, more subtly, their social behaviors. If you watch your dog, he gives you many clear signals before his aggressive threats elevate to a physical level. Regardless of the underlying emotion — whether dominance or fear — these signals are danger signals. Actual physical aggression, where teeth are applied to skin, is really only the final step in what is usually an elaborate progression of aggressive signals. These displays include:

✔ A prolonged direct stare

✔ Raised hackles

✔ Growling

✔ Bared teeth

✔ Body arching

✔ A stiff walk

✔ Tail curled between his legs or held very high over the back and fluffed out

✔ Pricked ears (if the dog has them) lowered to the side to look like a wide V or airplane wings

Many of these cues are seen long before a reaction actually erupts. Think back to puppyhood. Did you ever consider these actions cute? You're certainly not alone. The first time your puppy grabs a tissue and baits you with a gleeful expression, it's adorable. But antics like this soon lose their flavor, and before long, you may find yourself venting frustration over behaviors that you once laughed at. Of course, this reaction makes sense to humans, but it doesn't to a dog. And suddenly, the very one your dog turns to for interaction (namely you) is now turning on him, showing signs of what he interprets as aggression. Play growling and nipping in a puppy can appear to be "cute," or at least innocuous, but such behaviors may just be the tip of a growing iceberg that can sink your relationship with your dog. The answer is not to use force or rough handling to solve the problem, but rather to socialize and train him. (See Chapter 8 for more on living with a puppy.)

Human behavior

Human behaviors play an important role in canine aggression. Certain behaviors increase or decrease the likelihood of dog bites. For example, in 53 percent of dog bite fatalities, there was some suggestion that the dog was provoked by being struck or poked in the face, having things thrown at him, or otherwise subjected to human aggression. In the case of children, bites are more likely when they're running, shouting, or screaming. It is interesting to note that a one-hour class on "bite proofing" has been shown to reduce, by more than 80 percent, the likelihood that a child will be bitten by a dog.

The behavior of the dog's owners is also important. Dogs that are kept chained or confined in a small yard are approximately three times more likely to fatally bite people — and not just people who enter their territory, but people who they encounter when they escape or are released from their yard. Another important statistic is that dogs that have received obedience training (even just the simple beginners class where people stand around in a circle, and the instructor shows you how to get Rover to sit, come, and lie down) show nearly a 90 percent reduction in the likelihood of biting incidents. This result is probably due to the education, not only of the dog, but of the dog's owner as well.

What is unintentionally rough handling? Many people are unaware that chasing, yelling at, or hitting a dog can result in canine aggression. Each attempt to curb a dog's behavior in this manner is viewed as confrontational. A dog raised in this atmosphere often becomes defensive and guarded, which, as he matures, can lead to aggressive displays.

The problem is that once aggressive behaviors develop, they never disappear on their own. Dogs quickly become skilled at using aggression as a tool to get what they want or as a shield in stressful situations. If your dog is showing aggression or your young puppy is showing a propensity toward dominant behavior, do everything within your power to contain this behavior, then to reduce it, and finally to eliminate any reoccurrence of it. The first step is to know how to identify and acknowledge when and if your dog is showing signs of aggression.

Evaluating aggressive tendencies

We're often quite blind when it comes to flaws in the behaviors of those that we love. That is why children can sometimes be well on their way toward delinquent or unacceptable behaviors before we even admit to ourselves that a problem exists. The same goes for our dogs. It's psychologically difficult to admit that the dog that sleeps next to your bed could be a threat to anyone.

Now is the time to honestly evaluate the situation. Ask yourself the following questions:

- ✔ Does your dog growl at you, other people, or other animals?

- ✔ Has your dog ever snarled or shown his teeth to you or other family members?

- ✔ Does your dog snap, growl, or threaten when you try to take toys or other objects away from him or when you reach for or come near his food?

- ✔ Does your dog snap, growl, or otherwise resist when you groom or examine him?

- ✔ Does your dog growl, show his teeth, arch his body, cringe, or and curl his tail between his legs when petted, especially when your hand is raised over the top of his head?

- ✔ Does your dog nip at your ankles or those of children when playing exuberantly?

- ✔ Do you ignore nipping, chewing at hands, play snarling, or other mouthy behavior because you think that it's "cute" or because your dog is obviously too small to do anyone any harm?

- ✔ Does your dog force you to invent excuses for his socially unacceptable growling or pushy behavior?

- ✔ Do you feel worried or apprehensive as to whether your dog may react in an unfriendly manner when a stranger or another dog approaches him?

If you answered "Yes" to any one of these questions, then your dog has the potential to become aggressive. The fact that you're carefully reading this section at all may mean that you have some concerns about your dog's aggression level. It's important to read the suggestions in this chapter, however, if you find that your dog's reaction is escalating or anyone in your household is afraid. Call for professional help from animal behaviorists or dog trainers specializing in handling aggression problems.

Factoring in Breed Traits

Many dog breeds have genetic potential toward aggression. Terriers have been bred to fight other animals, and generally speaking are quite chippy around other pets, unless raised with them. Protective breeds, including Akitas, Great Pyrenees, and Rottweilers, have fewer inhibitions about biting people. Because of the breed specificity in these behaviors, the public has been led to believe that certain breeds of dogs are inherently bad. The negative image of

Pit Bulls is partly the result of sensationalized news reports, and it also is reinforced in movies and on TV.

The real question everyone wants answered is whether a dog's breed is the best predictor of its aggressive potential. A series of studies commissioned by the U.S. National Center for Injury Prevention and Control has been looking at deaths due to dog bites based on records collected over several decades. In this national database, clear trends are evident, but the fact that a certain breed ranks high on a list of problem dogs may not be significant.

Obviously, popular breeds will necessarily be represented in higher numbers for any given problem simply because there are more of them, so you need to take into account how many dogs of a particular breed are around. You can do so by looking at the number of dogs of each breed registered with the American Kennel Club and using it as an estimate of the percentage of dogs of each breed in the country.

It appears that compared to their popularity, certain breeds are significantly less likely to be involved in fatal dog bites, even though they're big and muscular. Leaving out the breeds that are simply too tiny to do fatal damage, the four breeds of dogs *least likely* to be involved in such incidents, although they have the bite strength and size to do so, are (beginning with the lowest proportional fatal bite frequency) the Labrador Retriever, Dachshund, Golden Retriever, and Bulldog. It may well be that the enduring popularity of Labrador Retrievers and Golden Retrievers as family pets is in part due to the fact that they're so safe.

Based on the national statistics on fatal dog bites, the eight breeds (starting with the most dangerous) that account for the majority of these tragic cases of aggression are

- ✔ Pit Bulls and Pit Bull-type dogs (defined here to include American Pit Bull Terriers, Staffordshire Terriers, American Staffordshire Terriers, and Bull Terriers)
- ✔ Malamutes
- ✔ Chow Chows
- ✔ Saint Bernards
- ✔ Siberian Huskies
- ✔ Akitas
- ✔ Rottweilers
- ✔ German Shepherds

Color coding

Sometimes genetic factors over and above breed identity predict aggression. For example, it's well known that certain lines of Springer Spaniels have a genetically inherited condition called *rage syndrome,* which causes them to suddenly, without warning, start biting and attacking anything near them. This fit of aggression may last only a couple of seconds or up to a minute, but after it's over, the dog acts as if nothing has happened. Now genetic and chemical markers can indicate whether this condition is in the dog's hereditary makeup.

A common genetic marker for some conditions is coat color in dogs. Some English Cocker Spaniels can suddenly bite without warning in what looks like a milder version of the rage syndrome in Springer Spaniels. Research done at Cambridge University demonstrates that this condition is partially predicted by the dog's color. Solid-colored English Cocker Spaniels are much more likely to have these conditions than are dogs with two or more coat colors. Furthermore, among the solid-colored dogs, those who are red or blonde colored have the strongest likelihood of biting.

Please don't assume that each dog of these breeds is born with an overblown aggressive instinct. All that the science gives us is the baseline probabilities. Whether any specific Golden Retriever or Rottweiler becomes aggressive depends upon who he lives with, how he was raised and socialized, and how he was trained and integrated into human society. There is no doubt that kissy-faced Rottweilers and nasty Goldens are out there, and humans and their actions must take responsibility for both the good and the bad outcome.

Ruling Out Medical Factors

If your dog is showing aggressive tendencies, especially if this wasn't a problem in the past, please rule out medical causes before addressing the problem behaviorally. Obviously, if an injury, disease, or some form of physical or neurological defect is the cause for the aggressive behavior, then no training or reconditioning of the dog's behavior will be effective until the problem has been controlled.

When aggression suddenly surfaces, an ailment, such as pain in the teeth, back, or joints, may be distressing your dog. If you move or touch a dog that is in pain, you can expect to be snapped at. The dog isn't trying to say anything with his behavior other than "Stop that! You're hurting me!" Make an appointment with your veterinarian immediately.

Here are a few more other medical conditions that may be behind your dog's sudden aggression:

✔ **Hypothyroidism:** Recent research has shown that fairly common conditions that cause the thyroid gland to produce abnormally low amounts of hormones may be associated with the onset of aggressive behaviors in more than 50 breeds of dogs. In addition to aggression, other subtle signs of imbalance are excessive shedding, bald spots, an increased number of infections, allergic symptoms, a tendency to gain weight, or (in intact female dogs) irregular heat cycles. Hypothyroidism is easily treated with appropriate medications and hormone supplements.

✔ **Encephalitis:** This disease can be caused by viruses or bacteria. Distemper and rabies are viral types of encephalitis. These conditions can appear in dogs of any age, and occasionally, although rarely, even in dogs that have been vaccinated. Sudden aggressive episodes are common with this condition. It's easily diagnosed by testing a bit of *cerebrospinal fluid* (the clear fluid in the brain and spinal cord) and is treatable with antibiotics and antiviral medications.

✔ **Hypoglycemia:** This is the medical term for low blood sugar. Hypoglycemia can cause major mood swings in humans as well and is often responsible for the moodiness and flashes of anger that people on severe weight-reducing diets show. In addition to aggression, the symptoms of hypoglycemia can include apparent weakness (staggering) and a glassy, dazed look. You can usually easily treat this condition with a change in the dog's diet and feeding schedules.

✔ **Head injuries or brain tumors:** A brain injury or swelling interferes with normal mental functions. Swelling, pressure, or even bleeding in the brain often results in a variety of neurological and behavioral symptoms and often aggression. If your dog's mood swings and aggressive episodes are also accompanied by other symptoms — including confusion or disorientation, irritability, increased episodes of whimpering or nonstop barking, or changes in activity level (either an apathy-like decrease or increased hyper-excitability — ask your veterinarian to examine this possibility. Other important signs include changes in the ways your dog moves, such as an alteration in his normal gait, abnormal postures, head tilt, trembling, staggering, excessive circling, frequent falling, or loss of balance.

WARNING!

Increased aggression can also be the result of *hydrocephalus*. This congenital condition occurs when the fluid-filled spaces in the brain (the ventricles) become enlarged. Because of the pressure placed on the brain, the surrounding brain tissue suffers from pressure similar to the swelling caused by injuries or tumors producing similar symptoms. This condition is more common in toy breeds and those dogs with a flattened face, such as Pugs or Pekingese. Symptoms occur when the condition becomes extreme, which may not be until adulthood.

✔ **Imbalances in brain chemistry:** Some dogs, like people, can have an imbalance of vital chemicals in their brain. Common human conditions, such as clinical depression, obsessive-compulsive disorders, anger outbursts, and mood swings, exist in dogs as well and may result from these chemical changes. *Serotonin,* a hormone that serves as a neurotransmitter, plays an important role in the chemical control of aggression and mood changes in the brain, especially when certain other conditions that affect impulsive behaviors are present.

Unfortunately, these imbalances have no easy solution because serotonin can't be administered with a shot or pill. In human beings, and now in dogs, however, there has been a good deal of success controlling these conditions with a class of drugs that keeps the serotonin already in the brain from being broken down and reabsorbed around the nerve endings, thus, in effect, increasing the amount of serotonin available for use by the neural system. The best known of this class of drugs is Prozac, which, in various forms, has been successfully used to treat some forms of aggression in dogs.

Altering your dog's angry brain

If your dog's brain chemistry is the cause of his aggression and mood swings, your veterinarian may well prescribe certain Prozac-type drugs to help increase the amount of serotonin in your dog's brain. However, if you suspect that your dog's brain chemistry is part of the cause of his aggression or as a supplement to behavioral treatments of aggression, you can do two things.

The first involves *5-Hydroxytryptophan* or 5-HTP, which is a naturally occurring amino acid that is used by the body in the manufacturing of serotonin. In the United States and other countries, it's marketed as a dietary supplement and is available over the counter in health-food stores and some pharmacies. It's designed for people who want an antidepressant and something that may aid in sleep, but it works by effectively increasing the production of serotonin in the nerve endings and therefore can help reduce aggressive tendencies in many dogs. As in the case of Prozac, the effects may not be seen until the treatment has gone on for up to six weeks, and if you stop administering it at anytime, you go back to ground zero. Doses of 5-HTP are often recommended as a "booster" along with behavioral treatment of aggression.

Another treatment of body chemistry for aggression is still being researched but appears promising. At Tufts University, a team of researchers looked at switching dogs to low-protein, preservative-free diets (although if the only preservative is vitamin E, that appears to be okay). This diet seems to reduce certain types of aggression in a sizable percentage of dogs. Changing your aggressive dog's diet in this way is worth a try because if it works for your pet, you'll see the effects within a week or so and you don't have much to lose.

Identifying Different Types of Aggression

At one time, aggressive behavior was considered to be a single problem, and therefore all dogs received the same treatment regime. Today, we know that aggression comes in many forms, each with its own cause and treatment requirements. It's extremely important for you to understand what's going on when your dog acts aggressively. Snapping at you because you touched him where it hurts is excusable behavior while snapping at you because you tried to move him off of the sofa is not and requires action.

Dominance aggression

The most common and treatable form of aggression relates to dominance issues. Dominance aggression involves a dog growling or biting family members in order to control their behavior and thus, effectively, move up in status in the pack or family hierarchy. While you may think that this aggressive behavior is sudden and unexpected, it's actually quite planned and deliberate and most likely first began to show up when your dog was an adolescent or young adult. Once a dog achieves sexual and emotional maturity, between 8 months and 3 years, many of the social restrictions associated with puppyhood are left behind. It's at this time that your dog tests authority to ensure that the most reliable "dogs" (which include him) are orchestrating group activities. This is the motivation for challenging those people or other family pets that he feels aren't as dominant as he is.

As your dog assesses your home life, he may start to try to climb the ladder of social control by picking on the most vulnerable family members — children and other pets. If successful, his behavior may escalate to include challenges to you. If your dog begins to block the entrance into rooms or growls at family members near his food, toys, or resting places, seek professional help immediately.

In your dog's eyes, if you're not authoritative and sensible, you're not good leadership material, and because someone must lead the group, he'll assign himself the role. The result? Your dog becomes aggressive to enforce his leadership. Unfortunately his threatening behavior may well have to do with your own personality and the way you interact with your dog. However, you are the easiest variable to change, provided that you're willing to modify your behavior for everyone's benefit.

Bite levels

Dogs, like people, control the level of aggression used to make a point. Not all bites are created equally, and scientists, such as Ian Dunbar, classify bite-related aggression into six levels.

Level 1: This is a threat and a deliberate miss — snapping at air — and it doesn't touch the skin. This "fair warning" snap is often given by well-socialized dogs as a "back off and leave me alone" signal.

Level 2: Involves teeth making contact, but the skin isn't broken. There may be pain and bruising, but no visible blood. This "hard threat" suggests that the next time, the dog will really use its teeth as a weapon.

Level 3: The first level where skin is broken. It involves a single bite, which results in one to three punctures with none deeper than half the depth of the eye-tooth (fang). It's meant to end the confrontation immediately because it threatens that the next stage of escalation may cause real damage. A dog producing Level 3 bites is well on the way to becoming a real aggressive threat and requires behavioral management.

Level 4: The dog is now trying to hurt his target. This bite is the result of a dog exerting heavy pressure, which results in one to four puncture wounds with one or more puncturing the skin to more than half the depth of the eye tooth. This bite may be accompanied by some tearing and bruising. Such a bite wound is likely to require medical attention. These injuries often result when the dog grabs and shakes what was in its mouth. It indicates a dog who is not inhibited about biting, and if no steps are taken, irreparable damage may be done to his next target.

Level 5: Involves multiple Level 4 bites. This dog is acting dangerously, perhaps because it feels that its life has been threatened, and he's now moved beyond his normal ability to reason his way through the situation. This dog is a real threat to his family and to society at large, and steps must be taken to treat the situation.

Level 6: The dog has killed a pet or person. This level requires no elaboration. It's the situation we're trying desperately to avoid.

The issue of dominance aggression has been confirmed by research done at the Western University of Health Sciences in California, which showed that owners, who are gentle pushovers when it comes to their dogs, are more likely to have to deal with dominance aggression in their dogs. Tip-off behaviors can be seen in people who treat their dogs like little children, giving in to their whims, giving them treats from the table, and allowing them to sleep undisturbed on sofas and beds.

Dominance aggression can escalate and, when aimed at children, can be quite dangerous. Most of the recorded dog bites are, in fact, family dogs who bite children. You have to understand that the dogs that are unsafe around children are usually dogs that haven't been well socialized. However, it's still important to monitor the interactions between dogs and children. A child may try to grab a toy or some other possession that the dog holds dear, and the dog may see this action as both a loss of his cherished item and a threat to his status, if he feels dominant over children. That is a setup for a biting incident.

Possessive aggression

The essence of possessive aggression is that the dog is telling you, "This is mine! You can't have it! You can't touch it!" This type of aggression is usually focused on food or toys and is most common in dogs that

- ✔ As puppies, had to compete with other pups for food

- ✔ Live in households with multiple pets, or even children, who may be viewed as coveting the dog's food or possessions

- ✔ Were shelter dogs, who may have been taken from a safe environment, but when thrust into a kennel surrounded by unknown situations, the dogs may vigorously guard their resources and space

---

Bite-proofing children

The first step in protecting children from dog bites is to learn to read the facial expressions and body language that a dog uses to convey threat, frustration, or fear and to teach these to children. This is just basic safety education, like teaching children to look both ways before crossing streets.

Because children naturally are attracted to dogs, you should teach them how to approach a dog. First, have them ask the dog's owner if they can pet the dog. Then the child should extend a hand. If the dog approaches to sniff it calmly, the dog is saying it would like to be friends. Calm petting can be supervised. If the dog turns away, growls, or lowers its head, the child shouldn't proceed.

If a child is playing and a dog approaches quickly, the "stand-like-a-statue" technique is effective in reducing the likelihood of being bitten:

- ✔ Teach your child that dogs don't chase statues.

- ✔ Ask him to think of a statue, and when approached to stand very still, to fold his arms across his chest and look up to the sky (discouraging all eye contact or interaction).

- ✔ Because statues are boring, the dog will eventually go away. When he does, back up slowly until he's out of sight.

The spoiled dog's dilemma

Not every wolf or dog wants to be leader of the pack, but he needs to know that someone is in charge and making decisions. It may seem strange to learn that a dog's anxiety can be increased when he gets what he wants without any responsibility for earning it. This is often the case with pampered dogs whose owners believe that giving their dogs everything they desire and asking nothing in return is a way of showing their love. Because only the leader usually has full access to all the pack's resources, this kind of treatment can lead a dog to feel that he must be in charge, meaning that he now has the responsibility to make all the decisions — even when the dog is uncertain as to what to do or when he may not understand what is actually happening. This uncertainty, combined with the fact that there is no one else in a leadership role evaluating the situation and making a decision, is bound to lead to fear and anxiety.

When you attempt to reassure this frightened dog, it often fails, because your reassuring voice tones and body posture can be read as fear by the dog, or simply because the dog hasn't learned to look to you for direction. The dog reasons that because you lack the stature of a leader, you're not in a position to make decisions or assessments of the situation for the rest of the pack, including her.

Don't wait until you have an adult dog with a food- or toy-guarding problem. Teach your puppy that being touched when he's eating is okay, and that your hands near the food bowl aren't there to take his food away. When you feed him, kneel down beside him while he eats. Now and then, interrupt his eating to offer an especially tasty treat, such as a piece of chicken or liver, which is bound to be more interesting than the kibble in the bowl. After he gets used to this, hide the treat in your hand, put your hand in his food bowl, and when he pushes his face close, open your hand and give him the treat. Then let him finish his meal with you still hovering close by. In this way, he learns that your close presence at mealtimes is a good thing, not a threat.

You can use a similar procedure with toys, bones, or other objects that he becomes possessive over. Offer to trade the object for a special treat and then return the object. This way, he learns that it's okay for you to handle his things because you don't intend to steal them permanently.

However, don't forget the principle of nonconfrontation in dealing with aggression. If your dog becomes persistently possessive over a toy or other object, then you must make it disappear from your dog's life, and it must never be seen again.

Fear-based aggression

The emotion that most commonly causes a dog to bite a stranger is fear. It is usually caused by a lack of early socialization. The early signs of potential fear biting aren't aggressive at all. Rather you observe that the dog starts out by hiding behind a person or dog when stressed, running away from human or canine contacts, or fearfully urinating in the face of what they perceive as threats — which can be just about anything. The problem is that later in life, these dogs will learn to use aggression frequently, because it seems to make the "threat" go away.

Your dog's acceptance of your leadership also helps to control anxiety and fearfulness because canines look to their leader to decide when a situation, visitor, or occurrence is a threat or challenge. If the leader isn't showing fear or concern, then the dog has no reason to worry. Please refer to the upcoming section "Controlling Aggression" to resolve your issues.

Territorial aggression

Dogs are most confident in their own territory (your home, yard, or car). Unfortunately, especially if a dog hasn't been well socialized to view all humans favorably, many dogs view any visitors as potential threats. They, therefore, bark to warn the rest of the pack or family that something is happening and also to threaten this stranger that they will use force, if necessary. From the dog's point of view, this technique is very effective. For example, when the mailman comes, the dog barks while he inserts letters into the mail slot, and the mailman goes away. In his mind, this outcome proves that this form of aggressive response really works! This outcome is rewarding enough to guarantee that he'll act even more aggressively next time.

Generally speaking, the easiest way to manage territorial aggression is to make sure that the postman, regular delivery people, and the garbage collectors aren't strangers. Introduce your dog to these people and have them give him a treat and perhaps a pat. This introduction won't stop your dog from alerting you that someone has arrived at your door, but it will tone things down and take away the aggressive territorial guarding behavior directed toward familiar people in your world.

Predatory aggression

Dogs evolved from swift running predators, and for some dogs, running and chasing are equivalent to dancing in humans — an enjoyable way to get into the rhythm of the universe. While for some dogs, the chase is all that is important, others enjoy pouncing at the end of the chase, which may mean nipping a cyclist, a child on a skateboard, or a jogger. In other words, these dogs are mimicking the aggressive patterns of the hunters in their evolutionary past. Certain breeds, including herding dogs, terriers, and hounds, are more likely to show these patterns of behavior.

As always, prevention is the best route. Early socialization and converting the puppy's desire to chase toys that are thrown for him to retrieve are the best ways to prevent predatory aggression. If your dog is already chasing joggers and bicyclists, then some form of aversion therapy is needed. Get some friends to engage in these activities around the dog, but first arm them with water pistols. When your dog chases them, something unexpected now happens. The jogger or vehicle stops, the dog gets a shot of water in his face and hears a shouted angry "No!" For most dogs, that response is quite adequate as aversion therapy.

If your dog is unimpressed by the water gun reaction or if his aggressive response is advanced, call for professional help. Keep a leash and training collar on your dog and correct him the moment he alerts to an inappropriate distraction.

Maternal aggression

It should be obvious that dogs that have just given birth will aggressively defend their puppies from anything that may threaten them. This reaction is a completely unrestrained use of force since a canine mother will do anything to protect her litter. Early socialization to a variety of different people can reduce the likelihood of such aggression when the female has puppies.

Unfortunately, dogs have an additional complication, which seems to set them apart from other domestic animals. It appears that whether they're pregnant or not, after ovulating, all female dogs go through a two-month period in which their body is flooded with the same hormones present during pregnancy. For some dogs, this experience even results in physiological changes that mimic pregnancy, such as lactating. In the last three or four weeks of this *phantom pregnancy,* the female may start acting in a strange manner around certain items, such as tennis balls, socks, soft toys, or shoes. Typically, she collects them and hides them under a bed or other piece of furniture. Furthermore, the female may become quite possessive and protective of these items and snap, growl, or bite anyone who comes near them or disturbs them. As in the case of a real pregnancy that results in a litter, the problem is reduced in a dog well socialized to people. However, the only real preventative is early spaying.

If this problem does occur in your dog, behavioral methods won't cure the aggression. Hormone treatments can eliminate it, or you can simply wait out the situation because it will usually disappear in a few weeks by itself. However, during the time that this form of aggression is likely, isolating the dog may be best, and certainly keep children or nonfamily members from approaching that pile of toys that the dog is protecting as she would a litter of new puppies.

Controlling Aggression

When dealing with aggression, the first step is to change the way your dog thinks about you — he must learn to respect you as a leader, not a follower or a playmate. Imagine meeting the president; though you may not like his political program, you still speak to him respectfully and, of course, you don't try to bite him. It is important that family members, including children, should be treated with respect. Your dog must learn that in his pack (family), all two-footed dogs are higher in status than all four-footed dogs.

To restructure your dog's thinking about his place in the family pack, he needs to learn to follow your lead, and to do so, you must act like a leader. There are behaviors that characterize the leader of the pack and distinguish him from his followers. The leader gets first choice of any food, can sleep anywhere he likes, goes first through any opening or into any new territory, and can demand attention any time he wants it. If your dog respects you (and your family), he is less likely to challenge you. However, you must reinforce your leadership.

Use a nonconfrontational approach when dealing with an aggressive dog. Attempts to confront a dog by using force will only cause the dog to respond in kind, which will ratchet up the level of aggression in the relationship. If the problem is based on fearfulness, confrontation, or dominance, your dog will view your retaliation as active aggression, causing him concerns about your authority and/or his own safety. Not only will a confrontational approach make the dog more reactive, but the dog's insecurity will be greatest when you — the person threatening him or hurting him — are near.

If your dog is showing signs of aggression, here are two actions you may take in reshaping his worldview. If the aggression persists, please seek professional help.

✔ **Hand-feeding:** One approach that encourages your dog's focus on your direction and presence is to hand-feed him. For the next month, and at every possible opportunity, hand-feed him his meals only after he has responded to a command, such as "Come," "Sit," "Stay," and "Down," mixing up the commands to strengthen his attention. The whole process should take a total of around 5 to 10 minutes.

If you're feeding your dog soft food, you can spoon out portions. Should your dog refuse to take part in your program by responding to your commands, postpone the activity a couple of hours until his hunger has taken hold.

Each time your dog responds to a command, give him his food as you praise him softly and touch his collar. (Remember, the leader gets to touch anyone that he wants.) If you're living with a spouse, partner, or kids, encourage them to take part in this activity.

After the dog has settled down and the aggressiveness and fearfulness have toned down, you can phase out the hand-feeding routine for his breakfast and dinner. He still has to come and sit, but now he gets the bowl put down as his reward. At first, the bowl will contain just a part of his meal so that he'll have to obey two or three commands before the meal is complete. Later on, it can contain a single serving.

✔ **Touching:** A simple method to strengthen your dominant position over your dog involves touching. Beyond daily strokes, this method involves systematic, full-body strokes that mimic the licking pattern a mother dog applies to her puppies. This "touch" not only helps to establish an emotional bond, but is also an expression of her dominance and control of the litter.

Make it a practice to touch your dog systematically on an almost-daily basis. Everyone in the family, *especially the children,* should be taught the following ritual because their position in the pack hierarchy is the most vulnerable. (Discontinue this procedure immediately if your dog shows aggression or rigidity. Get professional help immediately.)

The procedure to follow is quite straightforward. While talking in a soothing manner, saying the dog's name frequently, have your dog sit or stand in front of you. Take her head in both of your hands. Stroke or fondle her ears, neck, and muzzle in this two-handed manner, looking into the dog's eyes as you do. Next slide both hands down the dog's neck, back, and sides. Lightly slide your hands over the dog's chest and then all the way down each of the dog's front legs. If the dog is sitting, raise it gently to a standing position, lightly rub its belly and back, and then run your hands down the hind legs all the way to the tip of the paws. Finally, run your fingers quickly and lightly over the dog's tail (or tail region, if the dog has a docked tail). Finish by again grasping the dog's head momentarily and saying the dog's name in a happy voice.

The entire touching routine takes only about 30 seconds to a minute, and your dog will probably enjoy all the attention, but most importantly, she'll recognize that she's being subjected to being touched, which means that she's lower in social rank than the ones doing the touching.

TIP

If your dog is sensitive in a certain area, don't avoid touching your dog there unless she's showing aggression. (Seek professional help immediately.) Condition your dog's acceptance by offering her food or a lickable treat, such as peanut butter daubed on your finger, as you gradually increase your handling in this sensitive area.

Preventing Aggression

The goal is, of course, to prevent the onset of aggression. To do that, your dog must unequivocally and, in fact, quite happily accept your leadership and direction.

If your dog accepts you (and your family) as higher in the pack leadership, he'll be less likely to aggressively challenge you. However, your leadership can't be questioned. A good approach to ensure your dog's respect — a process you should initiate before your dog has shown aggression — is the *family cooperation system.*

The family cooperation system reminds your dog that he's part of a family structure, and not in charge or at the center of it. You outline what behaviors earn him rewards and use those rewards to shape his behavior. Using this system, your dog learns to look for and respect your direction.

Here's how it works:

✔ As the pack leader, you should never let your dog rush out of a door or through a gate ahead of you. Instead, use the "Wait" and then "Okay" commands.

✔ When the dog is resting in a favorite spot, make it move from time to time, using the phrase "Excuse me." Praise your dog for his cooperation, allowing him to return to its original position.

✔ Occasionally take an object or some food away from your dog. (Start doing this when your dog is still a puppy so that aggression is less likely and more easily controlled.) The moment you've done so, praise your dog for being unaggressive and return the object or give your dog an additional bit of food (see the early section on possessive aggression).

✔ Everything from toys, play, to attention should be offered only after your dog has responded to a simple direction, such as sit or down. Ignore all rude demands for your attention, including pawing, barking, or placing her forepaws on you. Either walk away, bring your arms over your face, or tug on his leash if he's wearing one. Immediately redirect him to "sit."

✔ Use the lessons outlined in Chapters 3 and 12 and the suggestions on including children to teach your dog to respond to everyone's directions. Choose two to ten word cues that you'll use to direct your dog throughout the day. Speak in clear, quick, bark-sounding tones, identifying what you want the dog to do (like *sit* or *come*) or where you want the dog to go (car, upstairs, kitchen). This gradually gets the dog into the habit of accepting your leadership and direction, which also helps eliminate any thoughts of aggression.

If your dog is already growling at you, get professional help. Your dog's aggression has escalated to a dangerous level and is beyond the scope of this book.

Figuring Out Whether Neutering Helps

As in humans, boys and girls are different, and it's not just a matter of different plumbing systems. When it comes to canine aggression, the most common culprit is a male adolescent dog, and the issue is usually related to dominance. Male dogs are 6.2 times more likely to bite humans, and sexually intact dogs are 2.6 times more likely to be involved in attacks than are neutered dogs.

Neutering is a way to take sex out of the picture by removing the sex hormone-producing apparatus, which are testicles for males and ovaries and uterus for females.

The male hormone testosterone is responsible for influencing a number of dog behaviors, from territorial urine marking, to dog-to-dog aggression, to roaming in order to stake territory and look for a mate. Neutering vastly reduces testosterone levels, thus curbing these behaviors.

Female sex hormones, on the other hand, affect her personality only during her heat cycles, which usually occur twice a year. It's then that she's most likely to urine mark and wander. Progesterone, a hormone involved with the female cycle, has a generally calming effect; however, it also stimulates a possessive or protective attitude toward her puppies, or anything that serves as a puppy substitute, such as her toys or young children. Neutering stops this twice-yearly potential for aggression.

Least you think neutering is a cure-all, it rarely affects fear biting, territorial aggression (the dog's natural defensive reaction when something comes near his home), or predatory aggression (which is the tendency to chase things that run and to nip or bite them).

Neutering does affect the dog's personality quite subtly in other ways. Neutered dogs seem to pay more attention to people because they're paying less attention to sex-related activities of other dogs. In addition, neutering a dog who is not yet an adult seems to freeze personality development at that stage, at least in terms of keeping certain puppylike traits in place.

Because the optimal time to neuter a dog is just before puberty, neutering becomes a useful tool if you have a dog breed where the adult tends to have pronounced aggressive tendencies. Generally speaking, the puppy is softer and less likely to show dominance and other tendencies that can lead to aggression later. Thus, if you have such a breed but like the pup's personality at the age of six months, subject to your veterinarian's approval, it appears to be a good psychological reason why neutering should be done at that age.

Part V
The Part of Tens

The 5th Wave   By Rich Tennant

"Diane—this stupid dog of yours is trying to tell us something again!"

In this part . . .

Because understanding your dog is paramount to loving her wholeheartedly, this part leaves you with our top ten tips for staying emotionally and psychologically connected to her. Use this information as a quick reminder and share it with other dog-loving friends.

Chapter 16

Ten Forms of Silent Communication

. . . .

In This Chapter

▶ Using your body posture, eye contact, and signals to direct your dog.

▶ Bonding with your dog through silence and serenity

. . . .

*I*f your goal is to share your life with a dog who enjoys minding you and prioritizes your opinion, you can influence your dog's behavior in many ways — all without saying a word.

Humans and dogs differ in communication style. People talk and talk and talk. We learn by listening. Dogs, on the other hand, learn by watching, taking direction by mirroring, and looking to others. Because your dog can't internalize your life experience, it's your responsibility to translate your message into a medium that she can understand and relate to. In other words, be quiet and start communicating silently.

Eye Contact

Your dog is clever, and she likes to interact and communicate with you. Your vocal responses, however, aren't an ideal indicator of your attention because you talk all day long. From her perspective, your eye contact is the surest determinant: eye contact, negative or positive, ensures your interaction.

If you're looking at your dog, she'll repeat the behavior that succeeded in getting your attention, again, 100 percent guaranteed.

Eye contact is so important that it influences your dog's behavior throughout the day. The following list shows you how simple eye contact acknowledgement influences your dog's behavior throughout the day:

✔ **Jumping:** If you look at your dog when he jumps, he'll jump again. In fact, the main reason your dog is jumping is to see whether he can get your attention. Whether you look at him when you're greeting him or when he approaches you while you're relaxing in your home, make sure that he has all four paws on the floor before you say hello.

✔ **Mealtime etiquette:** If you look at your dog while you're eating, you're inviting her to the feast. Is it any wonder that your dog can find the one person willing to share and park herself next to that chair? Better to feed your dog first, offer her a bed to rest in and a toy to chew, and encourage everyone to keep their eyes off the dog.

✔ **Barking:** If you look at your dog the instant she barks, guess what? You'll get a repeat performance. If you want a quiet dog, focus on your dog when she's quiet.

✔ **Walking manners:** Your leash walking goal is that your dog follows you on a loose leash and looks to you before responding to distractions in your environment. If you're following her, in her opinion, you're looking to her to interpret life experience.

✔ **Door manners:** Your door is the mouth of your den; whoever orchestrates this vital entranceway is the leader. If you're standing behind your dog as you exit or you're greeting friends in her shadow, then guess what? In your dog's mind, you're looking to her to lead. Your life will run smoother when you teach your dog the direction "Back" and praise her for responding to your lead.

✔ **Counter cruising:** Noting your interest in the counter, your dog will likely jump up to have a look as soon as her legs are long enough (or, if you have a large dog, she may be able to just look down at the counter!). If this normal reaction is met with immediate interaction, it will surely be repeated. Though your interaction is confrontational, it surely beats watching the clock tick. Focus on other behaviors, such as appropriate chewing or ball tossing, and discourage your dog's interest in the counter with a discouragingly sharp "No."

✔ **Furniture jumping:** If the idea of your dog on the furniture is less than appealing, take note of what your eyes may be encouraging. Whether your tone is pleasant or off-putting, if your dog can get your attention by jumping on the couch, rest assured it will become a daily amusement. Place a bed on the floor and calmly discourage her by tugging her off with a collar or leash. Focus your attention only when she's resting on the floor.

✔ **Chasing behavior:** If your dog runs after a child, cat, or car and you're left shouting after her, your eye contact and verbal attention are backing her up.

✔ **Chewing behavior and the grab-n-go:** The image is familiar: Your dog grabs a forbidden object, trots just out of reach, and waits for the inevitable chase. In the cartoons, it's funny; in real life, not so. But once again, your eye contact speaks louder than words.

✔ **Housesoiling:** Many dogs are so lively and bored that they'll do anything that gets a rise out of someone, including peeing. If your dog eliminates while staring you in the face and then hangs out to watch the cleanup, your eye contact (once again) is guaranteeing a repeat performance.

For more ideas on how to resolve these problems, please refer to Part IV.

Body Posture

Your dog is even more attuned to your body posture than another human is. Imagine seeing a loved one hunched over: Your immediate hesitation would be completely normal as you fumbled to help them or inquired as to their dilemma.

The moment you hunch your body, your dog must interpret what, if anything, is wrong with you and/or the situation. Other dogs hunch for one of three reasons:

✔ They want to play.

✔ They're scared.

✔ They're investigating something interesting.

Here's a quick tip to get your dog to come. Make a loud rancorous shouting noise to alert your dog's attention, but instead of beaconing or chasing her, simply hunch over and scratch the ground. Curiosity will ensure her participation.

Upright and relaxed is the ideal posture when directing your dog or trying to influence her calm cooperation in stressful situations.

Touch

No one can argue the influence of a loving touch. Furthermore, with dogs, touch symbolizes status: A respected, dominant dog is permitted to sniff or prod her group members for no other reason than a commitment to the group's well-being.

Choose a time when your dog is naturally calm and chaos is minimal. Flatten your hand like a paddle and stroke your dog in long, soothing strokes. Talk calmly as you do so and touch your dog's nose to tail. Though your dog's paws are sensitive to touch, stroke each individually; if she hesitates, treat your dog to ensure a more positive association to toe touches.

Your Demeanor

Attitude is everything! Your dog learns, judges, and respects you based not on what you say but how you act. This silent communication is ongoing 24/7: If you're successful in playing the role of a confident, self-assured leader, your dog will look to and respect your direction. Fake this attitude even when you're unsure what to do next.

When you're teaching your dog a new routine or introducing her to an unfamiliar circumstance, act comfortably familiar with the situation. Your assurance reassures your dog. Repeated directions, on the other hand, confuse and may frighten her. Your silent example will be all the reassurance she needs.

Plan your reactions to daily situations ahead of time so that you limit your befuddlement and thus give your dog the reassurance that you're knowledgeable enough to handle and direct her through all of life's events.

Unresponsiveness

Your attention is your dog's chief motivation in life, and he spends hours targeting the behaviors that ensure your interaction. Without this mutuality, your relationship couldn't exist. If you can embrace the power of your connection, then it's easy to deduce that withdrawing your attention can shape your dog's behavior for the better or worse.

Pay attention when she's stolen a slipper, but ignore her when she's quietly chewing a bone, and it's easy to predict which behavior she'll repeat. Ignore her when she calmly greets you with a toy, but react to her when she acts like a jumping bean — guess what she's going to repeat?

Outline the ideal responses to everyday situations, from chewing a bone while you're watching TV or fetching her ball when she wants your attention, and then focus on this good behavior!

Sometimes the easiest solution to remedy negative behaviors is to simply fold your arms in front of your face (which signals a withdrawal in group interaction) or leave (promptly ending interaction). The behavior that results in these responses will be quickly abandoned in favor of what works!

Mirrored Motion

If you want to rile up anyone, person or dog, all you need to do is jump around and act crazy. If you notice that your dog's behavior is often manic and out of control, look at your response. Does your blood pressure escalate? If so, you're mirroring your dog's reaction, which only makes matters more chaotic, not less. A better approach is to reverse the trend:

- ✔ List times or situations that excite or stress your dog.

- ✔ Ahead of time, work on the directions "Back," "Sit," and "Stay," as detailed in Chapter 12.

- ✔ Either attach your dog to a full-length leash or leave a hand leash on her for quick control (see Chapter 11).

If your dog is sensitive to sound distractions, such as the doorbell or the vacuum, lead your dog on a leash and ask a helper to simulate the sound periodically while you direct her nonchalantly. (If she's overexcited, read about red zones in Chapter 13.) Though she may react excitedly initially, she will soon mirror your calmer response.

Looking at Your Dog Less

If you follow your dog around, inside or out, she'll think you need a lot of direction. For example, if she grabs objects or gravel and you shout and chase her, in her mind, you're playing a game. Her object focus will not diminish, and neither will your frustration.

Your dog can learn by your example: Play with her toys, investigate appropriate obstacles, such as a wood pile or rock outcropping, or chase a squirrel. Choose an appropriate digging area or erect a sandbox and play there until she joins you.

Hand Signals

Dogs watch, people listen. Adjust your teaching to a medium your dog is most comfortable with — incorporating hand signals with your spoken directions. A dog who watches for direction is less likely to wander out of sight. Here are a few hand signals to try:

- ✔ **Sit:** A hand sweep from above your dog's nose to your eyes.

- ✔ **Down:** Pointing from your dog's nose to floor between her paws.

- ✔ **Come:** A broad sweep across your chest and then a directed point at your feet.

- ✔ **Follow:** A sharp slap of your thigh.

- ✔ **Good:** One or both arms thrown high in the air — the human exclamation point.

Body Position

Whoever stands in front is in charge. When walking your dog near roadways or in unfamiliar environments, teach her to follow your lead. When the unpredictable happens, such as the approach of a dog or stranger, she will automatically look to you and mirror your response.

In addition, teach your dog to respect your authority at the doorways — what she considers the mouth of your den.

Teach your dog "Back" (in Chapter 12), using it before greeting visitors. Always encourage containment and focus before entering and exiting.

Lure Touching

Imagine someone repetitively shouting directions at you — "Pass the ketchup, the ketchup, the ketchup." You'd neither want to listen or cooperate, and an escalating tone would only make matters worse. Your dog feels the same way!

A far better approach to teaching your dog a new direction is to be silent as you use food bits or a favorite toy to lure your dog into a chosen position, such as "Sit," or "Down," as described in Chapter 12. Once your dog is comfortable with the posture, you can associate a one-word cue with it. However, the real learning process occurred in silence.

Chapter 17

Ten Common Misunderstandings

*I*t seems that everyone believes that they understand dogs and dog behaviors — at least well enough to get along with their own pet. They base this belief on "facts" that they may have heard from their parents, friends, and acquaintances.

Unfortunately, acting on such misinformation can result in bad outcomes, a sharp deterioration in trust, and possibly increased aggression. In this chapter, we replace folk tales with fact.

True or false? In North America, one out of every four families lives with a dog! True, true, true!

Every Dog Wants to Be Leader of the Pack

Dogs don't have humanlike ambitions: Being No. 1 dog in their family pack is more of a burden than an honor. The truth is that dogs simply want their human pack members to assign them a rank number and to make the decisions. With someone else making the decisions, the dog doesn't have to ever be on guard and can now tend to the other matters on his agenda, such as an afternoon nap or a game of fetch.

The rank in the pack doesn't have to be earned by physical force. A strong pack leader controls access to food, resting spots, and water and has a stable mood. In fact, the only return this leader expects is attention and respect from his group.

The simple act of making a dog work for everything he wants, such as obeying a simple command like "Sit" before being given dinner, or even being given a pat, tells him that you're in charge.

Without an authority figure and adequate pack structure, your dog will become quite stressed. This stress is the source of many dog behavior problems. These problems come about because the dog thinks, "If no one in my pack is in charge, then someone must make the decisions, and the only one left is me." Thus, the unwilling dog is forced into a position of leadership. He must then be ever vigilant and becomes pushy, dominant, and even aggressive.

A Wagging Tail Means a Happy and Friendly Dog

A wagging tail signifying a friendly dog is one of the most common misunderstandings about dog behavior. Actually, the wag of a dog's tail can signal many things, depending upon its speed and the way the tail is carried.

A happy tail wag is actually a submissive gesture and one that is often paired with a lower rump, which seems to drag the hips with each swing. Translated, it says, "You have my respect, and I know that you won't hurt me." A dog giving this signal is quite approachable.

Contrast that broad tail wag with one where the dog's tail is held high over his back and the tail movements involve very short side to side swings at a high speed. This is the tail wag of a dominant dog who is saying, "Back off! Give me space!"

For a more thorough description of tail interpretation, refer to Chapter 3.

Dogs Understand Human Language

How many patient pets have listened to the constant diatribes of their well-meaning owners: "How many times have I told you not to get on the sofa? Behavior like that is simply not acceptable, and you're making me very angry. I don't want you to do that again."

Ask the person, and he may claim that his dog knows well and good what he's talking about. Ask the dog, but she'll likely be snoring.

Dogs can learn specific words that humans speak, with the average dog capable of learning around 165 words and/or signals. In addition, dogs are very attuned to tone of voice and instinctively pair it to an emotional state, thus people with deep voices are often given reverence, whereas doting, placating family members are often ignored.

A dog, no matter how intelligent, can't process full grammatical sentences.

A Fearful Dog Won't Bite

A dog cringing in fear is a sorry sight. The average person may feel drawn to the scene and eager to help, but few consider this frightened animal a threat. Approaching this dog, however, is a bad move. This dog fears for his life and will likely bite without warning or hesitation. When fear biters bite, they bite hard.

Fearful animals are, in fact, more likely to bite than dominant animals.

Panic drives fearful dogs to do anything to reduce the presence of a threat. Further, when you retreat from a dominant dog, he'll stop any further threat of aggression: In essence, you did what he asked. When you retreat from a fearful dog, however, he may still rush and snap as your presence is still a potential threat. He's afraid that you may still return to hurt him, so his emotions may well swamp any logical thinking about the situation.

You should view all frightened animals as potentially aggressive.

Dogs Know When They've Done Wrong

Here's the scene. You enter your home, and Rover looks at you, glances toward the kitchen, and then runs and hides. You walk into the kitchen, and trash is strewn all over the place — evidence that once again, your pet has been looking for edibles in the garbage. Your conclusion is obvious: Rover was feeling guilty because he messed with the trash can, and he knew that he'd done something bad, which is why he is hiding from you.

Unfortunately, your obvious conclusion is wrong. Remember, dogs have the mind equivalent of a 2- to 21/2 -year-old human.

Feelings of guilt don't appear until around 4 years of age in humans, and notions of right and wrong may not be fully formed even in adults.

So what's going on here? Your dog has learned that when trash is on the floor and you enter the house, bad things happen to dogs. He has no notion that he has any responsibility for the connection. He's simply showing fear for the punishment that he anticipates may occur.

 If your dog has such a trash problem and you still believe that your dog feels guilt, strew some trash on the kitchen floor yourself, let Rover see it, and then leave the house for five minutes. When you return, you'll see your dog cringing in the same manner that you call guilt, even though he knows that he's not responsible.

Dogs Sometimes Behave Out of Spite

Maggie has been out running errands all day while her dog Buddy was home alone. When she finally comes home, she finds the sofa cushions chewed to shreds. When her husband comes in from work, she explains, "Buddy was so upset that I left him for so long that out of spite and revenge, he destroyed our furniture."

It's a nice story, but wrong. Spite is another late developing emotion, like guilt, and the minds of dogs (equivalent to a human 2 year old) never reach that stage. Buddy chewed the cushions out of boredom. If he'd had something more interesting to chew on, like a beef shank bone or a peanut butter–filled chew toy, Maggie's sofa would still be intact.

 Another reason dogs choose to destroy or carry objects is that they may have your scent. Objects with the strongest scent are apt to be objects that you use frequently, so you naturally believe that the dog has deliberately chosen that object to distress or annoy you. However, this behavior is driven by a longing for your company, not a spiteful reaction to your departure.

Dogs Hate Cats

Dogs naturally chase cats, but this reaction isn't motivated by hatred. Dogs evolved from predators that chased, killed, and ate a lot of small animals, although their ready access to the food that we provide has diminished their killing instinct. Term it *call of the wild* or simple fun, dogs naturally chase any animal that runs from them — including cats. Sighthounds and terriers are the breeds most likely to chase cats.

Unlike other wild prey, however, when trapped, a cat will turn and fight. Such a confrontation is noisy and dangerous for both animals, and if you've experienced such an event, you'd certainly remember it. However, if you look at the statistics, you'll note 56 percent of dog owners also own cats, and they happily coexist, meaning that harmony between the species is within your reach.

Dogs Like It When You Hug Them

Most dogs don't enjoy being hugged. It's nothing personal, but as part of their wild heritage, dogs interpret any restriction of motion as threatening because running from trouble is their first line of defense. Though most dogs will tolerate a strong pat or quick arm hold, a full hug may be too restraining.

 Teach your children how to interact with dogs properly. Encourage your children to reach out their hands to allow a dog to sniff it. If the dog turns away, your children should, too. If the dog sniffs their hand calmly, show your children the appropriate way to stroke and pet them, but enforce absolutely no hugs!

Your Stress Has No Effect on Your Dog

Most people believe that their stress level has no effect on their pet's well-being and look to their pets as potential sources of stress relief for their human family. Though scientific data has confirmed that petting a dog does relieve stress, studies also show that your state of tension and anxiety can affect your dog as well.

When you're anxious, you emit scents called *pheromones* that signal your current psychological state to your dog. When stress scents are emitted, your dog will search for the source of danger that is causing your agitated state. His activity level may rise, as he becomes anxious and ill at ease. He may even think that your stress has been caused by something that he did. Your tension thus becomes your dog's tension, too.

Dogs are masters at reading body language, too. They can detect your mood by looking at your posture and the way that you move.

Avoid working with your dog when you're stressed. Use this time to relax or play games that may lighten your mood before you train or do other work with your pet.

Dogs' Licks Are Kisses

Probably one of the most enduring and widespread myths about dog behavior is that a dog's lick is the equivalent of a kiss. Actually, a dog's lick can have many meanings, and affection and greeting are only two.

Perhaps the most common meaning comes from a dog's early evolutionary history. In the wild, when a mother wolf returns from hunting, she has already fed herself. When she enters the den, the puppies gather around her and begin to lick her face. To a romantic, this gesture may look like expressions of love — with all the puppies overjoyed at mother's return. The actual purpose of this face licking, however, is much more functional.

Wild canines have a well-developed regurgitation reflex. Young puppies who are no longer nursing lick their mother's face and lips to cause her to vomit up food. This partially digested material is easy for the mother to transport and makes ideal dining for young puppies.

So the next time your dog is licking your face, ask yourself whether he's hungry. Perhaps he's simply asking for something to eat. Of course, humans, being easily flattered, often reward what they perceive as loving attention with a snack. And so it comes full circle.

Chapter 18

Ten Ways to Become Your Dog's Leader

. . . .

In This Chapter

▶ Discovering how a good leader communicates

▶ Understanding why every dog needs a trusted leader

. . . .

*L*eaders do more than boss their underling around; they set an example of good behavior and maintain a sense of calm authority, even in the face of excitement. If you're eager for more respect, try the simple steps in this chapter.

Control the Resources

In any group of dogs, the leader controls the resources, from food, to choice resting areas, to drinking locations. Because your dog views your relationship as though you (and your family) were other dogs, emphasize this authority by organizing structured feeding times, even hand-feeding a portion of your dog's meal to accentuate your authority.

Teach Your Dog to Mind Her Manners

Ordering anyone about, whether you're a dog or person, is poor form. "Get this, do that, scratch my back, over here!" — a person who made these epithets would be quickly put in their place, and yet many dogs get away with saying as much with their behavior.

Assess how your dog demands your attention: pawing you, whining, scratching your arm, or staring. You must stop these unruly interactions must stop; you're enabling your dog's incivility.

Before offering your dog anything she would consider a treat (food, your attention, toys), instruct her to sit. If she ignores you, position her calmly and then continue your interaction.

Each time she requests your attention, instruct her to sit until her manners improve to the level that she'll automatically sit whenever she wants something.

Reserve High Places for Humans

Woe is the temptation to invite your dog into your bed. An extra warm body on a cold wintery night — they didn't call them "three dog nights" up north for nothing! That said, however, your dog may read a lot into your resting positions. Young dogs and those who are showing aggression should be level trained. This formula highlights that you rest on higher sleeping ground — a bed or couch, in essence, being equivalent to a mound or hill. Your elevated level commands respect.

As your dog matures, and her respect for your direction improves, you may invite her to join you on permission. (Any sign of aggression would preclude this honor.) Teach your dog to "Sit and wait" and then encourage her to lie in one space by tapping that spot and saying "Up, up."

Your dog may inch her way up to your pillow or the back edge of the couch. Don't allow her to do so. Designate one area ahead of time. If she excites or rearranges herself, tell her "Off" and direct her back to her own bed on the floor.

Emphasize Your Right of Way

The most common and passive way dogs organize a hierarchy is through spatial definition. If you catch yourself stepping over or around your dog, or changing direction as not to avoid her, you're paying homage to her presence. Leadership (at this point) isn't within your grasp.

To reclaim your authority, teach your dog the definition of "Excuse me." Every time your dog crosses your path (on a walk, stairway, or about the house), calmly but clearly say, "Excuse me" and knudge her out of your way. You may need to bump your dog with your knees or scotch your feet under her body until she moves.

So be it. One of you must move about the other: If your goal is leadership, don't defer. As long as your dog cooperates, you don't need to do anything else other than just move along nonchalantly.

If your dog's chosen resting spots are blocking your footpath, the same rules apply. If you walk around her, you're saying that you are more aware of her than she needs to be of you. The result? Your dog will consistently place herself in your pathway in order to get attention and redefine your spatial respect. In this case, it's far easier to teach your dog to lie at the specified location or along the edge of the room.

 Does your dog trip you on the stairs, slide in front of you during a walk, or position himself in front of the TV or the stove? These actions are as rude as a loved one stretching out to work or exercise in the middle of your stairway or kitchen floor. You owe it to your dog to teach her better manners!

Use Time-Outs to Control Unruly Behavior

Bringing your dog to her crate, small room, or station calmly isn't punishment unless your inappropriate behavior makes it so. The calm act of escorting your dog to her kennel, station, or quiet room is a very acceptable way to handle normal frustrations. Losing your temper is far worse than to separate and regroup.

If you feel your frustration coming on, with no improvement in your dog's behavior, don't hesitate to put your dog in a time-out. Grab a favorite toy for your dog, direct him by voice or collar, and simply say, "Time out, my love," as you seclude him. Your authority to make these decisions and isolate your dog when she's unruly is both respectable and required. The duration of time out will be determined by how long it takes you to calm down, and whether your dog naps or is restless. These quiet times should not be more than 30 minutes, unless your dog is resting.

 You can also use time-outs to help children control their impulses around the dog/puppy, too. In this case, simply remind the children that when a situation gets out of hand, the dog will need to go to her quiet space (which in truth, she'll probably welcome), but that if they cooperate, you'll reward them with a sticker or other prize.

Here are several times when a time-out can help ease the situation:

- ✔ If your dog/puppy is getting overly excited with a situation. Isolate her with a displacement bone or toy.

- ✔ If an outdoor situation is overstimulating your dog, causing frantic barking, pacing or patrolling.

- ✔ When children interactions are getting out of hand.

- ✔ If you suspect that her inattention or poor behavior may be due to exhaustion. Puppies nip the hardest when they're overtired.

Empathize

Your dog wants to be understood and, above all, be respected for her life experience. An ounce of empathy can give you a special rapport with your dog. Once you can imagine life from her perspective, you can tailor your direction and become the leader you'd want to have if you were in the same situation.

Consider life from your dog's perspective. Why does your dog jump, for example? If jumping occurs during greeting, she's trying to get closer to your face, as is a normal canine ritual. Shouting or kneeing her introduces confrontational energy between you. Don't go there. Instead, consider your dog's reaction and what she may be trying to communicate and then comprise a direction that satisfies her needs while maintaining a structured home life. See Table 18-1 for examples of possible redirections.

Table 18-1   Possible Redirections for Problem Behaviors

Problem Behavior	Possible Issue	Leadership Redirection
Chewing furniture	Teething pain	Appropriate toys and bones
Jumping on countertops	Interest in odors, boredom, lack of structure and attention, mimicking your focus	Appropriate toys, fetching, giving dog her area in each room
Housetraining	Identifying location	Routinely taking your dog to one specified area at organized times.
Barking	Territorial alert	Calm interception, using the direction "Quiet" and redirection back to your side

Organize Space and Activities

A good leader, like a good team captain or parent, organizes the space and activities of those she's responsible for. Organization leaves little to question and provides a tremendous sense of security and calm.

Help your dog organize where to go and what to do in every situation, from family time activities, to meals, to a visitor's arrival. Consider your life's flow and organize a game plan for each situation. What should your dog do, for example, when you come in from errands? Where should she go, and what should she do when you're watching TV, or playing with the children on the swings? Consider Table 18-2 and copy it or add to it.

Table 18-2	Organizing Your Dog's Activities	
When . . .	*Space*	*Activity*
You eat	On a dog bed, under the table	Chew bone or toy
Visitors arrive	Stand back	Fetch toy or sit
Children/spouse arrives	Normal greeting posture	Fetch toy, stand on four paws, or roll for belly rub
Your children are playing with tempting toys in the playtime	On dog bed	Playing or chewing a toy
Visit a friend	Bring bed, bowls, crate	Keep your dog with you and lead him about on a leash until he's comfortable with his surroundings. Offer a toy or chew when he's expected to be still

Practice Full Body Handling

It's the leader's prerogative and responsibility to physically check her group members. Other dogs know this fact and will allow a dominant dog to thoroughly examine their body. In your vigil to assume authority, physically touch your dog each day, from head to toe.

Your daily attention to your dog's body allows you to note any growths, parasites, or skin alterations. Bring anything suspect to your veterinarian's attention.

Restore Predictability

Dogs enjoy predictability: Connecting to an experience when their role is defined. Your dog feels most safe in your home when predictability reigns, distractions are low, and your mood is stable. Though you may enjoy a more spontaneous schedule, your dog will not. Like a young child, he enjoys eating, toileting, and playing at similar intervals.

If you work during the day and your dog is left alone, hire a dog walker who you can call in case an emergency precludes you from getting home at your usual hour. Though your dog can't read the time, his biological clock highlights your arrival time. If you don't make it home, your dog may soil or become destructive.

Highlight the Positive

Consider playing on a team. Would you choose a captain that belittled your weakness or exalted your strengths? A benevolent leader plays a similar role: Emphasize your dog's good qualities and cooperative behavior, and she'll be a cheerful member of your family circle. For each negative behavior you encounter, establish a positive alternative.

Index

pointers, 85–86
recognized, 84
registration, 225
retrievers, 85
setters, 86
sociability, 93
spaniels, 86
spitz-type dogs, 88
sporting, 85–86
standards, 83
terriers, 89–90
territoriality, 92–93
toy, 90
vermin hunters, 89
working, 88
brow position, 33
brush-off technique, 30
bull baiting, 23
Bull Terriers, deafness in, 101
Bulldog, 225

• C •

Campbell, William (behaviorist), 65
cancer, detection by scent, 104
Canine Cognitive Dysfunction (CCD), 133–134
car, barking in the, 196
cataracts, 131
cats
  chasing, 252–253
  hearing ability of, 100
Cavalier King Charles Spaniel, 50
cerebrospinal fluid, 227
chain leashes, 144
chase recall, 25
chasing
  cats, 252–253
  curing overdeveloped instinct, 23–25
  a dog, 167, 223
  eye contact, 244
  as hunting behavior component, 22, 23
  predatory aggression, 233–234
chewing behavior
  curiosity, 196–197
  eye contact, 245
  teething, 197

children
  age-appropriate activities, 164
  biting, 223, 231
  encouraging participation and self-control, 163–165
  meeting, 120
  time-outs for, 257
Chow Chows, 225
civility, 54–55, 174
clicker, 140, 146–148, 151–152
coat color, deafness, 100–101
cochlea, 102, 127
cognitive enrichment program, 135
collars, 117, 141–142
colorblindness, 96–97
Come command
  clicker training, 147
  conditioning, 111
  daily uses, 13
  games, 183
  hand signal, 248
  human phrase equivalent, 160
  luring, 157
  meal association with, 152, 154
  overuse of, 154
  teaching, 154, 181–182
commands. _See also specific commands_
  human phrase equivalents, 160
  treat use in learning, 151
communication
  barking, 34–38
  body position, 248
  body posture, 38–42, 245
  demeanor, 246
  ear position, 42–43
  English to Doglish translation, 29
  eye contact, 30–33, 243–245
  facial signals, 43–44
  hand signals, 248
  lure touching, 248
  mirrored motion, 247
  silent, 243–248
  tail position, 44–45
  touch, 245–246
  unresponsiveness, 246–247
  vocal tones and intonations, 33–34
  words, 34

• T •

USINESS, CAREERS & ERSONAL FINANCE

Fundraising FOR DUMMIES
0-7645-9847-3

Investing FOR DUMMIES
0-7645-2431-3

Also available:
- Business Plans Kit For Dummies 0-7645-9794-9
- Economics For Dummies 0-7645-5726-2
- Grant Writing For Dummies 0-7645-8416-2
- Home Buying For Dummies 0-7645-5331-3
- Managing For Dummies 0-7645-1771-6
- Marketing For Dummies 0-7645-5600-2

- Personal Finance For Dummies 0-7645-2590-5*
- Resumes For Dummies 0-7645-5471-9
- Selling For Dummies 0-7645-5363-1
- Six Sigma For Dummies 0-7645-6798-5
- Small Business Kit For Dummies 0-7645-5984-2
- Starting an eBay Business For Dummies 0-7645-6924-4
- Your Dream Career For Dummies 0-7645-9795-7

OME & BUSINESS COMPUTER ASICS

Laptops FOR DUMMIES
0-470-05432-8

Windows Vista FOR DUMMIES
0-471-75421-8

Also available:
- Cleaning Windows Vista For Dummies 0-471-78293-9
- Excel 2007 For Dummies 0-470-03737-7
- Mac OS X Tiger For Dummies 0-7645-7675-5
- MacBook For Dummies 0-470-04859-X
- Macs For Dummies 0-470-04849-2
- Office 2007 For Dummies 0-470-00923-3

- Outlook 2007 For Dummies 0-470-03830-6
- PCs For Dummies 0-7645-8958-X
- Salesforce.com For Dummies 0-470-04893-X
- Upgrading & Fixing Laptops For Dummies 0-7645-8959-8
- Word 2007 For Dummies 0-470-03658-3
- Quicken 2007 For Dummies 0-470-04600-7

OOD, HOME, GARDEN, HOBBIES, USIC & PETS

Chess FOR DUMMIES
0-7645-8404-9

Guitar FOR DUMMIES
0-7645-9904-6

Also available:
- Candy Making For Dummies 0-7645-9734-5
- Card Games For Dummies 0-7645-9910-0
- Crocheting For Dummies 0-7645-4151-X
- Dog Training For Dummies 0-7645-8418-9
- Healthy Carb Cookbook For Dummies 0-7645-8476-6

- Home Maintenance For Dummies 0-7645-5215-5
- Horses For Dummies 0-7645-9797-3
- Jewelry Making & Beading For Dummies 0-7645-2571-9
- Orchids For Dummies 0-7645-6759-4
- Puppies For Dummies 0-7645-5255-4
- Rock Guitar For Dummies 0-7645-5356-9
- Sewing For Dummies 0-7645-6847-7
- Singing For Dummies 0-7645-2475-5

NTERNET & DIGITAL MEDIA

eBay FOR DUMMIES
0-470-04529-9

iPod & iTunes FOR DUMMIES
0-470-04894-8

Also available:
- Blogging For Dummies 0-471-77084-1
- Digital Photography For Dummies 0-7645-9802-3
- Digital Photography All-in-One Desk Reference For Dummies 0-470-03743-1
- Digital SLR Cameras and Photography For Dummies 0-7645-9803-1
- eBay Business All-in-One Desk Reference For Dummies 0-7645-8438-3

- HDTV For Dummies 0-470-09673-X
- Home Entertainment PCs For Dummies 0-470-05523-5
- MySpace For Dummies 0-470-09529-6
- Search Engine Optimization For Dummies 0-471-97998-8
- Skype For Dummies 0-470-04891-3
- The Internet For Dummies 0-7645-8996-2
- Wiring Your Digital Home For Dummies 0-471-91830-X

eparate Canadian edition also available
eparate U.K. edition also available

 WILEY

SPORTS, FITNESS, PARENTING, RELIGION & SPIRITUALITY

Golf FOR DUMMIES
0-471-76871-5

Baby Massage FOR DUMMIES
0-7645-7841-3

Also available:
- Catholicism For Dummies
  0-7645-5391-7
- Exercise Balls For Dummies
  0-7645-5623-1
- Fitness For Dummies 0-7645-7851-0
- Football For Dummies 0-7645-3936-1
- Judaism For Dummies 0-7645-5299-6
- Potty Training For Dummies
  0-7645-5417-4

- Buddhism For Dummies
  0-7645-5359-3
- Pregnancy For Dummies
  0-7645-4483-7 †
- Ten Minute Tone-Ups For Dummie
  0-7645-7207-5
- NASCAR For Dummies 0-7645-768
- Religion For Dummies 0-7645-526
- Soccer For Dummies 0-7645-5229-
- Women in the Bible For Dummies
  0-7645-8475-8

TRAVEL

Ireland FOR DUMMIES
0-7645-7749-2

New York City FOR DUMMIES
0-7645-6945-7

Also available:
- Alaska For Dummies 0-7645-7746-8
- Cruise Vacations For Dummies
  0-7645-6941-4
- England For Dummies 0-7645-4276-1
- Europe For Dummies 0-7645-7529-5
- Germany For Dummies
  0-7645-7823-5
- Hawaii For Dummies 0-7645-7402-7

- Italy For Dummies 0-7645-7386-1
- Las Vegas For Dummies
  0-7645-7382-9
- London For Dummies 0-7645-4277
- Paris For Dummies 0-7645-7630-5
- RV Vacations For Dummies
  0-7645-4442-X
- Walt Disney World & Orlando
  For Dummies 0-7645-9660-8

GRAPHICS, DESIGN & WEB DEVELOPMENT

Adobe Creative Suite 2 ALL-IN-ONE DESK REFERENCE FOR DUMMIES
0-7645-8815-X

Photoshop CS2 FOR DUMMIES
0-7645-9571-7

Also available:
- 3D Game Animation For Dummies
  0-7645-8789-7
- AutoCAD 2006 For Dummies
  0-7645-8925-3
- Building a Web Site For Dummies
  0-7645-7144-3
- Creating Web Pages For Dummies
  0-470-08030-2
- Creating Web Pages All-in-One Desk
  Reference For Dummies
  0-7645-4345-8
- Dreamweaver 8 For Dummies
  0-7645-9649-7

- InDesign CS2 For Dummies
  0-7645-9572-5
- Macromedia Flash 8 For Dummies
  0-7645-9691-8
- Photoshop CS2 and Digital
  Photography For Dummies
  0-7645-9580-6
- Photoshop Elements 4 For Dummie
  0-471-77483-9
- Syndicating Web Sites with RSS Fee
  For Dummies
  0-7645-8848-6
- Yahoo! SiteBuilder For Dummies
  0-7645-9800-7

NETWORKING, SECURITY, PROGRAMMING & DATABASES

Visual Basic 2005 FOR DUMMIES
0-7645-7728-X

Wireless Home Networking FOR DUMMIES
0-471-74940-0

Also available:
- Access 2007 For Dummies
  0-470-04612-0
- ASP.NET 2 For Dummies
  0-7645-7907-X
- C# 2005 For Dummies
  0-7645-9704-3
- Hacking For Dummies
  0-470-05235-X
- Hacking Wireless Networks
  For Dummies
  0-7645-9730-2
- Java For Dummies
  0-470-08716-1

- Microsoft SQL Server 2005
  For Dummies 0-7645-7755-7
- Networking All-in-One Desk
  Reference For Dummies
  0-7645-9939-9
- Preventing Identity Theft For Dummi
  0-7645-7336-5
- Telecom For Dummies
  0-471-77085-X
- Visual Studio 2005 All-in-One Desk
  Reference For Dummies
  0-7645-9775-2
- XML For Dummies
  0-7645-8845-1

Six Discipline Do's and Don'ts

Don't stare. Unless your gaze conveys deep affection, staring is perceived as confrontational and threatening. Don't confuse your dog. He'll learn to fear or challenge you.

Don't chase. Imagine rushing onto another person in the same manner. This technique induces fear or confrontation, not understanding. It's ineffective in communicating anything, except perhaps that you've lost your mind.

Don't grab, drag, or hold. When you grab, hold, or drag a dog, his only option is to defend himself. Though you may contain him in the moment or vent frustration, it will lead to out-of-control behavior.

Do stay calm, setting the example to model. You should be the one setting an example of how to act in all situations. Give your dog a good example to follow.

Do direct your dog. Your dog can't read your mind. In Chapter 11, you find easy-to-follow instruction on teaching your dog basic commands, such as to stay, follow your lead, and come.

Do provide alternatives. Give your dog every opportunity to behave well. Provide ample activities to occupy his energy and curiosity. When you discourage one activity (such as jumping), encourage something else, such as fetching a toy or sitting.

Simple Socialization Steps

Act like a confident leader: Stand tall and relax.

Say "Back" if your dog rushes forward. Bring him next to your side.

Retreat calmly if your dog seems overwhelmed.

Find your dog's red zone: the distance he can comfortably stand from a new distraction.

Brace your dog if he's afraid.

Teach the directions "Follow," "Wait," and "Stay" to direct your dog when he's engaged or stressed.

Understanding Your Dog For Dummies®

Reading Body Cues

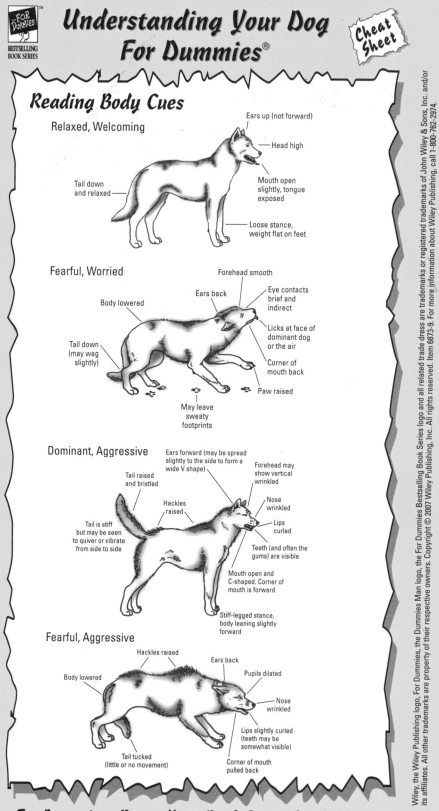

Relaxed, Welcoming
- Ears up (not forward)
- Head high
- Mouth open slightly, tongue exposed
- Loose stance, weight flat on feet
- Tail down and relaxed

Fearful, Worried
- Forehead smooth
- Ears back
- Body lowered
- Eye contacts brief and indirect
- Licks at face of dominant dog or the air
- Corner of mouth back
- Tail down (may wag slightly)
- Paw raised
- May leave sweaty footprints

Dominant, Aggressive
- Ears forward (may be spread slightly to the side to form a wide V shape)
- Forehead may show vertical wrinkled
- Tail raised and bristled
- Hackles raised
- Nose wrinkled
- Lips curled
- Tail is stiff but may be seen to quiver or vibrate from side to side
- Teeth (and often the gums) are visible
- Mouth open and C-shaped. Corner of mouth is forward
- Stiff-legged stance, body leaning slightly forward

Fearful, Aggressive
- Hackles raised
- Ears back
- Body lowered
- Pupils dilated
- Nose wrinkled
- Lips slightly curled (teeth may be somewhat visible)
- Tail tucked (little or no movement)
- Corner of mouth pulled back

For Dummies: Bestselling Book Series for Beginners